$65
1ᵉ Edition

Ethan Allen and
Allen & Wheelock

D1266371

ETHAN ALLEN
AND
ALLEN & WHEELOCK

their guns and their legacy

by
Paul Henry

MOWBRAY PUBLISHING • 54 EAST SCHOOL ST. • WOONSOCKET, RI 02895 • USA

LIBRARY OF CONGRESS
CONTROL NUMBER: 2005926473
Paul Henry
Ethan Allen and Allen & Wheelock
Woonsocket, R.I.: ANDREW MOWBRAY INCORPORATED — PUBLISHERS
240 pp.

ISBN: 1-931464-23-5

© 2006 Paul Henry

All rights reserved. No part of this book may be reproduced in any form or by any means without permission in writing from the publisher and the author, except for short excerpts used in book reviews.

To order more copies of this book, or to receive a free catalog of other fine antique arms publications, call 1-800-999-4697 or 401-597-5055, fax 401-597-5056

Email us at orders@manatarmsbooks.com or visit our web page at www.manatarmsbooks.com

Printed in China.

Opinions and other statements in this book are the author's own and do not necessarily reflect those of the publisher, its officers or affiliates.

9 8 7 6 5 4 3 2 1

American Society of Arms Collectors

Ethan Allen and Allen & Wheelock:
Their Guns and Their Legacy
by Paul Henry

The American Society of Arms Collectors is pleased to recommend "Ethan Allen and Allen & Wheelock: Their Guns and Their Legacy" by Paul Henry as a useful and valuable reference work.

William H. Guthman,
Chairman emeritus,
and Stuart C. Mowbray
serving Chairman
Publications Review Board

DEDICATION

This book is dedicated to my family. They are such a large part of my life and nothing would be worth doing without the love and strength that they give me every day.

Of course, none of this would have been possible without my great wife, Inga, for her years of understanding and tolerance. Inga has always been my best gun show Buddy and my best friend. She has spent many weekends watching my table while I searched for that rare Allen. The encouragement and help she gave me when I decided to write this book was priceless and I thank her from the bottom of this collector's heart.

Paul Henry

PREFACE

Although the firearms of Ethan Allen were not as popular as those of some other makers, his contributions to the firearms industry go much deeper than the products his companies made. Whether by design or by chance, it was Allen who gave many others the skills and knowledge to form their own gun manufacturing businesses. The impact that his companies had on the country's economy was enormous.

During Allen's years as an inventor and gun maker, he was credited with a total of 25 new patents and six reissues of his earlier patents. These patents had a major effect both on the firearms and on the early cartridge making industries. An understanding of the patent process is necessary for an understanding of some of Allen's manufacturing schedules and processes.

Most of the information about who worked for Allen and with whom he did business is found in the Allen & Thurber day book. Although it is very informative, it covers less than a year and a half of the company's operation, from October 1, 1846 to March 11, 1848. During this short period, however, we learn that some of the names that were associated with Allen during that time are still in the firearms related business to this day. We can only imagine how many others were associated with Allen before and after the period covered by the day book. This will be discussed further in the chapter on the day book.

Allen's first brother-in-law, Charles Thurber, was also his first partner in the gun making business. Little has been published on Thurber. Before he married Allen's sister, Lucinda in 1827, he graduated from Brown University and became a teacher at Milford Academy. He appears to have come from a wealthy family as his connection with Allen seemed to involve financial matters rather than gun matters.

Allen's long time friend, employee and also brother-in-law, Thomas Wheelock, became a partner with Allen when he became the "& Co." of Allen, Thurber & Co. This probably happened when Thurber was appointed to the Massachusetts State Senate late in 1853. Thurber did not return to the company after he finished the term and in 1856 Wheelock became a full partner and the firm name was changed to Allen & Wheelock. Although he did not become a full partner until 1856, Wheelock had been a major part of the daily operations of the companies for many years. There is no other name that appears in the day book more often than his. As early as 1844, he was signing invoices and receipts for the company.

The day book is also the source of information on the production of guns at the end of Norwich operations and the beginning of those in Worcester. The recorded purchases of materials, orders and invoices were often more interested in totals than the exact specifications of the items sold, so it is necessary to make some general statements regarding their physical properties. Previous attempts to qualify the numbers of the different kinds of guns made by the various companies have been based on observations made of surviving specimens and, for the most part, have been far from the actual production numbers.

Allen's use of the term "revolver" for his pepperbox pistols has caused some confusion among the collectors of the late-twentieth century. The modern collector has sometimes failed to remember or even to learn the history of his field. The U.S. Patent Office used the term "revolver" for almost any weapon with a part that revolved, including revolving cylinders, revolving barrels or even revolving firing pins. Also be aware that he term "pepperbox," while it was widely used in the second half of the 19th century, took a while to catch on with the public.

There is no doubt that Allen's early guns had assembly or batch numbers rather than serial numbers. At first it was thought that the low numbers seen on most of Allen's firearms indicated limited production, but sales numbers taken from the Allen & Thurber day book have proven that some of the pistols thought to have been made in the hundreds were actually made in the thousands. For convenience in this book, the numbers found on the guns will simply be referred to as numbers, not serial numbers.

Very few of Allen's guns have exact barrel lengths. They are usually found to be slightly shorter than stated. For instance, a four inch barrel will more likely measure out to three and seven eighths and an eight inch barrel might be seven and seven eights, etc. To avoid having a book full of fractions, measurements have been rounded to the nearest one-fourth inch. Pepperbox barrels are measured for their entire length and would normally be about a half inch shorter if measured to the center of the nipple or down the bore.

The use of the word "identical" means similar as there are very few parts made by Allen that are interchangeable with other guns, since they were still being hand fitted.

It is not possible to determine when production of a certain model started from the patent date, as it has been proven many times that an improvement on a gun may have been in production long before the patent was granted. One such case in point is that Allen patented the lipfire cartridge a full year before the first lipfire revolver was patented. It would not make sense that he would make a cartridge and the machinery to produce it for a gun that didn't exist. There are more examples of this throughout the book.

Since, at this writing, no production records from the Allen & Wheelock factory have surfaced, so much about the sequence of production is speculation or an educated guess, if you will. However, once a collector becomes familiar with some of Allen's ways, it becomes a little easier to determine which is early and which is late. This can be accomplished by observing the shape of the grips, the type action, the configuration of the butt plate on rifles and in several other ways that will be covered in the book.

Another case in point is that most Allen & Wheelock guns have steel grip escut-cheons up to a little over halfway through production and brass after that.

Regardless, it is not the author's primary goal to necessarily determine which came first, the chicken or the egg, but rather to point out the differences of the many models and variations of the guns produced by Allen & Wheelock.

As some of the different models of guns manufactured by Allen & Wheelock are identical except for size, you will notice that the photos of the pistols are in front of a grid of one-inch squares for size reference. However, this system was not practical for the long arms.

All guns, pictures and advertisements that are not credited to another collector or institution are from the author's collection.

ACKNOWLEDGEMENTS

To personally acknowledge everyone who has contributed to this book would be impossible, as so many have been helpful over the many years of collecting bits of data, pieces of information and the guns themselves.

I have never laid claim to being an author, but with the help of many very good friends and my family, I offer these writings as my contribution and appreciation to the gun collecting world for the countless hours of enjoyment that I have spent at gun shows enjoying the wonderful world of gun collecting.

I consider these writings as a continuation of the book *The Story of Allen & Wheelock Firearms* written by my dear friend and fellow collector Mr. H. H. Thomas in 1965. Mr. Thomas made the gun collecting world aware of the Allen & Wheelock arms that so little was known about previously.

Although he has been gone for many years, I will be forever grateful to the late Sam Smith who was instrumental in convincing me to collect Allen & Wheelock firearms and who put me in touch with other Allen collectors.

I cannot say enough about the special help that I received from my good friends Les Bassinger, Bart Richards and Norm Szymonik. None of this would have been possible without their help and I will never forget it.

I would also like to give special thanks to Rick Sullivan and Nancy MacLean, who are descendants of both Thomas P. Wheelock and William Onion for sharing so much family information with me that was previously unknown.

To Piet Broekzitter, Ken Budny, Tom Carter, Johann Freundorfer, Perry Hansen, Frank Harrington, Pete Kiefert, Dick Littlefield, John Matson, Les Miller, Lee Norris, Nick Penachino, Billy Puckett, Richard Rosenburger, Doug Stack, Bud Stock, Phil Van Cleave, Jas Van Driel, Paul Wellborn and Chuck Worman, who have helped make gun collecting such an enjoyable part of my life, I thank you all.

A special thanks to the great people at the Worcester Historical Museum who spent many hours going through their records looking for every shred of information available.

In addition, I would like to give extra thanks to my wife Inga, daughter Paula and my friend Roger Muckerheide for the many hours they spent helping me with these writings.

Finally, yet importantly, a very special thanks to Frank and Karen Sellers for their help. Frank has taken many precious hours away from his busy work schedule to further edit and share his vast knowledge of gun collecting with this author. The amount of information he has added to this book is outstanding and demonstrates his unselfish commitment to the great hobby of gun collecting and I will forever be grateful.

To the many others that I have neglected to mention by name who have helped me in my years of collecting, I thank you very much.

I can think of no other hobby that has been as rewarding and fulfilling as gun collecting. Of the many hundreds of individuals that I have encountered in the 37 years that I have enjoyed this great hobby, I can count on one hand the ones that I can not consider my friends or that I regret knowing.

I am of the old school and believe that a picture is worth a thousand words, so I will keep the text as short as possible and hope the pictures will tell the story.

PAUL HENRY

ETHAN ALLEN, SEPT 2, 1806 – JAN 7, 1871

Meet the Boss. In 1831, Ethan Allen started his first business in Milford, Massachusetts, making cutlery tools for the shoe making industry. This picture was apparently taken after 1847.

THOMAS P. WHEELOCK, OCTOBER 5, 1813 – MAY 21, 1864

After nearly 30 years of searching for a photo of Thomas Wheelock, the late Herb Peck Jr., better known as "The Professor," gave this picture to the author a few weeks before he died. The signature in the lower left of the photo is actually that of T.P. Wheelock, but the name that is scratched on the back of the photo is T. Wheelock. As no other pictures of him have surfaced, it cannot definitely be confirmed that this is actually Thomas P. Wheelock.

TABLE OF CONTENTS

Chapter 1
HISTORY

Ethan Allen was born to Nathaniel Allen[1] and Lucy Daniels on September 2, 1806, in Bellingham, Massachusetts. Little is known about Allen's early years but it is assumed that he led a normal childhood with his parents and four sisters. At some time in his youth, the family returned to his father's origin in Medway, about five miles down the Charles River. The map below shows the location of the many towns involved in Allen's life.

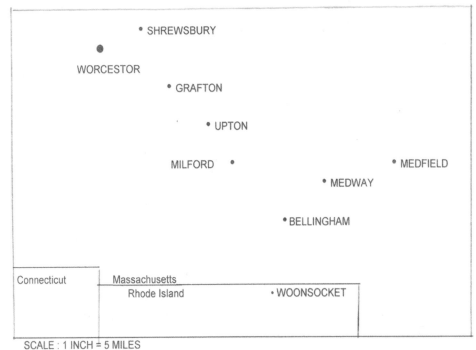

SCALE : 1 INCH = 5 MILES

This map is of Ethan Allen's manufacturing life. Except for his brief appearance in Norwich, Connecticut, fifty miles to the southwest from Worcester, all of Ethan Allen's cutlery, guns, cartridges and other manufactured articles were made within this thirty mile circle in south central Massachusetts.

Bellingham was a farming community across the border from Woonsocket, Rhode Island, a manufacturing town. Another family that lived in the area was that of the brothers Benjamin and Barton Darling. The Darlings had owned land on the Bellingham/Woonsocket border since early Colonial times. Aside from farming, they also manufactured rotary pumps, valves, sluices and other iron items, including their patented pepperbox pistols. It is quite possible that Allen spent some of his younger years around their small factory, as he had to learn his future trade somewhere. It would be too much of a coincidence that he later made a similar product if there had not been some contact. The Darling brothers patented their pepperbox on April 13, 1836, a little over a year and a half before Allen was granted his first patent on November 11, 1837.

1.Harold Mouillesseaux, *ETHAN ALLEN, GUNMAKER*, p. 1, speculated that his name was Nethaniel and Ethan was a shortened form, but there are examples of his using the normal spelling. Hereafter cited as *Mouillesseaux.*

Allen's first known business venture was in Milford, Massachusetts, around 1831, where he was involved in the manufacture of cutlery and tools for the shoe making industry. Milford was a mill or manufacturing town about five miles above Bellingham and the same distance west of Medway. The fact that his brother-in-law Charles Thurber had a substantial home in that town, with outbuildings suitable for making the products that Allen was making, was probably not an accident. Perhaps Thurber was involved in Allen's business sooner than we have previously thought.

Allen married Mary Harrington of Shrewsbury, a town north and west of Millbury. Allen was listed as a resident of Medway on the marriage license, which was recorded in Shrewsbury May 31, 1831. This could probably be evidence that Allen was not established well enough on his own and was still living at home when he got married. There has been no evidence presented for the date of the move, but it is generally accepted that Allen moved his factory to Grafton about 1836. On February 8, 1837, the following advertisements appeared in the *Worcester Palladium.*

WANTED,
A MAN with a SMALL FAMILY, to take charge of a Boarding House;—Also, on the 1st of April next, a number of *Gunsmiths,* or *Machinists,* to work at the manufacture of *Pocket Rifles.* Liberal wages will be given, and references as to good moral character required. Enquire of E. ALLEN, New England Village, or at this Office.
Feb. 8, 1837.   3t

Wanted,
ON the 1st of April next, a number of GUNSMITHS, or MACHINISTS, to work at the manufacture of *Pocket Rifles.* Liberal wages will be given, and references as to good moral character required.
Enquire of E. ALLEN, New England Village, or at THIS OFFICE.
Feb. 8, 1837.   tf

At the time of the move, Allen's address was shown as New England Village. This name was given to the industrial area in Grafton but did not survive long. All of the surviving guns, long and short, carry the name Grafton if they have Allen's name on them. Shortly after Allen moved to the Grafton area, Charles Thurber quit teaching at the Milton Academy and also moved to Grafton.

It has been reported previously that Allen's first product in the firearms line was the Lambert cane rifle, which was made about 1835 as a sideline to his modest cutlery tool business. This gun was invented by Dr. Roger Lambert of Upton, Massachusetts, only a few miles up the road from Milford on the way to Shrewsbury. These guns are reasonably well made and were certainly within the capabilities of Allen, but no evidence has been discovered to show that he actually made them.

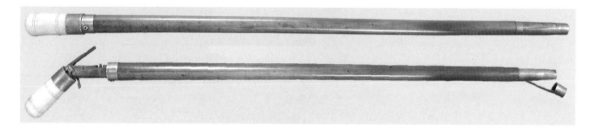

This Lambert Cane gun shown above has a 30 inch 44 caliber barrel, a red stained wood cover and an ivory knob. To operate, the handle is pulled back, which moves the mechanism into firing position. It also pulls the barrel back, releasing the spring loaded tip or cover at the front end to clear the muzzle. Bending the handle downwards forms the pistol grip, cocks the hammer and lowers the folding trigger. Note the flat hammer which was later used by Allen on his pepperboxes and single shot pistols. Frank Sellers collection.

After moving to Grafton, Allen began the manufacture of an underhammer single shot percussion pistol with a saw handle grip that he called his undercock pocket rifle. This style of pistol, often called a boot pistol, was very popular in New England and was made by many of the smaller gun makers who worked there. They also proved to be popular in larger cities and many dealers ordered them in quantity from Allen. There was no patent on this form of pistol as all of its features had been in common use for many years. As Hershel Logan pointed out in his book *Underhammer Guns,* this form was known in the early eighteenth century and possibly earlier. Allen made his underhammer pocket rifle in a variety of calibers and barrel lengths.

In 1837, Allen was doing well enough to form a partnership with one of his brothers-in-law and formed the company of Allen & Thurber. As mentioned above, Thurber was not primarily interested in the gun making end of the business. He was educated in the fine arts and was a poet of some note. He was also a schoolteacher, but showed some interest in the mechanical fields by inventing what he called a "writing machine" to assist the handicapped in writing. (See below.) This form of a typewriter was very early and not many were made, but a few can be seen in New England museums.

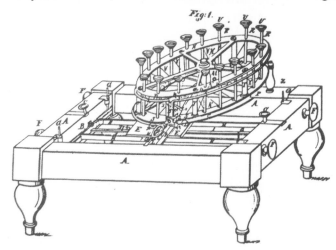

Shown above is U.S. patent number 3,228 issued August 26, 1843 to Charles Thurber for his writing machine. It was intended as an aid for the handicapped and was 30 years ahead of the first typewriter. Only a few were made.

With new blood and probably new money, Allen & Thurber developed an entirely new line of products but Allen's original pocket rifle continued to be made under his own name. The new line of firearms included a single shot pistol based on Allen's first patent, number 461 of November 1837, called the tube hammer by today's collectors, a variety of pepperboxes using the same cocking mechanism and a few long guns.

Late in the Grafton period, they started making a new style under-hammer pistol that was also referred to as a pocket rifle, but production was limited.

Another important change in Allen's life after the move to Grafton was the starting of his family. Ethan and Mary had two daughters. Laurette was born March 17, 1838, and Angenette was born August 19, 1840. Both were married in 1860, Laurette to Henry Wadsworth and Angenette to Sullivan Forehand. Both grooms were employed by Allen & Wheelock.

Shortly after the birth of their second daughter, Ethan and Mary decided to go their separate ways. The divorce was not a surprise as there had been difficulties for some time. According to testimony in court, Mary had refused to move into the new house that Allen had purchased in Grafton and there had been some vocal expressions made that widened the gap between them.

4

Notice.

WHEREAS it has become impossible to live with my wife, MARY ALLEN, and I have therefore made ample provision for her support at suitable boarding places; and whereas she may be induced to contract debts under the impression that I will pay for the same—I hereby give notice that I will not hereafter pay any debts of her contracting, or incurred for her support, except such as I may personally contract, and all persons are cautioned not to trust her on my account.

ETHAN ALLEN.

Grafton, Dec. 16, 1840.   49

Ethan's marriage to his first wife Mary ended in what appears to have been a bitter divorce on December 16, 1840. This is the notice that was published on the front page of the Worcester newspaper called the "*National Aegis*" on January 6, 1841.

Allen's major competitor at that time was Colt, with his five shot, single barreled revolvers. Although not nearly as accurate as the Colt, Allen's pepperbox offered six quick shots and cost one fourth as much. In 1841, when Colt's Patent Arms Manufacturing Co. went into receivership, it gave Allen a virtual monopoly on American-made multi-shot weapons. In 1842, the company moved to Norwich, Connecticut to take advantage of the plentiful labor market. Although pepperbox and single shot bar hammer pistol production was increased, only a very few long arms were produced at Norwich.

Thomas Prentice Wheelock was born October 5, 1813, to Gershom Wheelock of Medfield, Massachusetts and his second wife, Priscilla Mason. Gershom's first wife, Abigail Adams, was the mother of his first son Nathan. She did not survive the birth of their second child, a daughter, who also did not survive. Priscilla was the mother of his remaining seven children: Eleazar, Abigail, Mary, Thomas, Sally, Amos and Sarah. Several of Thomas' siblings became involved with the various Allen companies. This will be covered in some detail in the next chapter.

On October 26, 1839, Thomas Wheelock and Ethan Allen's sister, Mary, filed their intention to marry in the city of Grafton. Mary's middle name, Adams, shows the connection that both families had with the Adams family, one of the most famous families in Massachusetts. The three children that resulted from that union were Ellen Augusta, Charles Prentice and Mary Kate. On July 30, 1847, Charles Prentice, the 26 month old son of Thomas and Mary Wheelock, died. He was their only son.

Another result of the move to Norwich was Allen's second marriage. He married Sarah Johnson of Norwich on June 12, 1843. It was the second marriage for both. Two children were also born into their marriage. Helen, his third daughter, was born May 12, 1849, and William Ethan, his only son, was born November 22, 1856. Both were born after Allen & Thurber moved back to Massachusetts, this time to Worcester, a few miles northwest of Grafton. Helen married John Marble, a prominent Worcester physician, on April 8, 1873. William Ethan never married and it appears that he was never involved in any of Allen's various companies. He died of Bright's disease in 1893.

The entry for July 6, 1847 in the Allen & Thurber day book simply had the word Worcester next to the date, and the absence of any entries for four days is the only clue that the company had moved from Norwich, Connecticut to Worcester, Massachusetts where production would eventually be greatly increased. City of Worcester records show that the company set up shop in the Merrifield industrial complex at Union Street.

The product line at Worcester was considerably different than it was at Norwich. Several of the pepperboxes were eliminated and a new single shot pistol, designated as the No. 6 rifled pistol, was added. This pistol had a shotgun-type spur hammer that was easy to cock and fire, making it a more accurate pistol, and it cost a fraction of Allen's special order target pistols. It also appears that Allen's undercock pocket rifles were eliminated from production.

Total sales for the first quarter at Worcester showed a drop of less than 10% from previous quarters. This is an amazing number considering that several days were lost in moving the factory fifty miles and setting up new work facilities in Worcester. Part of the sales were undoubtedly made up by sales of pistols that had been made at Norwich as many of the early Worcester pistols are identical to the same pistols made in Norwich, only marked differently

On June 14, 1854, the Merrifield industrial complex where Allen, Thurber & Co had set up their factory burned to the ground, putting them and other manufactures that had been located there out of business. By the end of the year, however, Allen, Thurber & Co had built a new factory at what was called "The Junction." This is probably the same property they had purchased in 1854 on Lagrange Street. The 1855 Worcester street map shows that Lagrange was a short street that was located on the south edge of town and ran between Main and Beacon streets.

FIRE ARMS MANUFACTORY, FOREHAND & WADSWORTH, WORCESTER, MASS.

Although the company name on the building says Forehand & Wadsworth, this is the same factory that Allen built in 1854 after the fire destroyed his original factory at the Merrifield complex and is the same facility that the firm of Allen & Wheelock occupied from 1856 to 1864.

The new factory consisted of three buildings: a small two story office building, a three story factory building and a single story forge building. This last building was separated from the others, as the fires and hot metal made there were a definite hazard for the period and probably was the cause of the Merrifield fire. This new factory is shown above as it appeared after Allen's death.

It is not known exactly when longtime employee and an another of Allen's brother-in-laws, Thomas P. Wheelock, became a partner in the company, but a letter from Lane & Reed that was addressed to Allen, Thurber & Co. was dated April 1, 1854.[2] (Wheelock was the "& Co") This is the earliest known evidence that Thomas Wheelock was actually a full partner in the company and places the beginning of their partnership sometime between January 1 and April 1, 1854.

After moving into their new factory, the company not only continued with their tried and true line of single shot pistols and six shot pepperboxes, but also brought online a new, smaller five shot pepperbox that was obviously very popular. It was made during the rest of the Allen, Thurber & Co period and into the Allen & Wheelock era before any changes was made to the pistol. Long arms production, which had been nearly nonexistent at Grafton and Norwich, increased with a variety of field grade rifles, shotguns and a few high quality target rifles.

William H. Onion was the son of Allen's sister, Clarissa and her husband, Leonard Onion. He was born on April 4, 1826 and was seven when his father died in 1833. In 1840, Clarissa and her family were living with Allen in Grafton. In 1850, Clarissa and her daughter were living with the Allens in Worcester.

Although William worked at the Allen factory, there is no indication that he was ever classified as an apprentice. Payroll records show that in December of 1846, he had worked a total of 75-3/8 days in the last quarter of the year, but no payment was shown. On March 30, 1847, two days before his 21st birthday, he was paid $94.68 for 71.5 days work or slightly more than $1.30 per day. On the first payroll at Worcester, his wage had increased to $1.50 per day and he received $109 for 73 days work. On the same day, he received a bonus payment of $18.25 with the explanation of "25 cents extra for 73 days work." Before his first paycheck, there would be periodic entries in the day book for $10.00 to $20.00 cash payments made out to him with no explanation.

In 1850, William Onion established an importing business at 99 Maiden Lane in New York City. William was only 24 years old at that time, so it is certain that Allen put up the money for him to open the business and appointed Thomas Wheelock to help him get the business going. Since the A.W. Spies hardware store was located at 91 Maiden Lane and carried a full line of Allen's products, one has to wonder if there was some kind of a feud going on for Allen to open a business just a few doors down from Spies, one of Allen's best customers.

The 1851-52 Trow's New York City directory listed William Onion as an importer at 99 Maiden Lane. The same issue listed Thomas Wheelock as an importer at 9 Maiden Lane. The address was surely meant to be 99 Maiden Lane as the 1852-53 directory, listed them together as Onion & Wheelock, Importers. Wheelock's residence was listed as 44 Barclay Street and Onion's residence at 17 Barclay Street.

In 1856-57, the same directory listed Onion & Wheelock, as *"manufactures & importers of guns, rifles & pistols, sportsmen's cutlery, gun material & sporting apparatus, 99 Maiden Lane. Depot for fire arms, etc. manufactured by Allen & Wheelock."* The business of Onion & Wheelock would occupy the 99 Maiden Lane address until moving to 366 Broadway in the early 1860s and would remain there until 1864, the year that Wheelock died.

---

2. *Mouillesseaux,* p. 108.

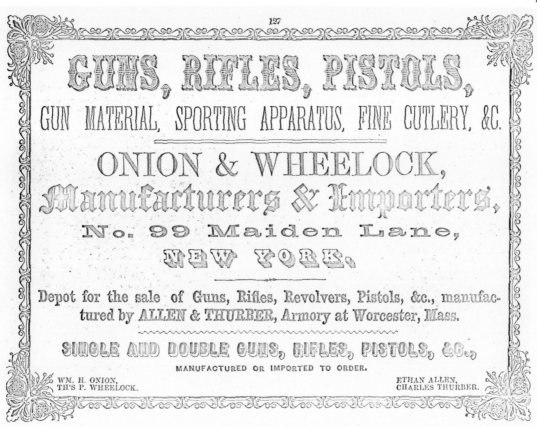

This early Onion & Wheelock advertisement shows they were the depot for ALLEN & THURBER. This dates the ad sometime before 1854. It appears that there was a four way partnership between Onion, Wheelock, Allen and Thurber at that time.

186   GUNS, RIFLES, PISTOLS,

GUN MATERIAL, SPORTING APPARATUS, &c. &c.

Onion & Wheelock,

MANUFACTURERS & IMPORTERS,

99 MAIDEN LANE, NEW YORK.

Depot for the Sale of Guns, Rifles, Pistols, &c. manufactured by ALLEN, THURBER & Co., Armory at Worcester, Mass.

GUNS, RIFLES, PISTOLS, &c. &c.,

Wm. H. Onion.   } Ethan Allen.
T. P. Wheelock. }   Manufactured or Imported to order.   { Charles Thurber.

This is a later Onion & Wheelock advertisement than the preceding one. The address is the same but they were now depot for ALLEN, THURBER & Co. This dates the ad between 1854 and 1856, as those were the only two years that the company was known by that name.

After 1853, the directories show Wheelock's residence as Massachusetts, indicating that he had returned to Worcester either when Onion was able to take care of the store by himself or he was called back by Allen to help at the factory. It is obvious that Charles Thurber was not contributing much to the operation of the company as he had become deeply involved in other ventures. In 1853, he was director of the City Bank of Worcester, a County Commissioner, a Trustee of Brown University and had been chosen to replace State Senator John S. Knowlton who had resigned. To add to his very busy life, his wife, Lucinda (Allen's sister), had died a year earlier in 1852. On March 1, 1853, he married Caroline E. Bennett, the widow of Reverend Joseph Bennett. With all of the activity in Thurber's life, there was little time left for him to contribute much, if anything, to his company. In 1856, Charles Thurber retired and the company became Allen & Wheelock. Thurber died in 1886 at the age of 83.

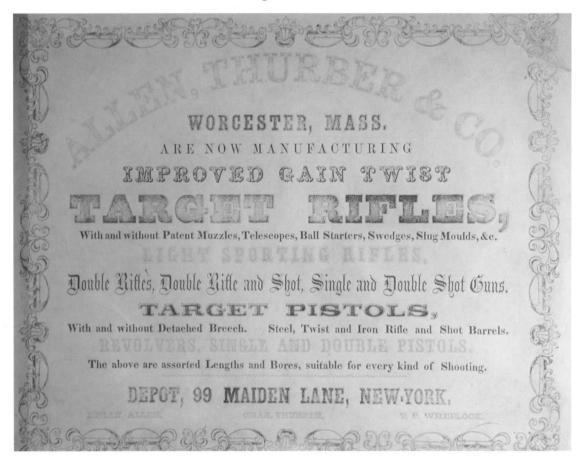

This advertisement for the period of 1854 to 1856, boasts that Allen, Thurber & Co were manufacturing improved gain twist target rifles, with and without patent muzzles, telescopes, ball starters, swedges, slug molds, light sporting rifles, double rifles, double rifles and shot, single and double shot guns, target pistols with and without detached breech, steel, twist and iron rifle and shot barrels, revolvers, single and double pistols in assorted lengths and bores that were suitable for every kind of shooting.

The Allen, Thurber & Co poster shown above shows that their "DEPOT" was at 99 Maiden Lane, the same as the directory ad shown on the preceding page. This suggests that the poster was intended for distribution in the New York City area, as anyone beyond that could write to Worcester just as easily.

It is obvious that Ethan Allen was a very successful businessman. In 1850, he owned property amounting to $60,000 and by 1860 that had increased to $150,000 in real estate and $50,000 in personal estate. In 1870, his worth had increased to $200,000 in real estate and $70,000 in personal property. The census reports for those years also show that he always had two domestics working for him but never the same two.

Allen bought his first home in Worcester in 1847. It was originally built by Levi Dowley in 1842 when the address was shown as 770 Mail Street. In 1853, the address became 322 Main Street. American Antiquarian Society photo.

Allen's second and last home that was built on Murray Avenue in Worcester. After Allen's second wife Sarah died in 1896, their daughter Helen and her husband, Dr. John Marble, would inherit the home. From F.P. Rice's book *The Worcester of 1898.*

Beside his great success as a gun manufacturer, Allen had formed a very successful cartridge making business and had designed and patented new machinery that was superior to anything else that was available at that time.

In 1859, a former Allen employee, Horace Smith, and his company Smith & Wesson, brought a lawsuit against Allen & Wheelock for infringing on Rollin White's patent for the bored through cylinder. Among the claims by the plaintiff's lawyers over the course of the trial was that Allen & Wheelock had illegally manufactured and sold 25,000 cartridge revolvers over a four-year period starting in 1858. As Allen's lawyers did not dispute their claim, the number was probably much higher and production more than likely started before 1858. The suit was based on 1858 as that was the year Smith & Wesson purchased the rights to use White's 1855 patent.

On November 12, 1863, after almost four years in and out of court, an injunction banning Allen & Wheelock from the manufacture and sale of all revolving cylinder arms with chambers bored through was handed down. The injunction did not include single shot cartridge rifles, pistols or percussion revolvers, and their production continued.

On May 21, 1864, Thomas Wheelock died at the age of 51 from apoplexy. He was buried in the Allen section of Rural Cemetery in Worcester.

In 1865, Allen formed E. Allen & Co., to include his two sons-in-law, Sullivan Forehand and Henry Wadsworth. This company lasted until Allen's death on January 7, 1871, when the company was reformed as Forehand & Wadsworth. They remained partners until Wadsworth's death in 1890. The company name was then changed to Forehand Arms Co., which would last beyond his death on June 7, 1898, until his heirs sold the name and stock on hand to Hopkins & Allen in 1902. They continued to use the name until the stock was gone. Hopkins & Allen was one of the gun making companies formed by former employees of Allen.

In 1858, Charles W. Hopkins, Samuel S. Hopkins and Charles W. Allen founded their company to take advantage of the expiration of Colt's patent. Between 1847, when Allen left Norwich, and the formation of their own company, they probably worked with Thomas Bacon, another former Allen employee that had started his own company after Allen & Thurber moved to Worcester.

The eight years that he and Ethan Allen were partners in the firm of Allen & Wheelock were Allen's most productive. Eighteen of his twenty-five patents and all of his reissues were granted during this period. Two more patents were issued the same year that Wheelock died. Although Thomas Wheelock had been an important employee for over 20 years, his name does not appear on any of the patents.

William Onion had learned his trade well and after Wheelock and Allen had both died, he founded the company of Onion, Haigh & Cornwall, but only Cornwall would be listed as his business partner in later years.

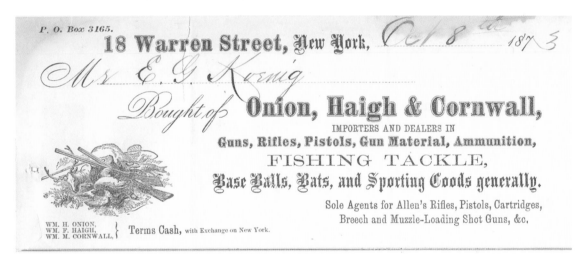

This Onion, Haigh & Cornwall letterhead dated Oct 8, 1873, shows them as sole agents for Allen's Rifles, Pistols Cartridges, Breech and Muzzle-Loading Shot Guns & etc. In later years, the name was changed to Onion & Cornwall. It is not known what became of Haigh but the business stayed at the same address as late as 1977. William Onion died November 1, 1895 at age 69.

In 1865, William H. Onion's Son, Leonard William Onion, married Marion Abbott, the granddaughter of Thomas Wheelock (Ellen Augusta Wheelock's daughter). They had four sons who would become the first four brothers in America to become Eagle Scouts. In May of 1920, the Onion family legally changed their name to Allen, thus assuring that the relationship of Ethan Allen & Thomas Wheelock would be united forever.[3]

---

3. This information is courtesy of Rick Sullivan and Nancy MacLean, who are decedents of Thomas P. Wheelock and William H. Onion.

Chapter 2
THE DAY BOOK

Although this book was referred to earlier as THE Day Book, it has now been identified as the fifth in a series of Day Books. It is marked on the first page as "E / Allen & / Thurber / Norwich / Conn" in five lines. A verification of this is found on the first page, shown below, where an entry refers to "from Old Day Book, p. 436." The series probably started in Norwich but could have covered Grafton as well.

Day Book E, which we will continue to refer to as "the Day Book" was a standard leather bound ledger 12 and three quarters inches tall and eight inches wide. It originally contained 700 pages but the pages from 470 to 575 have been cut out with a razor, leaving only a small segment of each page along the bottom of the spine.[1] The last 124 pages were blank. This book covered the daily operation of Allen & Thurber from October 1, 1846, to March 16, 1848, and has an interesting history.

In April 1924, Allen's mansion on Murray Avenue in Worcester was torn down to make way for an apartment building. Among the items discarded were all of the papers, memorabilia, etc. abandoned by previous generations. Only one tattered Day Book is known to have survived and the other years of Allen's history have been lost.

Through a series of events, the Day Book eventually found its way into the hands of Harley J. Van Cleave and his son Philip, pioneer Allen Collectors. The Van Cleaves published an article titled *"Gleenings from the Allen & Thurber Day book"* that briefly describes the contents of the Day Book.[2] This was the first time in nearly one hundred years that actual facts and figures on the company's daily business records had been reported. It gave the collector and historian a glimpse of the internal workings of Allen & Thurber as well as how this very successful business carried on its daily activities, and reveals who some of the company's employees, suppliers and subcontractors were. More importantly, it reveals the importance of Thomas Wheelock and how he fit into the company long before he became a partner.

Thomas Wheelock's name was first mentioned in Day Book E on October 1, 1846, the first day the Day Book covers. The third entry for that day was a payment to Wheelock for the amount of $11.36

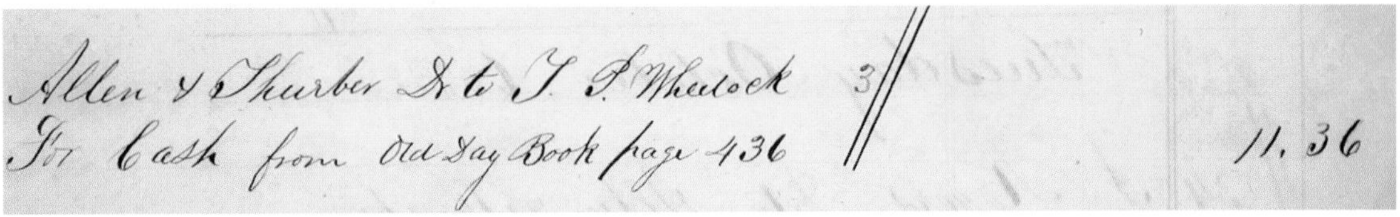

Above is the third entry from the Allen & Thurber Day Book on October 1, 1846 showing that T. P. Wheelock was paid $11.36 for items from the previous Day Book.

There is hardly a page that does not have at least one entry concerning Wheelock. Most of the transactions were cash returns for the purchase of miscellaneous items that were mostly connected to the business part rather than the manufacturing part of the company. It can be said with certainty that Thomas Wheelock was a very important part

---

1. This should be p.469, but there is a duplicate p.292, throwing the succeeding pages off by one.
2. *Hobbies,* January, 1940, p.103.

of the company and had more to do with the daily operations of the company than either Allen or Thurber. Company documents from the early 1840s have been seen with Wheelock's signature on them.

Besides the information regarding the sales, purchases, pay rolls and general costs, there is also information on the financing of this moderately sized business in the first half of the nineteenth century. Among the thousands of entries, there are many that cannot be related to the business a hundred and fifty years later. A trained accountant could probably put some items in place, but it really doesn't matter today. Costs and profits tell us what we need to know even if they are not item specific. Two such items were entries dated November 14 and 16, 1846, which seemed to be accounts paid to Charles Thurber in the amount of $912.69 and to Ethan Allen for $1,843.52. It was speculated that these were profit payments and probably represented the irrelative shares of the business. A careful reading of the entries showed that they were not actual payments but a balancing of what had been paid for by Allen & Thurber that were actually individual debts of the two men.

Although the Day Book precedes the Allen & Wheelock era by some eight years, there is so much valuable information that relates to Allen, Thurber, Wheelock and so many others that it would be unjust not to include some of that information in these writings. Of special importance is that it covers the company's last nine months of operation at Norwich, Connecticut, and their first eight and a half months of operations at Worcester, Massachusetts.

After spending a little time with the Day Book, it becomes apparent that previous estimates of sparse production at the Norwich factory were far from correct. During the period at Norwich covered by the Day Book, they sold 5,484 pepperboxes and 577 pairs of single shot pistols or a total of 6,898 pistols, an average of 782 pistols per month. This included 155 pairs of Ethan Allen's undercock pocket rifles, which were credited to Allen's account rather than Allen & Thurber's.

How did they make that many pistols? They had a factory with many employees and a series of independent workers or contractors who furnished parts or did specific jobs on specific guns. The easiest item to figure was the employees. From the payroll, we know how much each employee was making, but not necessarily what he was doing.

Payday was quarterly, falling on the last day of March, June, September and December. The work week was Monday through Saturday with Sunday being the only day off. Work continued through Christmas, New Year's Day and all the other holidays we have today if the fell on a weekday. The first payday in the Day Book was 31 December, 1846, and covered work done in October, November and December. There were fourteen people on the first payroll. The chart on the following page shows how many days each employee worked during the quarter, how much they were paid per day and a total of their quarterly pay. The following quarters only show the total pay, as that is the only figure germane to calculating the overhead of the factory. Generally, they seem to have been loyal employees and all but one worked the entire period covered in this Day Book while the company remained in Norwich, and half of them made the move from Norwich to Worcester with the company.

NAME	DAILY WAGE	DAYS WORKED	DEC 1846	MAR 1847	JUNE 1847	SEPT 1847	DEC 1847
Thomas Wheelock	$2.00	78	$156.00	$142.00	$154.00	$150.00	$171.00
George Stewart*	1.41	65 7/8	93.36	88.56	108.18	89.16	48.75
Fred Allen*	1.33	(1)	40.50	29.33	56.63	78.67	145.89
Charles Worthington	1.25	70	87.50	94.84	88.75	96.00	100.87
Jonas Greenwood	1.00	70 5/8	77.72	77.17	74.37	(2)	35.25
William Onion	---	75.3/8	(3)	94.68	111.00	109.50	133.00
Horace Smith	2.00	62-1/2	125.00	---	---	---	---
Henry Hopkins	1.66	58 5/8	97.14	105.75	115.92	64.53	---
John C. Howe	1.57	36 6/8	57.87	94.12	17.25	---	---
Dennison Geer (4)	1.50	39	58.50	33.75	14.81	---	---
Thomas Bacon*	1.50	27 1/8	41.76	89.64	14.80	---	---
Charles Allen	1.42	58 5/8	85.06	85.54	56.63	---	---
Norman Wales	1.00	47 5/8	47.62	71.75	53.62	---	---
A. S. Benchley	1.50	---	---	3.93	---	28.63	---
John P. Holmes	1.33	---	---	4.00	---	53.96	93.00
Alonzo Howe (5)	1.25	---	---	---	76.25	10.00	---
E. F. Farewell (6)	1.61	---	---	---	---	58.33	102.91
Samuel Waters	1.00	---	---	---	---	21.00	75.00
Theo Mayo (7)	1.00	---	---	---	---	16.83	78.13
M. M. Hall	1.50	---	---	---	---	66.10	116.48
S. Arnold Whipple	1.50	---	---	---	---	---	36.00
J. W. Albee	1.64	---	---	---	---	---	49.17
Pat Butler	.84	---	---	---	---	---	44.36
Joel Bolster (8)	.50	---	---	---	---	---	46.00

*   These people also furnished parts or worked part time for hourly wages.

1.   Fred Allen was paid on an hourly basis, the daily rate estimated. He also picked up paychecks for a number of subcontractors.
2.   Not listed on the payroll but cashed a check for $40.69.
3.   Onion was not on the payroll even though he worked 75 3/8 days.
4.   Also Gees, Gies, etc.
5.   His job was bluing barrels. One of the few whose actual job is known.
6.   Paid for 36 days, 8 hours on 7 March, possibly his last day.
7.   Theo was terminated in January after they deducted $5.00 from his pay for using their tools.
8.   Joel was the first night watchman to appear as such on the payroll.

The next group of people involved in the manufacture of Allen & Thurber pistols are the individual contractors, those who did a specific job on a piece work basis, so much for each item done. These are divided into the type of work they did.

FITTERS: (Assembled parts and were paid 88¢ to $1.00 for pepperboxes and 75¢ per pair of single shot pistols.) Oliver Beckwith (75¢), H. W. Beckwith (88¢), H. B. Benchley (88¢), J. W. Benchley (88¢ to 95¢), L. H. Carey (88¢), E. C. Hall (89¢), E. H. Hall (88¢), Nathan S. Harrington (75¢ to 88¢), J. C. Howe (88¢), E. H. Hall (88¢) William H. Jewel (88¢ to $1.00), Alexander Stocking (89¢), G. H. Wright (88¢) and G. W. Wright (88¢).

POLISHER: Charles H. Allen was paid 16¢ per pepperbox or pair of single shot pistols and 14¢ per flask.

14

STOCKER: Amos Wheelock, Thomas' younger brother, made grips for 16¢ per pepperbox or pair of single shot pistols.

ENGRAVERS: George H. Martin, J. Walter Martin and C. D. Hedge did the engraving for an average of 12¢ per large pistol and 8¢ for small pistols.

HARDENER: Fred Allen.

The supplies of individual parts to go to the fitters are arranged in two categories, large parts and small parts.

LARGE PARTS; BARRELS: Edwin Prescott borrowed $100 from Allen & Thurber at 6% interest on 30 October, 1846, and shortly began furnishing barrels at 50¢ for 4 inch, 60¢ for 5 inch and 80¢ for 6 inch. This continued until December of 1847. On February 5, 1848, he was paid $10.27 for 6 1/2 days work, his last appearance in the Day Book. A. S. Benchley, later Benchley & Hopkins, started furnishing single shot barrels the same time as Prescott started the pepperbox barrels. The price for single shot barrels was 7.5¢ for 2 inch, 9.5¢ for three inch, 12¢ for 4 inch, 15¢ for 5 inch and 18¢ for 6 inch. In November 1847, Benchley and Hopkins undercut Prescott's pepperbox barrel prices to 42¢ for 4 inch, 50¢ for 5 inch, 60¢ for 6 inch and by the end of the year, Prescott was no longer furnishing barrels. As an interesting sidelight, both were paid for the barrels that blew up in testing!

SMALL PARTS: (All other parts, see chart on following page for prices.) Fred Allen, Thomas Bacon, A.S. Benchley, Benchley & Hopkins and J.G. Loomes furnished thousands of parts for pennies. Among the smalls, are the mysterious items. "Cones" were sold to Allen & Thurber for 16 2/3¢ each by Prescott and Benchley & Hopkins while at the same time Fred Allen was selling them for just over 2¢ and Thomas Bacon was selling them for 2 1/2¢. What were they? Norwich pepperboxes had integral nipples so the immediate thought is out. Perhaps they were nipple shields? J.C. Howe delivered "bands" for 2¢ each. What were they? Joel Dewing, Thomas Wheelock's brother-in-law delivered thousands of "knobs" at a penny each. Ends for cleaning rods? Cases were furnished by J. Rogers at 37.5¢ each or $4.50 per dozen. Molds were made by Joel Dewing for 11¢ and 12¢, and flasks by A.S. Benchley for 25¢ and George Stewart for 20¢.

The only recognizable components delivered by outside suppliers were "briches" which were delivered at 16¢ per pound. These presumably are breeches or frames for the various pistols. The smaller frames would be cheaper as they would weigh less. Unidentified "castings" were delivered regularly but only one large delivery of steel, just under ten tons, was made during the period covered by the Day Book. Items such as files, vises, wheelbarrows, lamps, stoves are all covered and must be included in overhead along with rent, power and repairs. Consumables such as gun powder, oil, alcohol, vitriol, dragon's blood, soap, coal, ink, old shoes, rags, potash, bones appeared regularly. There was even an entry for a container of urine.

All of this allows us to calculate the approximate cost of the pistols produced. The following chart will show the cost for both the most popular pepperbox, the No. 2 with 4 inch barrel (Norwich standard) and the No. 9 pistols with 2 inch barrel. (Muff pistol)

| | PARTS COST | | | LABOR COST | |
	PEPPERBOX (EACH)	No. 9 PISTOLS (PER PAIR)		PEPPERBOX (EACH)	No. 9 PISTOLS (PER PAIR)
Barrel	50¢	15¢	Fitting	88¢	75¢
Frame	33¢	20¢	Stocking	16¢	16¢
Hammer	5¢	2¢	Polishing	16¢	16¢
Trigger	4¢	2¢	Engraving	12¢	8¢
Trigger guard	4¢	2¢			
Springs	6¢	5¢		OVERHEAD	
Screws	3¢	3¢	Payroll	50¢	35¢
Spangles	.002¢	.002¢	Supplies	45¢	30¢
Mainspring link	1¢	1¢	Rent	45¢	30¢
Lever	3¢	3¢	Misc.	35¢	25¢
Escutcheons	1¢	1¢	Total Cost	$4.162	$2.892

The chart above shows a breakdown of the cost to make a standard Norwich pepperbox with four inch barrel and a pair of No. 9 bar hammer single shot pistols with two inch barrel.

These costs could vary slightly due to a different combination of parts, finish, type of grips or even the weather, but at even a sizable increase, it demonstrated that Ethan Allen could make a profit selling his undercock pistols at $4.00 per pair. It is obvious that Allen & Thurber were making substantial profits selling small single shot bar hammer pistols at $5.00 per pair and standard size pepperboxes at $8.00 each.

Over one hundred individual customers bought guns from Allen & Thurber in the period covered by this Day Book. Some only bought one or two but most bought in quantity. The top ten customers bought over half of the production.

MAJOR DEALERS AND LOCATION	PEPPERBOXES BOUGHT (ALL TYPES)	NO 9. PISTOLS BOUGHT (ALL BARREL SIZES)
William H Smith, Norwich, Ct	1,353	101-1/2*
A.W. Spies, New York	805	59-1/2*
James Eaton, Boston	573	174
Francis Tomes & Son, New York	421	51
Wolf & Gillespie, New York	421	10
J.C. Grubb, Philadelphia	401	51
William Huntington (Location not known)	350	29
Lane & Read, Boston	331	24
John C. Bolen, New York	297	52
E.K. Tryon, Philadelphia	281	18
TOTAL	5,333	601 PAIRS

*Since these pistols were sold in pairs, a half an order is actually one pistol.

The chart above lists only the top ten dealers that are recorded in the year and a half that the Day Book covers. Note that the dealers were located in major markets.

Shown below is a drawing of the parts that are in the standard Worcester six shot Allen pepperbox with the 1845 type action. This is the same as all Allen & Wheelock five and six pepperboxes but differs slightly from the four shot pepperbox.

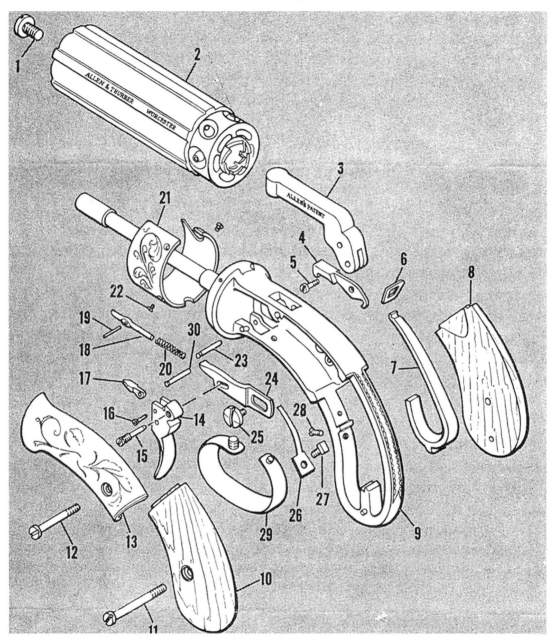

PARTS LEGEND

1. Barrel retaining screw	11. Grip screw	21. Nipple shield
2. Barrel group	12. Side-plate screw	22. Shield screws
3. Hammer	13. Side-plate	23. Trigger pin
4. Sear	14. Trigger	24. Hand
5. Sear screw	15. Hand operating pin	25. Hand retaining screw
6. Mainspring link	16. Barrel latch screw	26. Hand spring
7. Mainspring	17. Barrel latch	27. Spring retaining screw
8. Right grip	18. Detent pin	28. Mainspring tension screw
9. Frame	19. Detent retaining pin	29. Trigger guard
10. Left grip	20. Detent spring	30. Hammer pin

As seen on the invoice, not all pistols were sold at the same price. Some dealers paid $8.00, some $8.25 and some $8.50 for the same pistol. Some dealers received discounts on their purchases, others did not. This was not based on the quantities purchased but on the timeliness of payment. Those who issued sight drafts, (those which would be paid immediately by the bank) received a 3% discount. Those whose accounts were paid within a month usually got no discount but were not charged any interest. Those who took longer than a month were charged from 2 to 5% depending on the period.

On October 22, 1846, the following order to Samuel Sutherland of Richmond, Virginia was entered into the Day Book. This is typical of the way that all orders are recorded in the Day Book.

Shown above is a typical order that has been taken directly from the Day Book. This order was placed on October 22, 1846 at the Norwich factory. The first item consisted of 24 pistols; No. 2-4 inch shows the price at 8-1/4 or $8.25. The No. 2-4 inch pistol was the standard 6 shot pepperbox with nipple shield and four inch barrels. The second item was for 3 of the same only with ivory grips for $10.50 each or $2.25 extra. The next five items are for various standard size pepperboxes and are priced the same. The eighth item is also a Norwich standard but with silver grips that cost $1.25 extra. The next item is for 3 pairs of No. 9-2 inch pistols for $5.25 a pair. The No. 9 pistols were the single shot bar hammer percussion model and the small muff pistol was the only bar hammer with a two inch barrel. The next three guns were also bar hammer single shot pistols with three and four inch barrels. Two molds were included with one of the three inch pistols. The last item consists of 12 molds and the total order was for $316.25.

Ivory and silver grips were available for an extra $1.25 to $2.25. It appears that Allen gave different buyers different prices for the grips but the average charge was $2.00. Quite a few were sold with ivory but not very many with silver. Water buffalo horn grips were also available but only a few were noted in the Day Book.

To this point, most references have been made only to pistols that were made by Allen & Thurber, but the Day Book shows they made and sold other items. Oliver Allen bought 41 "whale guns" for $32 each and 25 molds for them for 75 cents each. Francis Farewell bought a shotgun for $12. Several people, including Horace Smith, bought "ivory rules" for 63 cents each and many of the dealers bought "paper cases" for their pistols. When was the last time you saw a pistol made by Ethan Allen in a cardboard box?

On July 1, 1847, the last day at Norwich, it was business as usual other than the fact that ten of the twenty entries in the Day Book for that day involved various payments to Wheelock for expenses he had incurred including postage, freight, labor payments and rental for a horse and buggy.

The absence of any entries in the Day Book for four days and the name Worcester next to the July 6, 1847 entry was the only indication that the company had moved to Worcester, Massachusetts, where business would continue.

Since early Worcester pepperboxes resemble the late Norwich pepperboxes, with the exception of the markings and a slightly different grip angle, these guns were probably all made in Norwich and marked Worcester. Single shot bar hammer pistols were also made in the Norwich style but did not have grip spangles. Regardless, the company obviously had a good supply of pistols on hand when they arrived at Worcester and sales continued with only a minimum of delay.

The Day Book reveals that quite a few future firearm manufacturers obtained at least part of their gun making and business skills from Allen. The names of Thomas Bacon, (Bacon Firearms Co.) Charles Hopkins, Samuel Hopkins, Charles Allen, (Hopkins & Allen) Horace Smith, (Smith & Wesson) Edwin Prescott, John C. Howe and Alexander Stocking appear in the Day Book. All were either employed by Allen & Thurber or were suppliers or sub-contractors.

This brief review brings to light some of the names from the past that were associated with Allen and helped him form a successful business that would remain in operation under one name or another for over 65 years. Some of the familiar names that were associated with Allen during his early years are still in business today. In 1991, through another series of events, and with the help of some very good friends, the author obtained possession of this rare treasure of early American history. To totally illuminate the contents of the Day Book would be a book in and of itself, so only a few of the highlights are touched upon at this time.

On the right is the Allen & Thurber Day Book number "E." Although it is torn and tattered, it is a treasure chest of valuable information.

Chapter 3
EARLY ALLEN SINGLE SHOT PERCUSSION PISTOLS

Although this book will focus upon the firearms that were manufactured by Ethan Allen and Thomas Wheelock between the years of 1856 and 1864, this chapter provides a short review of the evolution of Allen's single shot percussion pistols before the Allen & Wheelock period. Hopefully, this will give the reader a little more insight of the early years and some to the changes that were made during that period of production.

It is a fact that Ethan Allen's claim to fame is his pepperboxes, but the single shot pistols were where he got his start. After moving to Grafton, Massachusetts, in 1836, Allen's first venture into the pistol market was what he called his "under cock pocket rifle." The underhammer mechanism was extremely popular in New England and were made by over a hundred gunsmiths there. Allen's version featured a saw handle design, which allowed for a longer sighting radius and thus more accuracy than a standard pistol grip stock and were available in barrel lengths from five to ten inches and in calibers from 28 to 44, but all first models were made using the same frame and grip. A thin iron plate covering the whole top of the action was used to carry the maker's information, the retailers information, or both. The one shown below has the typical marking: "E. ALLEN / GRAFTON / MASS" and POCKET RIFLE / CAST STEEL / WARRANTED". The two sets of three line markings were normal but each line was an individual stamp and the markings could vary. Note that the engraving was applied after the marking and partially obscures Allen's name.

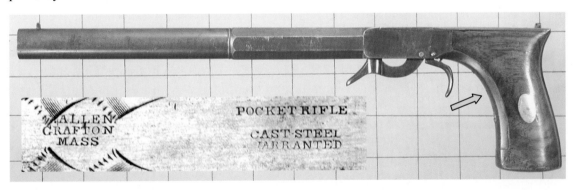

Allen's first signed firearm was a single shot underhammer pistol like the early one pictured above. It has an octagon and round, 32 caliber 8 inch barrel and is marked E. ALLEN / GRAFTON / MASS and POCKET RIFLE / CAST STEEL / WARRANTED on the top strap. (See inset.) Note the thick steel front tang strap that is only used on Allen's first model underhammer pistols. (See arrow.) Number 16, from the Don Greschaw collection. Inset photo of markings is courtesy of James D. Julia Auction Co.

Production of the pocket rifles started in the spring of 1837. One of the legends attached to Allen is the "fact" that New York hardware dealer Adam Spies was so impressed with Allen's creation that he agreed to buy all of the guns that Allen could make for $4.00 a pair. Since very few of these guns have been seen marked A.W. Spies and the names of other dealers are found today, it is obvious that no actual agreement was ever reached between the two.

In the preface, brief mention of the numbering system used by Allen was made. To illustrate the point, notice that the two pocket rifles shown on the next page, like most of Allen's single barrel pocket pistols, were sold in pairs and had the same batch numbers.

The pair of underhammer pistols shown above are both numbered 71 on the underside of the barrel. In order to tell them apart, one pistol has a period or punch mark after the batch number. (See arrow.) Photo is courtesy of James D. Julia Auction Company.

A few of the agent's names that will appear on these pistols include: A.W. Spies, Mead & Adriance, Wolf & Gillespie, etc. These and others were verified by the Day Book. A number of specimens will also be encountered with no name at all, whether due to wear or lack of original marking. Unmarked first model Allen pocket rifles are easy to identify by the heavy beveled tang that runs down the front of the grip. No other maker used this identical strap and mechanism.

On December 1, 1847, the last recorded sale of an undercock pistol was made to Joseph Grubb. As these pistols were sold in pairs, the actual invoice was for 1/2 an undercock, rather than just one, but it was a special order with a 12 inch barrel. As this was the only confirmed sale at Worcester during the eight and a half months that the Day Book covers, it appears that Allen had discontinued the pistol. Although these pistols were sold at all three locations, all were marked Grafton.

Allen kept the manufacturing and marketing of his pocket rifles separate from the Allen & Thurber part of the business and all proceeds from sales of the pistol went to him rather than to Allen & Thurber. When an underhammer was in a combined sale with Allen & Thurber pistols, a separate payment would be made to Allen for the undercock pistols. As an example, on March 16, 1847, Allen & Thurber gave Ethan Allen a check for $104 from the sale of 26 pairs of undercock pistols. In turn, all parts and labor for the pistols were billed to Allen. Finally, on December 11, 1847, Allen sold the remaining supply of parts to Allen & Thurber for $286.44.

There are actually two entirely different Grafton underhammer pistols and both were referred to as pocket rifles. The second model shown below was the first pistol to bear the

This second model Grafton pocket rifle has a four inch octagon and round 32 caliber barrel that is marked CAST STEEL / WARRANTED / POCKET RIFLE ALLEN & THURBER / GRAFTON, MASS. on five barrel flats. It has the early wide Grafton-style back strap and grip spangles. The carving on the grips is not factory. Number 63.

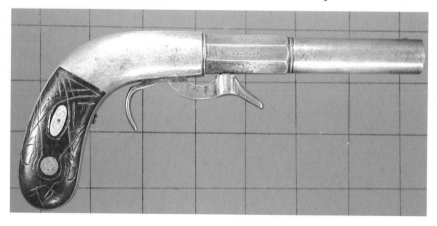

Allen & Thurber name after Allen had formed the partnership with Charles Thurber in 1837. It was a more streamlined pistol that had a rounded frame and bag type grips. As very few Grafton-marked second models have been seen, it is obvious that production was very limited. There is no indication that any were made late at Norwich, but production did resume later at Worcester.

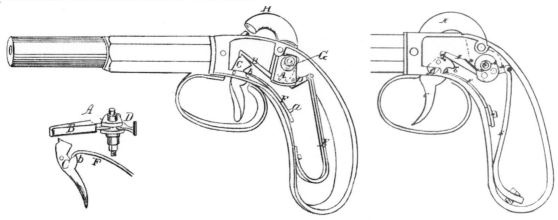

The pistol on the left above is shown on Allen's first patent number 461, issued on November 11, 1837. On January 15, 1844, reissue patent number 60 covering improvements of the main spring, trigger cam and the hammer tumbler was granted. On August 3, 1844, reissue patent number 64 was granted. It did not include any additional improvements but goes into more detail of the workings of the action. The trigger, trigger spring, hammer tumbler and the link of the second reissue are shown in the lower left inset.

It appears that when Allen was granted his patent number 461 on November 11, 1837, the company decided to direct their attention to making the new single shot tube hammer pistol. This patent covered the action that allowed the pistol to be fired with a pull of the trigger, thus eliminating the need to cock the pistol. This is the same cocking and firing mechanism that was used in all of Allen's early pepperboxes.

Allen was authorized by the Commonwealth of Massachusetts to be a prover of firearms in 1936.[1] Some have thought the "P.M." markings as seen on the tube hammer

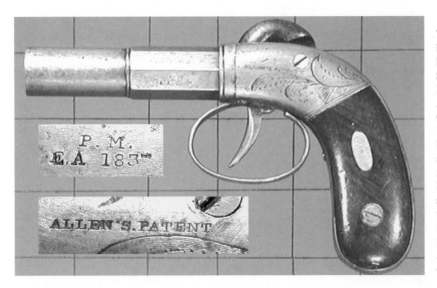

The two and a half inch barrel of the little tube hammer is marked CAST STEEL / WARRANTED / POCKET RIFLE / ALLEN & THURBER / GRAFTON / PM / EA 1837. Allen was authorized by the State of Massachusetts to be prover of military firearms in 1836, but proofs are not usually seen on civilian pistols, so the meaning of the P.M. mark remains an unsolved mystery at this time. Allen's Patent is marked on side plate. (See inset.)

---

1. J.V. Puleo Jr., *Notes on the proof of New England Militia Muskets*, p. 19, Man at Arms, Lincoln, Rhode Island, March / April 1985.

single shot pistol and early pepperboxes means "Proof Massachusetts," but proofs are usually only seen on military firearms, so the full explanation for the mark is unclear.

As simple as the action was, it was a major advance in firearm technology of its day. To have a small pistol that could be carried in one's pocket and fired with one quick pull of the trigger was a vast improvement as the majority of pistols made by others at that time were larger and had to be cocked by hand before they could be fired.

Up to this point, Allen's pistols had been made with fixed barrels, but with the introduction of the tube hammer single shot pistol came the screw-type barrel that could be removed with one of Allen's combination barrel wrench/bullet molds. The screw off barrel was standard for the remainder of bar hammer single shot percussion production.

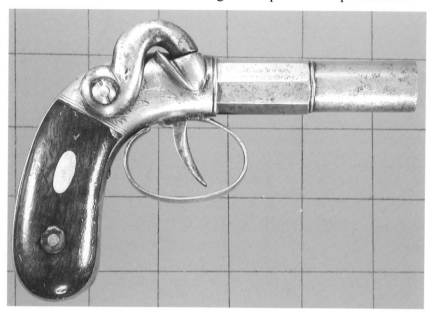

Allen's barrel wrench / bullet mold.

The right side view makes it obvious why it is called the tube hammer. This is the later model that has a one screw side plate and a straight main spring.

The tube hammer was soon replaced by the more conventional bar hammer style that would be used on all but a few of Allen's pepperbox and single shot models.

Allen & Thurber's new bar hammer self-cocking mechanism was used on all subsequent single shot bar hammer pistols and all but a few pepperboxes. This early Grafton pistol has a two and three quarter inch octagon and round rifled 36 caliber barrel and the early wide back strap. Later Grafton bar hammer pistols have the narrow back strap as described on the following page. Number 11, from the Lee Norris collection.

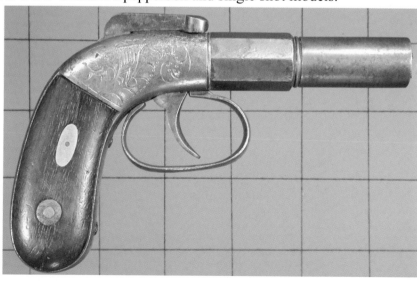

All Grafton tube hammer pistols have wide grip straps, but only a few of the very early Grafton bar hammer single shots have wide straps and were soon replaced with a new frame with a much narrower grip strap. It is possible that Allen figured out that wood was cheaper than steel and so the change was made early in production. The narrow design was used without change through the remainder of production on all bar hammer pistols and pepperboxes as well.

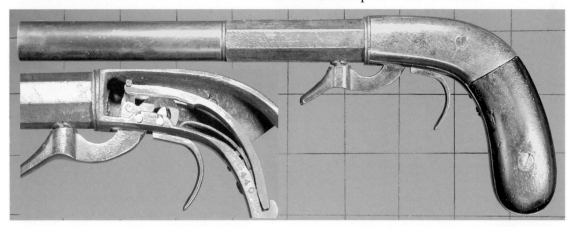

The wide back strap on the right is just under one half inch wide and the narrow back strap is one fourth of an inch wide.

In 1842, the firm of Allen & Thurber moved to Norwich, Connecticut, where production of the single shot bar hammer continued without physical change. However, about midway through the Norwich period, the action was changed from the 1837 to the 1845 type, but the 1837 patent markings would be used well into the Worcester period. With the exception of the under hammer pistols, the different actions can be determined by the location of the main spring tension screw.

In 1847, the company of Allen & Thurber moved to Worcester, Massachusetts, where production of the bar hammer pistol continued. The underhammer single shot that had not been made since the early Grafton days was reintroduced, but with a narrow back grip strap and minus the oval silver grip inlays that had adorned Allen's pistols for years. The action of the second model Grafton and the Worcester underhammer pistols are identical.

The Worcester underhammer single shot pistol is basically the same as the Grafton with the exception of the barrel markings which now read ALLEN & THURBER / WORCESTER / CAST STEEL on three of the barrel flats. Because it uses the same action (see inset) and wide main spring as the Grafton models, the front grip strap remains the same width as the Grafton model but the back grip strap has been narrowed from three eighth to one fourth of an inch. These are the only Allen firearms that use this type of action. The silver grip spangles are not seen on Worcester single shot bar hammer pistols. Robert Avery collection. Number 440.

24

The changes of the bar hammer single shot pistol from early to late can be seen in the three photos shown below.

Early Worcester single shot bar hammers had the early quick drop grips but the silver spangles that adorned the grips on Allen's pistols for many years are gone. The 1845 action can be identified by the high location of the main spring adjusting screw. (See arrow.) Number 23.

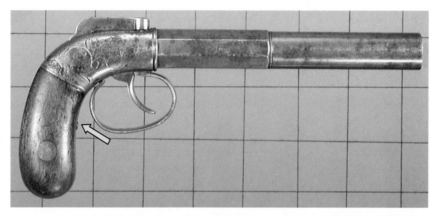

Although absent of any makers name or location, the pistol on the right is of early Worcester vintage. The grips are now at a more gentle angle and are refered to as the semi-dogleg grip. Number 216.

This late single shot bar hammer pistol has a set of very rare pewter grips that are engraved and numbered to the gun. The angle of the newly designed rounded bag-type grips was the final style change. Although this is a late pistol, the 1837 patent marking was still used. Number 480.

The final design change during the Worcester era was the introduction of the new, longer frame with better grip angle as shown in the above picture. Although the No. 9 self cocking pistol had gone through quite a few changes over the approximately 25 years of its existence, Allen's basic mechanical principles remained the same from the early Grafton days to the Allen & Wheelock era. Allen's designs and mechanics were so successful that other manufacturers would copy them for many years.

Chapter 4
ALLEN & WHEELOCK SINGLE AND DOUBLE SHOT PERCUSSION PISTOLS

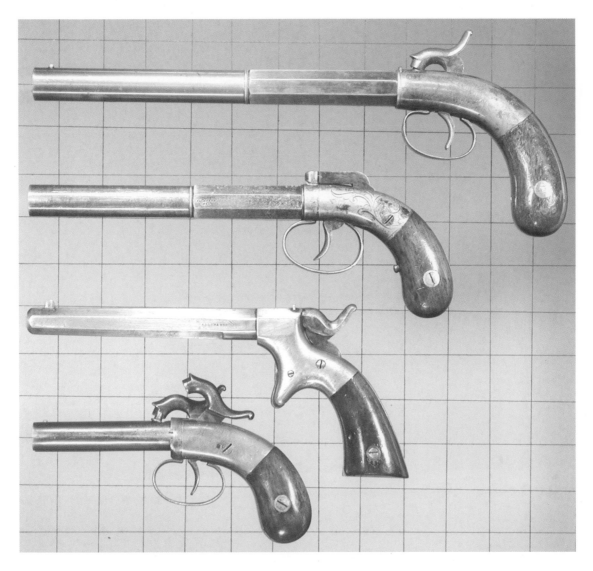

The pistol at the top of the picture is a shotgun hammer boot pistol that has an eight inch octagon and round 36 caliber rifled barrel and was referred to by Allen & Thurber as the No. 6 rifled pistol. Number 42. The second pistol is a bar hammer that is referred to as the No. 9 single self cocking pistol. It has a six inch 36 caliber octagon and round barrel. Number 803. The third pistol is called the inline or straight line because the nipple is in line with the bore. It has a five inch 32 caliber octagon barrel with deep rifling. Number 510. The bottom pistol is a double barreled single trigger pistol with rifled three inch 36 caliber barrels. Number 231.

Single and double Allen & Wheelock pistols were carried over from the Allen, Thurber & Co. era with the exception of the inline. Production of the No. 6 rifled or boot pistol started sometime after the company move to Worcester in July 1847. It is seen with Allen & Thurber and Allen, Thurber & Co. as well as Allen & Wheelock markings and was unchanged throughout production.

The No. 9 single self cocking pistol is actually a refined version of Allen's early Grafton and Norwich single shot pistols that had gone through several changes. Although the No. 9 pistols were made prior to the Allen & Wheelock era, they are identical to the later Allen & Thurber / Allen, Thurber & Co. pistols although the barrel and hammer markings will vary slightly on later Allen & Wheelock-made pistols.

The inline pistol is an exclusive Allen & Wheelock product. Later versions of this pistol consisted of the frame that was made to accept short pieces of rejected barrel stock.

The Allen & Wheelock double pistol is a Worcester product and was also marked Allen & Thurber / Allen, Thurber & Co.

Shown below is a copy of an Allen & Thurber price list that was sent to J.A. Harris on May 15, 1849 and shows the prices of several different pepperbox pistols as well as the bar hammer and shotgun hammer single shot pistols.

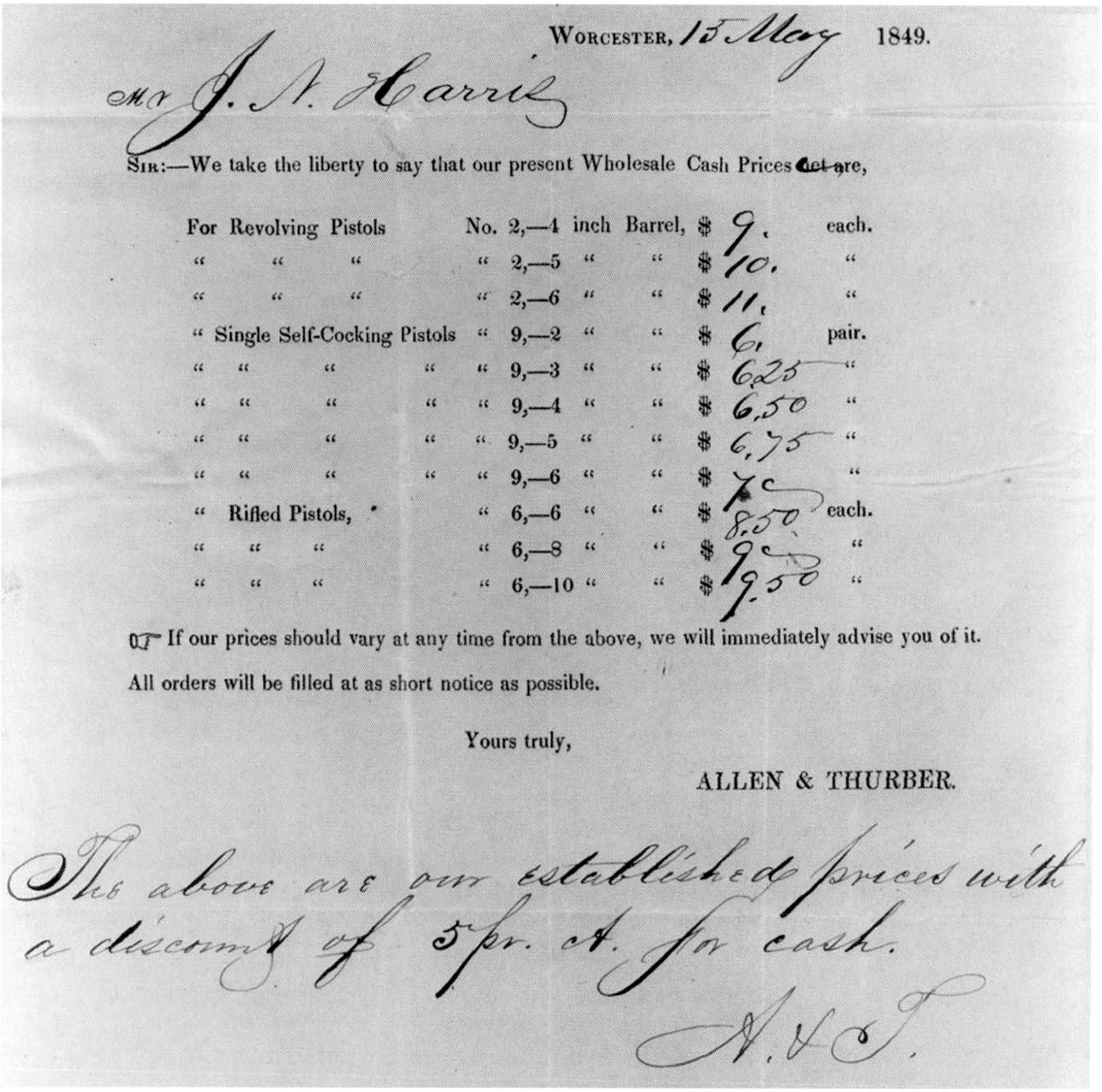

WORCESTER, *15 May* 1849.

Mr J. A. Harris

SIR:—We take the liberty to say that our present Wholesale Cash Prices ~~del~~ are,

For Revolving Pistols	No. 2,—4 inch Barrel,	$ *9.*	each.
" " "	" 2,—5 " "	$ *10.*	"
" " "	" 2,—6 " "	$ *11.*	"
" Single Self-Cocking Pistols	" 9,—2 " "	$ *6.*	pair.
" " "	" 9,—3 " "	$ *6.25*	"
" " "	" 9,—4 " "	$ *6.50*	"
" " "	" 9,—5 " "	$ *6.75*	"
" " "	" 9,—6 " "	$ *7.0*	"
" Rifled Pistols,	" 6,—6 " "	$ *8.50*	each.
" " "	" 6,—8 " "	$ *9.0*	"
" " "	" 6,—10 " "	$ *9.50*	"

☞ If our prices should vary at any time from the above, we will immediately advise you of it.

All orders will be filled at as short notice as possible.

Yours truly,

ALLEN & THURBER.

The above are our established prices with a discount of 5 pr. ct. for cash.

A. & T.

One of the few surviving Allen documents is this May 15, 1849 copy of a list of prices that was sent to customer J.A. Harris from the Allen & Thurber firm. The No. 2 revolving pistols are for Allen's pepperboxes. The No. 9 self cocking pistols are the bar hammer single shots and the No. 6 rifled pistols are the shotgun hammer boot pistols. **Mouellesseaux, p. 96**

Chapter 5
ALLEN & WHEELOCK BAR HAMMER SINGLE SHOT PISTOLS

This young man is holding an Allen bar hammer single shot pistol with a six inch barrel. (Nice tie!)

One of the cornerstones of Allen's business was the single shot bar hammer percussion pistol referred to as the Number 9 self cocking pistol. Although Allen's April 16, 1845 patent number 3,998 generally relates to a double action pepperbox, it is the same basic action that is used on all Allen & Wheelock bar hammer single shot pistols.

Having gone through several major changes prior to the Allen & Wheelock period, these guns were carried over unchanged from Allen & Thurber / Allen, Thurber & Co. period other than the name. The very early Allen & Wheelock marked pistols have ALLEN'S PATENT / 1845 on the hammer or barrel in two lines and later pistols are marked PATENTED / APRIL 16, 1845, on the side of the hammer, also in two lines.

This photograph illustrates the five No. 9 pistols in barrel lengths from two to six inches that were referred to in the Allen & Thurber price list shown on page 26.

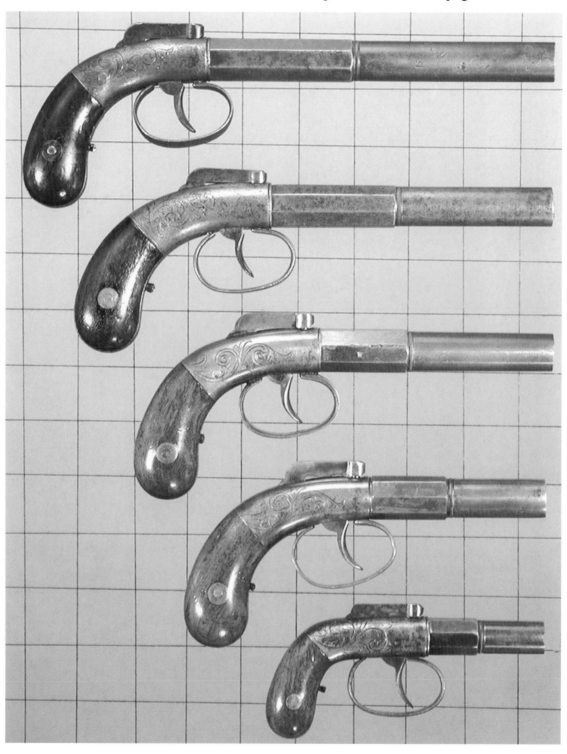

The above pistols and their prices are listed from top to bottom. The six-inch pistols were priced at $7 per pair. Number 170. The five-inch pistols were priced at $6.75 per pair. Number 299. The four-inch pistols were priced at $6.50 per pair. Number 227. The three-inch pistols were priced at $6.25 per pair. Number 298. The pistol on the bottom has a two inch 30 caliber barrel and is generally referred to as the muff pistol. They were priced at $6.00 per pair. Number 608.

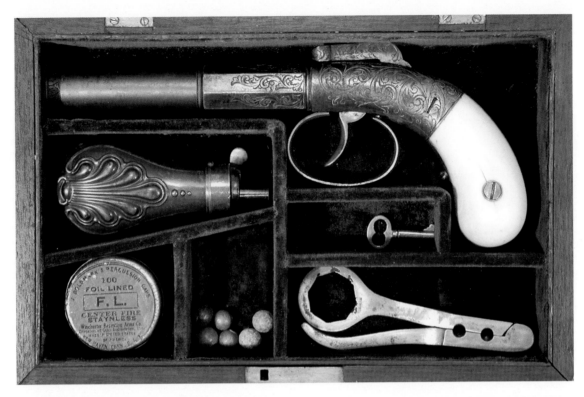

This No. 9 pistol with a four inch barrel has extra fine engraving on the frame, barrel, hammer and trigger guard and is cased with accessories. Note the combination bullet mold / barrel wrench. The shell-type flasks are commonly seen in Allen cased sets. Number 796.

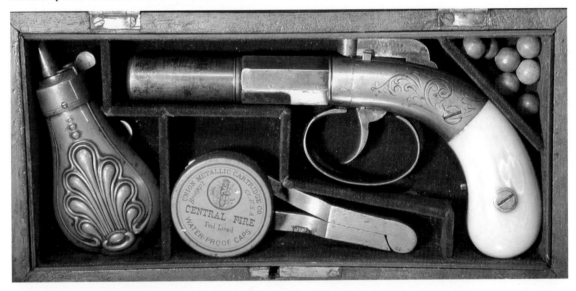

Above is a No. 9 single shot Allen & Wheelock bar hammer pistol with a three inch barrel and ivory grips that is nicely cased with accessories. It is equipped with an interesting hammer safety device.

On the left is a close up of the pistol shown above. It is fitted with a hammer safety that will keep the hammer from resting on the percussion cap when the pistol was loaded. (See arrow.) By raising the hammer slightly, the safety lock could be pushed under the hammer and is held in place by the pressure of the hammer. When the hammer was raised, the spring loaded safety lock would spring to the side and allow the hammer to strike the cap. It is not known if this was one of Allen's experiments or someone else's clever idea. Number 527.

Standard size bar hammer pistols are most common with 36 caliber octagon and round barrels that will be found in lengths of three to six inches but the Day Book does reveal an order for a No. 9 pistol with a seven inch barrel that was probably a special order. The smaller muff pistol is standard with a two inch octagon and round 30 caliber smooth bore barrel.

As these guns could either be loaded from the muzzle or by unscrewing the barrel from the frame, Allen offered a combination bullet mold/barrel wrench. (See page 22.)

Other than doing away with the frame engraving and rounding off the top of the hammer, there were no changes during the Allen & Wheelock period of production.

The late single shot No. 9 pistols were made without frame engraving, which saved Allen 8 cents per unit. The top pistol has a four inch 36 caliber octagon and round rifled barrel. Number 98.

The muff pistol on the bottom is also unengraved and has a two inch 30 caliber smooth bore barrel. Note the round top hammers on both pistols. Number 203.

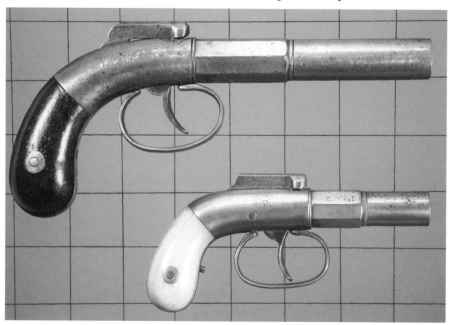

The small muff pistol is also included in Allen's No. 9 category. Although none has ever been seen bearing the maker's name or place of manufacture, any Allen pistol that has the PATENTED / APRIL 16, 1845, date stamped on the hammer, is definitely from the Allen & Wheelock period. As with its larger counterpart, the muff pistol would eventually succumb to cost and would also lose their modest frame engraving in later years. As with large frame No. 9 pistols, unengraved muff pistols also have round top hammers. An entry in the Day Book shows that Allen & Thurber were selling muff pistols as early as October 20, 1846 at the Norwich factory.

On the right is a muff pistol with solid silver grips that are numbered to the pistol. It has a two-inch, 30 caliber smooth bore barrel and is marked Allen's patent on the hammer. Number 929.

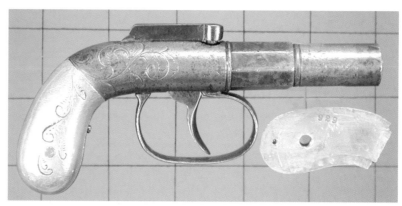

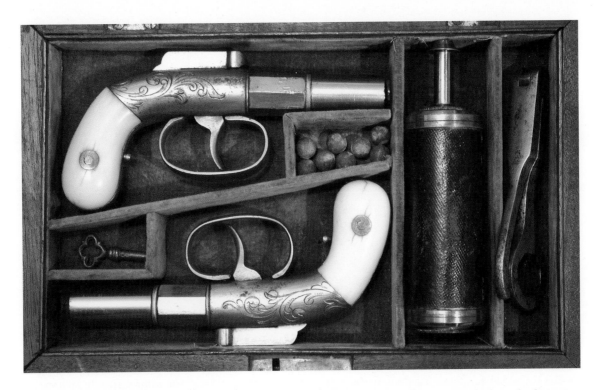

Shown above is a double cased set of No. 9 muff pistols with ivory grips. They are marked on the hammers PATENTED / APRIL 16, 1845 in two lines, which is the Allen & Wheelock-type patent date. They are in a typical wooden case with an Allen barrel wrench / bullet mold, a plunger-type powder flask with a compartment in the bottom for percussion caps, a few round balls and a key. Numbers are 127 and 620.

This is a rather unusual double cased set of Allen & Wheelock muff pistols. Although the case is not the typical type used by Allen, and does not have the accessories normally seen in cased sets, the pistols do have consecutive numbers. Numbers 320 and 321.

Members of the rescue party which, in 1859, freed Dr. John Doy, (seated) from the jail at St. Joseph, Mo., after he had been kidnapped and jailed for stealing slaves and setting them free. The rather friendly man that is standing second from the right has an Allen muff pistol on a cord around his neck (see arrow). The photo is from the Kansas State Historical Society, Topeka, Kansas.

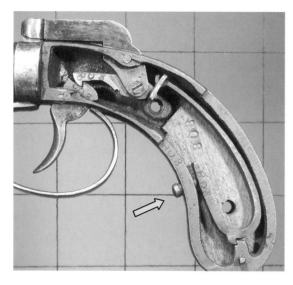

On the left is a view of the 1845 type action used on the bar hammer single shot pistol. It is always advisable to keep the main spring tension adjustment screw (see arrow) as loose as possible.

Shown above is an enlarged view of the side plate screw from the pistol on the left. It is absolutely necessary that the flat spot be properly aligned with the internal workings. If the action of a pistol does not work freely, possibly a slight turn of the screw one way on another might correct the problem.

Shown below are the three different types of hammer marks that will be seen on Allen & Wheelock single shot bar hammer percussion pistols and pepperboxes.

Standard flat top hammers on engraved pistols have the Allen & Wheelock marks.

All early flat top hammer models with engraved frames have late Allen & Thurber marks.

Late hammers on non-engraved pistols are marked the same but are rounded on the top.

Chapter 6
SHOTGUN HAMMER BOOT PISTOLS (THE NO. 6 RIFLED PISTOL)

This Civil War soldier is armed with a musket and a No. 6 Allen shotgun hammer boot pistol in his belt.

34

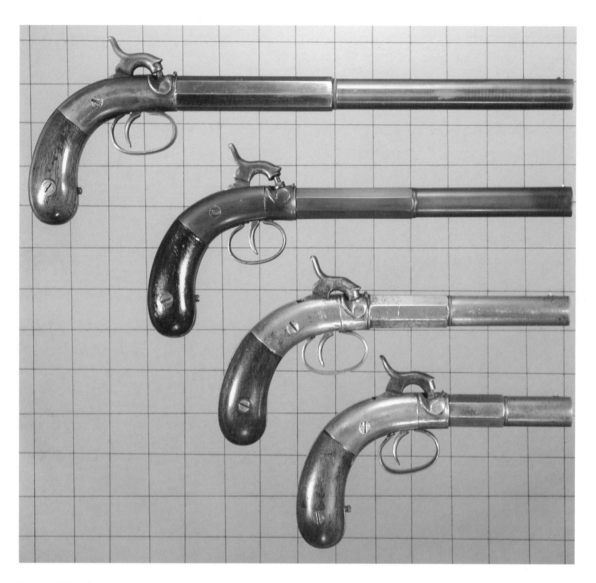

The first No. 6 pistol on top has a ten inch octagon and round, 36 caliber, rifled barrel. Number 747. The second pistol has a rare seven inch octagon and round smooth bore, 34 caliber, barrel. Number 2. The third pistol has a very large 45 caliber, five inch rifled barrel. Number 21. The bottom pistol has a short three inch barrel that is also 36 caliber. Number 274.

The No. 6 rifled pistol or shotgun hammer boot pistol was carried over from the Allen, Thurber era and remained unchanged throughout the entire production.

A rather plain looking pistol, it is standard with blued finish, varnished walnut grips, and a very simple single type action that had no half cock. Because of the lack of a safety position, one can imagine that there must have been a lot of accidental discharges.

It was not a very glamorous gun, but was an effective way to have self protection or a reasonably accurate target pistol at a reasonable price.

Although commonly referred to as the boot pistol or shotgun hammer single shot pistol, Allen's official name for these guns was the inside cock, No. 6 rifled pistol. They were available in part octagon barrel lengths of three, four, five, six, seven, eight, and ten inches and in calibers from 32 to 44, but 36 was the most popular.

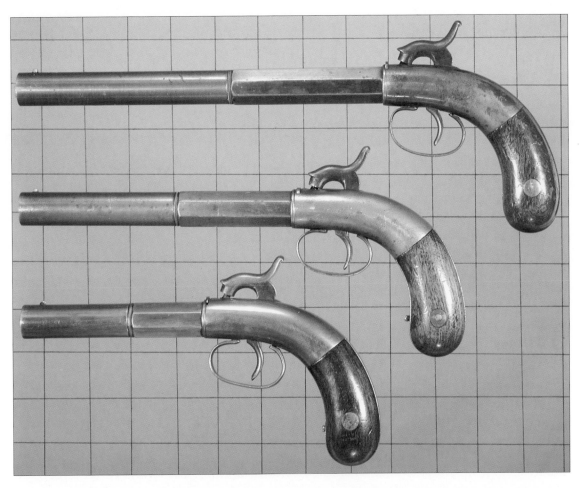

The pistol on the top has an eight inch 36 caliber rifled barrel. Number 421. The middle pistol has a six inch 36 caliber rifled barrel. Number 110. The pistol on the bottom has a four inch 32 caliber rifled barrel. Number 586.

This is an unusual boot pistol that was modestly engraved after it left the factory. Although it is not the typical Allen-style engraving, it was nicely done. It has a 36 caliber octagon and round five inch barrel with an unusual blade front sight. Number 397.

All pistols are marked on one of the top barrel flats "Allen & Wheelock" in one line with the batch number on the bottom barrel flat. Occasionally, a pistol will be seen with Worcester marked on the barrel, but with no consistency. As they also had screw off barrels, the need for a ramrod was eliminated.

As illustrated on page 26, the May 15, 1849 price list quoted the number 6 rifled pistol at the following prices:

- With six inch barrel ---- -$8.00
- With eight inch barrel ---$9.00
- With ten inch barrel---- $10.00

Although the price was more than double that of the single self cocking pistols, they were larger and much more powerful than the self cocking bar hammer pistols and cost about 50 cents extra per barrel inch.

It is also interesting to note that they were priced only slightly less than the standard 6 shot pepperboxes.

As these pistols are equipped with both a front and rear sight, they seem to be a generic version of Allen's more expensive target pistols.

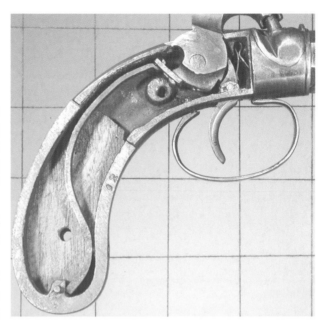

Shown above is the simple action of the No 6 rifled pistol.

The term "boot pistol" seems to be an abused definition. It really does not seem appropriate to call a gun with a three or four inch barrel a boot pistol, unless you are wearing sneakers. To be politically correct, it would seem that a pistol should have a barrel length of at least six inches to qualify as a boot pistol, but that is simply the opinion of the author.

Included in this chapter is a little shotgun hammer muff pistol that is illustrated below. As common as these little pistols are, the vast majority are unmarked and it is very rare to see one bearing the Allen markings. At this writing, only two have been reported that were marked Allen & Thurber and one marked Allen & Wheelock.

This little shotgun hammer single shot pistol was brought on line in the early days of Worcester. Although only a few examples bearing Allen marks have ever been found, they do exist. The Allen pistols will always have grip escutcheons where others will have a small wood screw holding the grips together. This pistol has a three inch 30 caliber smooth bore round barrel and is unmarked. Number 305.

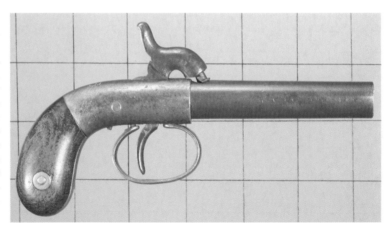

From the number of look-alikes that are on the antique gun market today, there is no doubt about the success that not only Allen but also others enjoyed from this design that was so simple it could not be patented.

Chapter 7
SINGLE SHOT INLINE PISTOLS AND THE MINIE BALL MOLD

The inline or straight line single shot was so named because the nipple is in line with the barrel. The inline was definitely a no frills firearm with a very simple action that was made to accept just about any kind of barrel that could be threaded and screwed into the frame. An early and a late style can be distinguished by the angle of the grips and the types of barrels used.

It was originally thought that the inline pistol was made specifically to utilize rejected or obsolete barrels when Allen was ordered to stop making cartridge pistols with bored through cylinders in November, 1863. That is partially true, but most early pistols have octagon and round barrels that fit the frame perfectly. As shown in the top photo below, the barrel fits the frame so precisely that it is almost impossible to see where the frame ends and the barrel begins.

It was originally thought that the early octagon and round barrels were from the bar hammer single shot pistol but those barrels have inside threads and the inline barrels have outside threads that screw into the frame and are of a different dimension.

Early inline pistols were fitted with octagon and round barrels that were made to fit the frame perfectly.

This later second model is fitted with a percussion revolver barrel that has a sharp angle at the front of the barrel spacer. (See arrow.) This is a typical Allen 32 caliber barrel that is probably from a side hammer percussion belt model.

The barrel on this late second model has been machined to eliminate the sharp step of the barrel spacer. (See arrow.) The deep rifling indicates that the barrel is from a percussion pistol.

Later inline models will be found with more streamlined-style grips that are often referred to as the slow drop, or the Smith & Wesson-type grips.

Many different types of barrels will be seen on the later variation and although there is no doubt that many are indeed reject pieces of barrel stock, not all came from the Allen scrap pile as Allen was known to have bought at least some rejected barrel stock from other gun makers.

The top three early pistols illustrated on the following page show that the barrels are mated to the frame perfectly and were made for the pistol and there can be little doubt that the barrels were made to fit the frame.

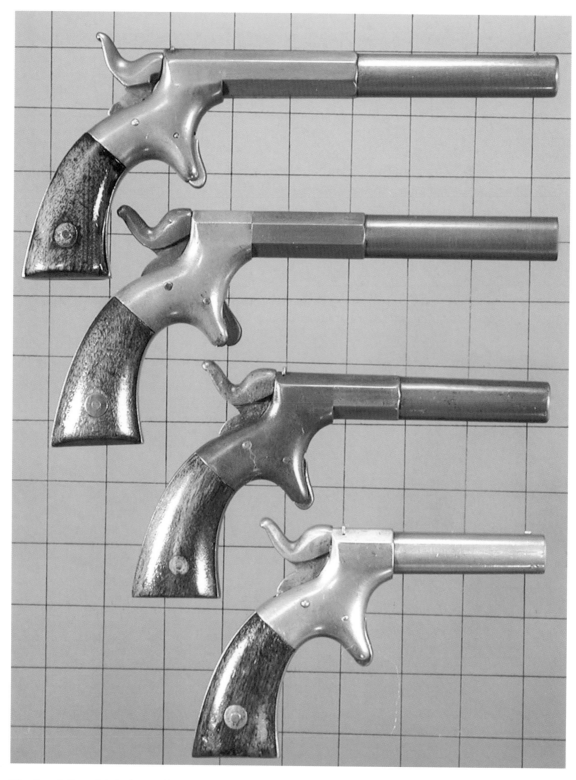

The four inline pistols shown above are all early models with quick drop grips. The top pistol has a six and a fourth inch octagon and round 38 caliber rifled barrel. Number 925. The second pistol has a brass frame with an unmarked six inch rifled barrel. It is not equipped with sights and is likely a prototype. The only marks on the pistol are a 0 marked on the frame and grips. The third pistol has a short four and a half inch 38 caliber octagon and round rifled barrel. Number 141. The pistol on the bottom has a short three and a half inch 36 caliber round smooth bore barrel that is from an unknown source. Number 314.

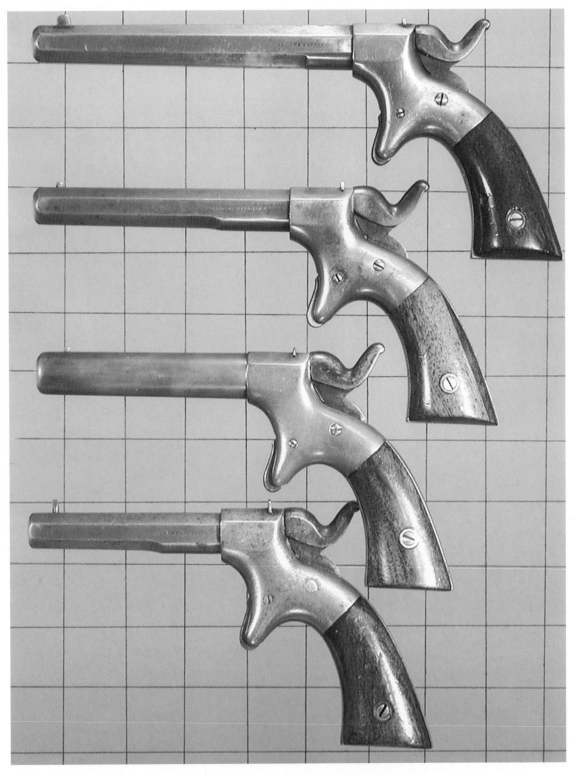

The four inline pistols shown above are all late models with the slow drop Smith & Wesson-type grips. The top pistol has a rifled six inch 32 caliber Allen barrel. Number 310. The second pistol has a five-inch octagon barrel. Number 139. The third pistol has a four-and-one-fourth-inch round tapered 36 caliber smooth bore barrel from an unknown source. Number 78. The pistol on the bottom has a smooth bore four inch 34 caliber octagon barrel. Number 352. All are marked ALLEN & WHEELOCK except the round barrel pistol and it is unmarked.

ALLEN'S MINIE BALL BULLET MOLD

On July 29, 1856, Allen was granted patent number 15,454 for a new and improved bullet mold for hollow projectiles. In his patent application, Allen makes the following description of his improvement.

"My improvements relate to molds for that class of bullets known as the "Minie ball" and other analogous forms. These heretofore have been cast with the sprue at the point, which, when cut off, left a flat end instead of a point, rendering it necessary to swage or pare it by another operation to make a perfect-ball and no little inconvenience has arisen from the sticking of the ball in to mold, whereas by my improvements, these faults are entirely remedied, making the ball perfect in form and delivering it freely."

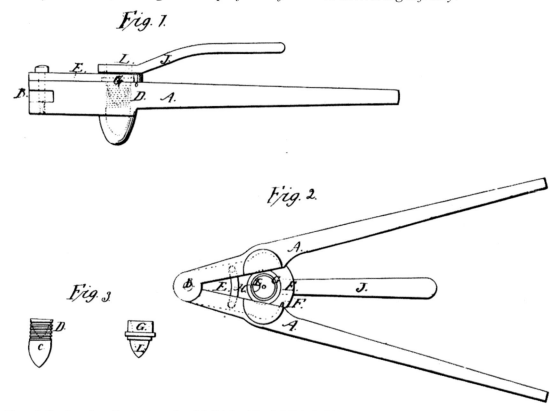

Above is the drawing of patent number 15,454 for Allen's Minie ball mold for hollow projectiles.

It is not known if any of the molds were manufactured as none have ever been reported. Since this improvement came at the end of the percussion age it is possible that Allen scrapped the idea and focused his attention on his newly formed company of Allen & Wheelock.

Regardless, after a full page of Allen's typical rambling description of how his simple bullet mold works the final claim of his patent is as follows:

"Cutting off the sprue by means of a cutter working on the curve of the inner surface of the ball, so as to leave the ball smooth and symmetrical, substantially in the manner and for the purposed of above set forth and described."

Chapter 8
DOUBLE BARRELED SINGLE TRIGGER PERCUSSION PISTOLS

This man holding an Allen double barreled pistol would look right at home sitting at a poker table in the Long Branch Saloon.

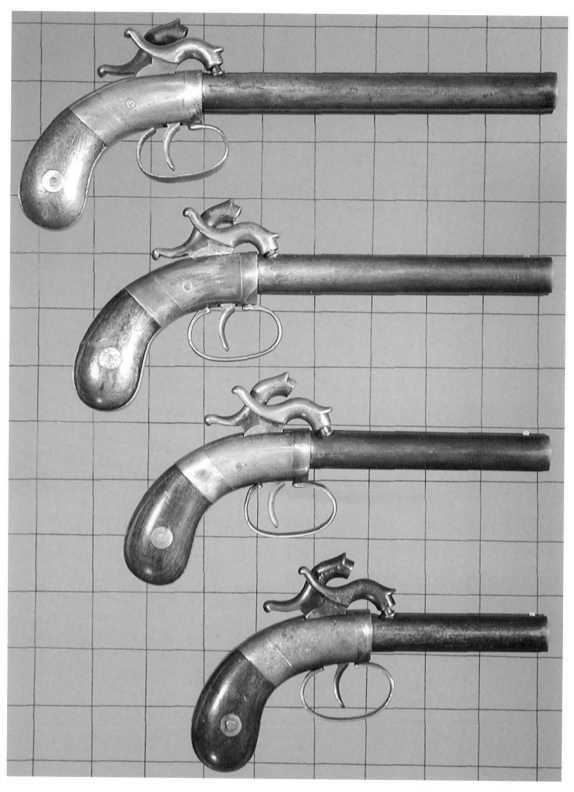

The four double barrel single trigger pistols pictured above are identical except for the barrel lengths. All are marked ALLEN & WHEELOCK between the barrels. The top pistol has six inch barrels. Number 944. The second pistol has five inch barrels. Number 690. The third pistol has four inch barrels. Number 681. The bottom pistol has three inch barrels. Number 23. The barrels are deeply rifled.

The Allen & Wheelock double barrel single trigger pistols were another carry over from the Allen & Thurber / Allen, Thurber & Co. period and are of Worcester vintage. They will be seen with all three company names.

Early Allen & Thurber models had a U-shaped main spring that could be distinguished from later models by the presence of the main spring tension adjusting screws that are located on the inner grip frame just behind the trigger guard. (See top photo on page 44.)

Soon, new straighter main springs without adjustment screws became standard and the pistol would remained unchanged for the remainder of production. There is no indication that they were made after the Allen & Wheelock era.

All are standard blued 34 caliber barrels and frames with case hardened hammers and triggers. Varnished walnut grips are standard but, as shown below, at least one double pistol was made with ivory grips and nicely engraved.

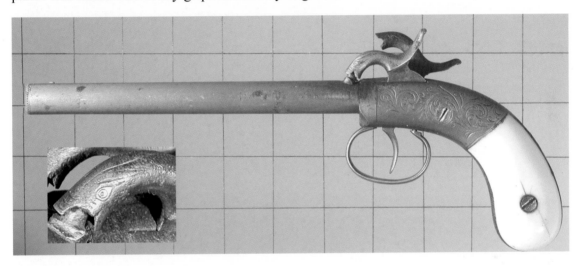

This very rare engraved double pistol has 34 caliber six inch barrels, ivory grips and serpent head hammers. (See Inset.) Number 4.

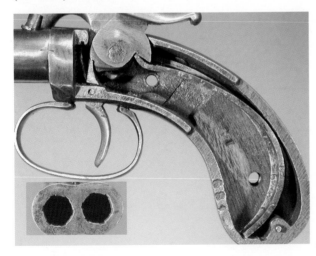

The action of the double barreled pistol is basically the same as the No. 6 rifled pistol with no half cock position. There is no connecting link between the main spring and hammer. Note the deep rifling in inset photo.

Double pistols marked Spalding & Fisher are very similar to the Allen & Wheelock and also have a plain unengraved frame. However, Bruce & Davis marked pistols are engraved and are equipped with ramrods. It is hard to understand why Allen's own single and double shot percussion pistols were not all made with ramrods.

Since Bruce & Davis, as well as Spalding & Fisher, were distributors and not manufacturers, Allen more than likely made at least the frames and actions for both of them.

All Allen & Wheelock double pistols are marked on top of the barrels.

One can only imagine how it would be possible to fire the first barrel without setting off the second barrel. As these specimens all have a rather hard trigger pull, it would make it extremely difficult to stop halfway through the cycle with only one charge detonating if both hammers were cocked at the same time.

Regardless of the disadvantages, it is obvious that these pistols were very successful as they are frequently seen at gun shows bearing the markings of Bruce & Davis, Spalding & Fisher and Blunt & Syms, as well as Allen & Thurber, Allen, Thurber & Co. and Allen & Wheelock.

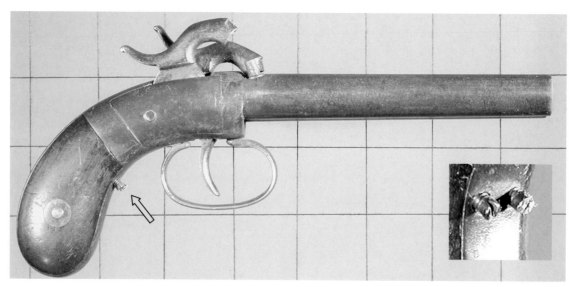

Pictured above is a very early Allen & Thurber double pistol that has main spring tension screws (see the arrow and inset). These early pistols have U-shaped main springs. Number 610. From the Jay Drelinger Collection.

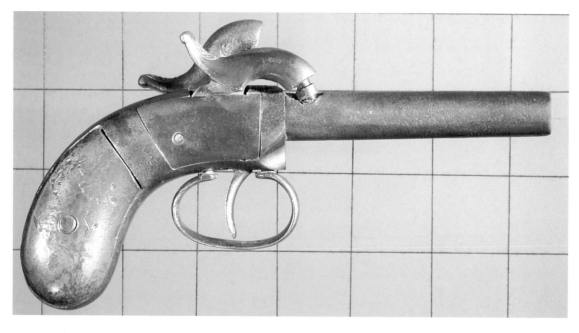

Pictured above is a rather tattered Allen look-alike that has brass grips that look to be original. The frame is very similar to an Allen but the barrels are different and originally had a ramrod thimble. It has deeply rifled three and a half inch 34 caliber barrels and is marked B&S (Blunt & Syms) CAST STEEL, NY on top of the barrel rib. Number 70.

Chapter 9
EARLY ALLEN & THURBER PEPPERBOXES

A young Civil War soldier is armed with two Allen pepperboxes, a sword, a shotgun and a determined look. Photo is from the Herb Peck Jr. collection.

THE RING OF PEPPERBOXES

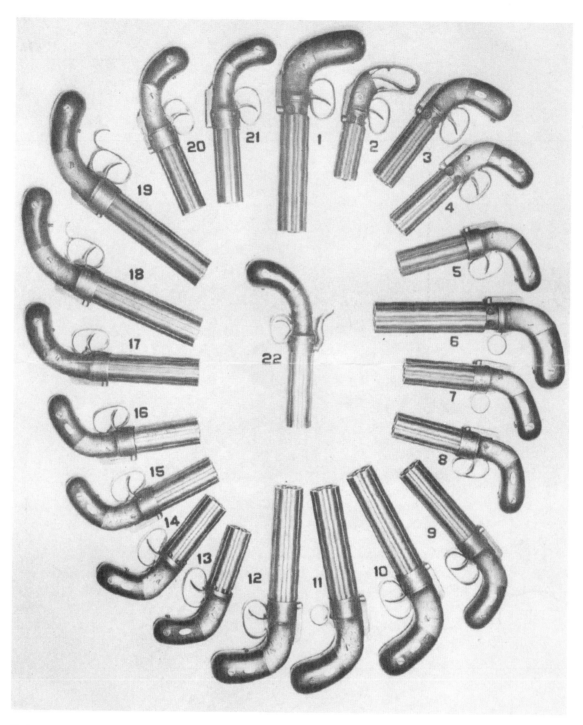

Referred to as the ring of pepperboxes, this photo shows some of the different models and variations of the Allen pepperbox. A brief description of each piece appears on the following page. This photo of the ring of pepperboxes originally appeared in the November 1950 issue of *The Gun Collector,* Whitewater, Wisconsin and was from the collection of Harley J. Van Cleave at that time.

Harley Van Cleave spent most of his life collecting firearms made by Ethan Allen but his favorites were pepperboxes. His names for the various models have long since been revised by modern day collectors but it is a great opportunity to see some of the different pepperboxes made by Allen in one picture and hopefully it will not be confusing to the reader. The following is a list of the pepperboxes and the way that he had them categorized over 50 years ago. All descriptions are those of Harley Van Cleave.

1. THE PRIMITIVE MASSIVE GRAFTON 6 (Large, no inlays in grips; no grip pins)
2. THE DAINTY GRAFTON 6. (28 cal; no grip pins; very small)
3. THE PRIMITIVE SLIM JIM 6 (31 cal; no grip pins; wide back strap; only spring bolt for cylinder stop)
4. THE LIGHT SHIELDLESS GRAFTON 6 (Similar to #3 but with narrow back strap and thicker grips with grip pins)
5. THE LIGHT SHIELDED GRAFTON 6 (On bar hammer in small letters "ALLEN'S PATENT", period for apostrophe and between words)
6. THE PRIMITIVE MASSIVE NORWICH SHIELDLESS RING TRIGGER 6. (Differs from Massive Grafton #1 in having grip pins and from all others in Massive series in lacking nipple shield)
7. THE DOG LEG SLOTTED NORWICH 6. (Note shape of handle)
8. THE LIGHT ANGULAR SHIELDED NORWICH 6 (similar to #5 except side plate is distinctly longer)
9. THE LIGHT TRANSITIONAL SHIELDED NORWICH 6 (Tension screw above level of grip screw)
10. THE EARLY MASSIVE NORWICH SHIELDED 6 (Tension screw below grip screw)
11. THE TRANSITIONAL MASSIVE NORWICH STANDARD SHIELDED 6. (Tension screw well above level of grip screw)
12. THE PERFECTED MASSIVE NORWICH STANDARD SHIELDED 6 (Accessory trigger spring omitted but its notch remains in front edge of grip frame.)
13. THE EARLY HAMMERLESS ALLEN 6 (Low tension screw; no external hammer)
14. THE IMPROVED WORCESTER ALLEN HAMMERLESS 6. (Tension screw above level of grip screw)
15. THE LATE LIGHT TRANSISITIONAL SHIELDED WORCESTER 6 (Nipple shield stamped with open rose design)
16. THE IMPROVED LIGHT SHIELDED WORCESTER 6 (Newly designed frame lacking spring notch inside rear edge of grip frame)
17. THE LIGHT WIDE RIBBED WORCESTER 6. (Cylinder ribs wide; frame not narrowed laterally; without inlays in grips)
18. THE RIBBED MASSIVE SPURRED WESTERN 6. (Broad flat cylinder ribs; curved finger spur welded to lower corner of guard)
19. THE FLUTED MASSIVE SPURRED WESTERN 6. (Cylinder fluted)
20. THE STANDARD LIGHT FLUTED 6. (Nipple shield with curled plume design; fluted cylinder; engraved frame)
21. PLAIN LIGHT FLUTED 6. (Without frame engraving; side plate screw reduced in size)
22. THE EARLY THUMB HAMMER 6. (Single action; grip screw on left side, side plate screw on right)

Harley Van Cleave spent most of his life collecting Allen pepperboxes. After his death, the collection was maintained and added to by his son Philip, until 1991, when the collection was sold. Between Phil and his father, they represented 75 years of researching and collecting of Allen firearms.

If there were any firearms that can readily be associated with Ethan Allen, it would be his pepperbox pistols. The Allen pepperbox played an important part in American history and gained popularity during the California gold rush days. Although never noted for their accuracy, the massive size of the dragoon pepperbox with its six quick shots was enough to ward off many potential claim jumpers.

Based on his November 11, 1837, patent number 461, Allen produced a large variety of pepperbox pistols. Although his original patent actually had nothing to do with a pepperbox, it did cover its basic action. (See page 21.) It was not until April 16, 1845, that he obtained patent number 3,998 that related directly to a pepperbox with a newly designed action that eliminated several parts and improving its operation. (See page 51.)

During the early years of Grafton and Norwich manufacture, no other product of Allen's was made in as many different models and variations as his pepperbox pistols, as many changes were made over the years to improve the firearm.

This 28 caliber Dainty Grafton is one of the earliest pepperboxes produced by Allen. It has removable nipples, wide back strap and fluted ribs on the three inch six shot barrel. The hammer is marked ALLEN & THURBER / GRAFTON, MASS. in two lines. ALLEN'S PATENT is marked on the left side of the frame. Production was limited and very few have survived. Number 123. From the Perry Hansen collection.

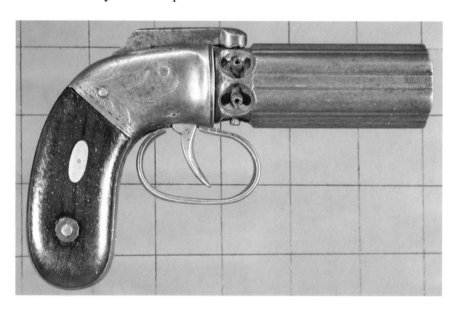

This early Grafton six shot pepperbox has a four inch barrel group that has gold inlaid flutes, a hand engraved nipple shield and solid silver frame. ALLEN'S PATENT is marked on the hammer in one line and the initials M.R.-Mc.C.C. are inscribed on the left side of the frame. It has the early Grafton-style wide back strap and ivory grips and is unnumbered. This is the finest known Allen pepperbox and is from the Roger Muckerheide collection. Photograph by Stuart C. Mowbray.

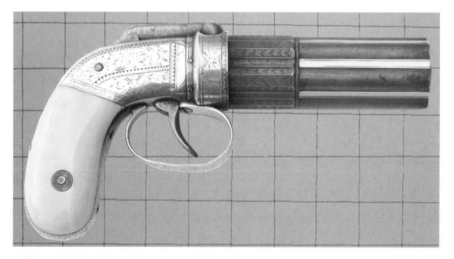

It is not known when Allen started producing the dragoon size pepperboxes, but as with all Grafton marked products, they are quite rare. Although seldom seen, there are no less than four variations, but all are basically the same.

Very early Grafton dragoons have no frame engraving or grip spangles and a spring type detent located between the barrel and the frame to keep the heavy barrel from rotating past its point of alignment. Later models have grip spangles and eventually frame engraving that would remain standard on all Allen dragoons. The final variation consisted of adding a nipple shield.

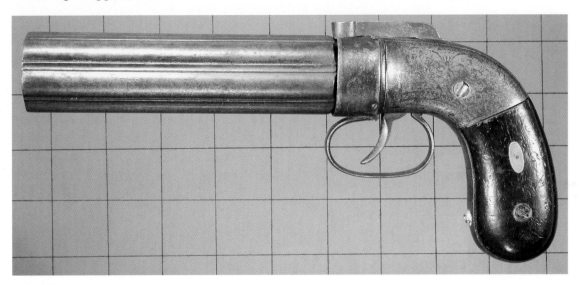

This late Grafton or very early Norwich dragoon pepperbox has an etched nipple shield. Very few early Allen pepperboxes were made with shields. Note the early fluted barrel ribs. The pistol is unmarked with the exception of the Number 2 on major parts. From the Ronald J. Navratil collection.

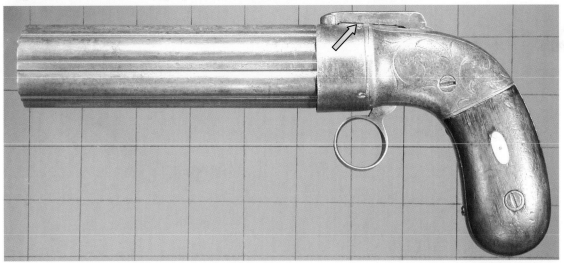

This intermediate Norwich ring trigger dragoon pepperbox is made with a shield. It is marked ALLEN'S PATENT on the hammer in one line and has the 1837 date on the barrel. The low location of the main spring tension screw indicates that it has the 1837 action. Note that the bottom of the hammer has been filed down. (See arrow.) This was a rather common practice as after continued use, the nipples would wear down and the hammer would strike the frame before the nipple. Filing off the lower part of the hammer was a quick and easy fix. Number 76. From the Elon Yurwit collection.

This early Norwich ring trigger has the distinctive dogleg type grips, early 1837 action and fluted barrel ribs. The hammer is marked ALLEN & THURBER / NORWICH C-T in two lines. The four inch barrel group is 32 caliber. Number 26. From the Perry Hansen Collection.

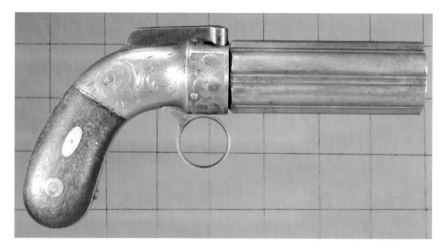

This seldom seen concealed hammer ring trigger pepperbox has the early 1837 action and is of intermediate Norwich vintage. The 32 caliber four inch barrel group has flat ribs and is marked ALLEN'S PAT-ENT / PATENTED 1837 CAST STEEL on two of the barrel ribs. Number 17. From the Robert Avery collection.

This concealed hammer pepperbox with conventional trigger guard is also of intermediate Norwich vintage and still retains the 1837-type action as indicated by the low location of the main spring tension adjusting screw and the flat barrel ribs. Number 6. From the Perry Hansen collection.

Up to this point, all of Allen's pepperbox revolvers incorporated the same early 1837-type action that had been used on all single shot bar hammer pistols as well. On April 16, 1845, Allen was granted patent number 3,998 that covered a new type of action that eliminated several springs and moving parts.

The main changes consisted of a new U-shaped main spring that was more flexible and a new one-piece sear (see arrow below in the patent drawing) that connected the main spring to the hammer and trigger. This eliminated the trigger return spring and the sear spring.

E. ALLEN.
Revolver.

No. 3,998.   Patented April 16, 1845.

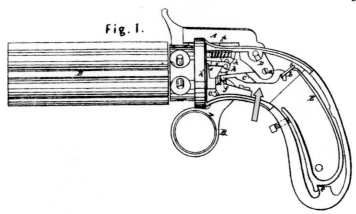

Allen's patent number 3,998 shows the new improved 1845 action. This patent also applies to the bar hammer transitional revolver and the single shot bar hammer pistols as well. It is interesting to note that the action is actually designed to be double action. It is obvious that the strange looking "horn" on the hammer was for cocking purposes. Although not a practical looking design, several Allen pepperboxes with this type of hammer have been observed but none were double action and had to be cocked manually.

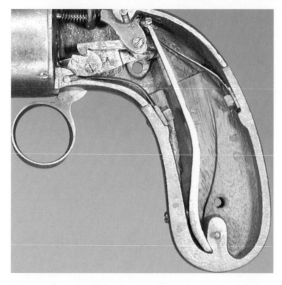

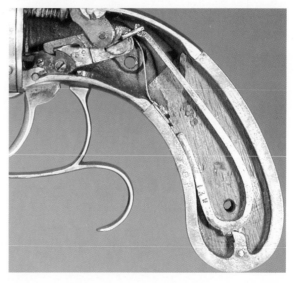

Shown above is the action from an early ring trigger dragoon pepperbox. This is typical of all pistols that have the 1837-type action.

This is the 1845 action from a late Worcester dragoon. All Allen & Wheelock pepperboxes have this type of action.

Allen's new action was put into production during the late Norwich years, but the 1837 patent date would continue to be seen until well into the Worcester period. It was not until Allen & Thurber replaced the ribbed barrels with fluted barrels that the 1845 patent date would be used.

Only late Worcester-marked Allen & Thurber, Allen, Thurber & Co. and Allen & Wheelock pepperboxes have fluted barrels.

This late Norwich standard six shot pepperbox has a 32 caliber five inch ribbed barrel group. Although it has the late 1845, action, it still retains the 1837 patent date. The high location of the main spring tension screw indicates the 1845 action. (See arrow.) Number 32.

This early Worcester six shot pepperbox has a different grip angle than the Norwich but still retains the grip spangles. The nipple shield now has a rose vine-type engraving and has the 1845 action, but is still marked with the 1837 patent date. Number 26. From the Perry Hansen collection.

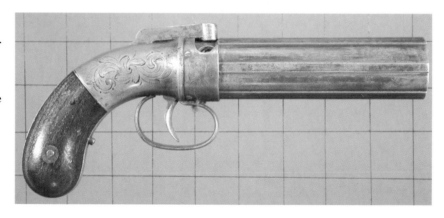

This often overlooked Worcester baby dragoon differs from other Worcester pepperboxes in that it is 34 caliber and has a five inch barrel group. The late bag-type grips are made without the grip spangles that had been standard since early Grafton days. Number 68. From the Elon Yurwit collection.

All Allen & Thurber pepperboxes made during the Grafton and Norwich period had six shot barrels. It was not until Worcester production began that Allen would bring out a five shot in an effort to make his products more appealing to an ever growing population, and to keep up with competition that was constantly increasing. A new, more compact four shot pepperbox would be patented and manufactured later during the Allen & Wheelock era that featured a different method of attaching the barrel to the frame.

Pepperbox manufacturing was still a high priority in 1856, at the inception of Allen & Wheelock. Production of the basic line of six shot standard, dragoon size and five shot pepperbox revolvers continued virtually unchanged from the Allen & Thurber period.

Although Allen had obtained his new patent in 1845, it was well into the Worcester era before the new patent date was used on pepperboxes. As frugal as Allen was, it is quite possible that he simply wanted to use up the existing 1837 dies or perhaps the 1845 dies were not available yet. Whatever the reason, Allen certainly got his money's worth since it is not uncommon to see a 1837 stamp that is actually fractured.

About the time that the full fluted barrel group became standard, Allen & Thurber introduced their new lighter more compact five shot pepperbox.

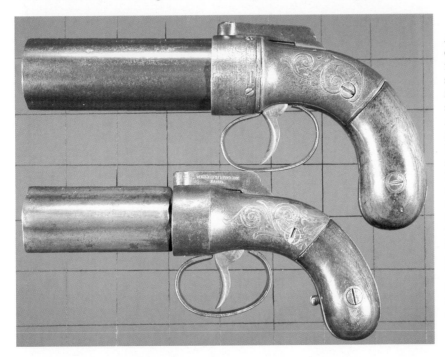

Allen changed the barrel design of his pepperboxes from ribbed to fluted sometime after production at Worcester had started. Only the late Allen & Thurber marked pepperboxes have fluted barrels but they are standard on all Allen, Thurber & Co. and Allen & Wheelock pepperbox models. The six shot on the top is marked Allen, Thurber & Co. and has a four inch 32 caliber barrel group. Number 104. The five shot on the bottom has a three inch barrel and is marked Allen & Thurber. Number 194.

During the Allen & Wheelock era, as the popularity of the pepperbox dwindled and competition increased, Allen found it necessary to cut production costs any way he could without sacrificing the performance or integrity of the firearm. This was done by eliminating the frame engraving on the four, five and six shot pepperboxes. Later, a new design for the five shot pepperbox did away with its nipple shield.

With the introduction of Allen's new line of large caliber percussion revolvers, production of the 36 caliber dragoon size pepperbox was probably the first to end. It is rare to see an Allen & Wheelock-marked dragoon pepperbox indicating that their production was limited.

Due to the total absence of any Allen & Wheelock factory records known to the author at this time, it is not possible to accurately determine the time of production or the number of units produced by Allen & Wheelock. Some models are rather common and some are quite rare, but the main effort is to point out the primary differences and variations within each major group of pepperboxes. Patent information is of little help as Allen was noted for using an improvement long before he was issued the patent.

As the popularity of Allen's percussion revolvers and his new line of cartridge revolvers increased, the beloved pepperbox that had been the cornerstone of his business died a slow death, thus ending production of one of the most important firearms in American history.

Allen memorabilia is rare, to say the least, but shown below are two items that have survived the rigors of time. The envelope has the Allen & Thurber return address on the back flap.

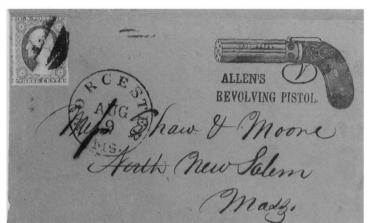

This rare envelope with an image of an Allen & Thurber pepperbox is postmarked 1851. From the Perry Hansen collection.

Shown above is the back flap from the envelope on the left.

Shown below is a tin case that is for Allen & Thurber percussion pepperbox revolvers. It has two separate compartments for the storage of shooting supplies, such as lead balls, caps or patches. It was found in an antique shop in London, England and measures three and one forth inches by two and one quarter inches. It is obvious that it was either made in England or for the European market, as Allen was exporting a few firearms at that time. It is interesting to note that the word "pepperbox" is printed in two words and they are referred to as revolvers.

This Allen & Thurber tin case was recently found in an antique shop in London, England.

Both compartments are hinged at the back and are the same size.

This has been a short review of some of the changes that the Allen pepperbox revolvers went through before the Allen & Wheelock period of production.

Chapter 10
ALLEN & WHEELOCK PEPPERBOXES

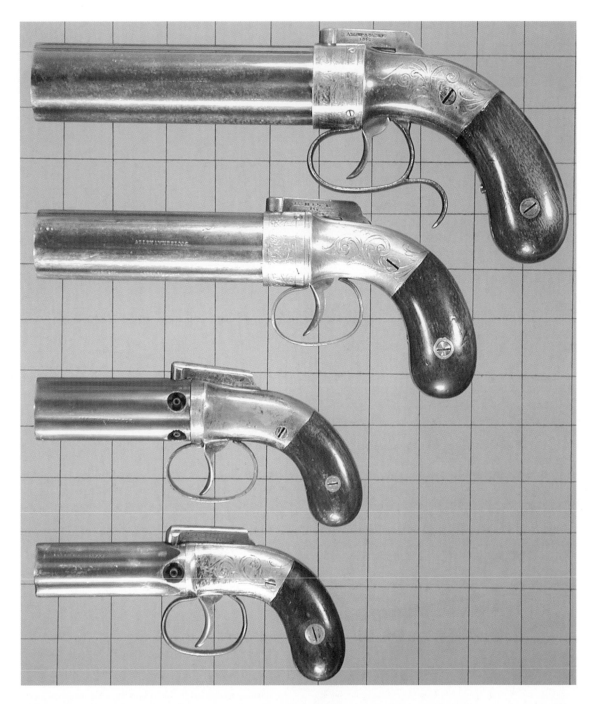

Allen & Wheelock pepperbox revolvers were made in four distinct frame sizes. At the top is a six shot 36 caliber dragoon with six inch barrels. Number 39. Second is a standard six shot 32 caliber with five inch barrels and engraved frame. Number 426. Third is a five shot 32 caliber with three inch barrels that was made without a nipple shield. Number 482. The bottom is a four shot 34 caliber with three barrels. Number 12.

Pepperbox production would not continue beyond the end of the Allen & Wheelock period of manufacture. The useful life of Allen's pepperbox ended, not only because of

56

increased competition from others, but also because of his own success with other types of percussion and cartridge pistols.

Most Allen & Wheelock pepperbox revolvers have three rows of notches cut into the rear of the barrel group. The innermost row of notches is for the barrel latch to lock the barrels in place when the trigger is pulled. The middle row of teeth is what the operating hand connects with to turn the barrel. A spring loaded detent pin fits into the shallow outer notches to keep the barrel from freewheeling when the trigger is released.

Shown above is a barrel from an Allen & Wheelock pepperbox. All pepperboxes have the same type of rotation and locking system. This is the same basic action that Allen used on all of his early pepperboxes.

The inner row of teeth are for locking the barrels in place. The middle row is for rotating the barrels. A spring loaded pin fits into the outer notches to keep the barrel from free wheeling when the trigger is pulled.

The photo on the right shows the three different components that are involved in the normal operation of the pepperbox. Directly under the hammer is the spring loaded detent pin (part number 18 on the illustrated parts list on page 16 of the Day Book chapter) that keeps the barrels from rotating after the trigger has been released. To the left of the stem is the operating hand (part number 24 on the parts list) that rotates the barrels when the trigger is pulled. Directly under the stem is the barrel lock (part number 17) that locks the barrels in place when the trigger is pulled all of the way. Although the action is the same, the method of attaching the barrel to the frame differs on the four shot models. It should be mentioned that the stem or shaft that the barrels rotate on is actually part of the frame casting and cannot be unscrewed or removed.

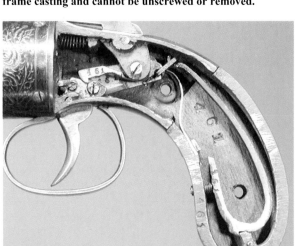

On the left shows the 1845 action from a late six shot Worcester standard that is the type used on all Allen & Wheelock pepperboxes. Although smaller in size, it is identical to the 1845 dragoon action illustrated on page 38. All major parts should have the same number as the frame. This action is also similar to the bar hammer transitional revolver. Notice that the main spring adjusting screw has been over tightened and should be backed off.

Chapter 11
THE DRAGOON PEPPERBOX

The 36 caliber dragoon pepperbox had gone through many mechanical and style changes before it become known as the "49er" due to its use during the California gold rush of 1849. Any person who was man enough to carry this massive side arm would surely be worthy of any claim jumper's respect.

The final major change came during the Allen & Thurber period when the barrel design was changed from a flat ribbed to a fully fluted barrel group. It was at this time that Allen, for some unknown reason, decided to start using the 1845 patent date, although the improvement had been in use for many years. Although the dragoon was surely manufactured during the Allen, Thurber & Co. period, no collector has ever reported seeing a dragoon pepperbox with those markings.

Frame engraving varied slightly from gun to gun, as did the shield engraving. The rose-vine type is the most common but occasionally a simple scroll and vine design can be encountered. All dragoons are 36 caliber and the standard barrel length is six inches, although shorter lengths can be seen. The barrel and frame are blued and the hammer, trigger and trigger guard are casehardened. Varnished walnut grips are standard but an ivory stocked specimen will occasionally be seen.

With the introduction of Allen & Wheelock's line of large 36 and 44 caliber revolvers, it is reasonable to believe that production of the dragoon pepperbox was halted long before the smaller pepperbox models. This is partly evident in the fact that a correct unengraved dragoon has never been noted. (This is not to say they do not exist.)

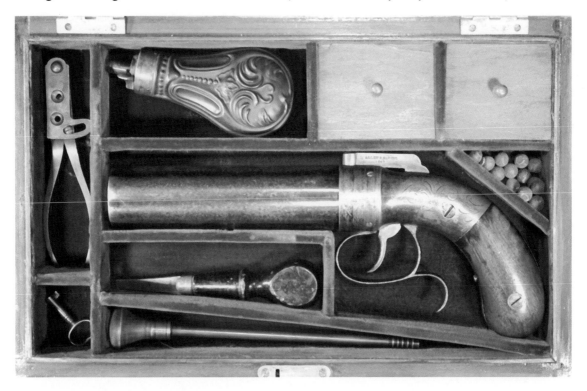

This early 36 caliber Allen & Wheelock dragoon pepperbox is cased with accessories in a box that is of a later vintage than the pepperbox. Number 26.

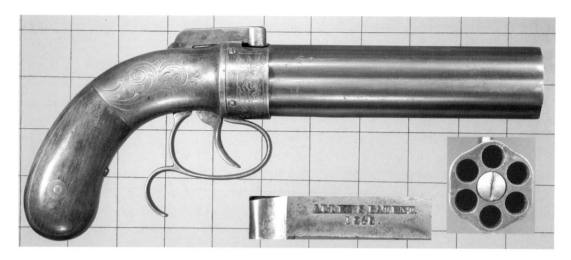

This early Allen & Wheelock Dragoon is marked on the hammer ALLEN'S PATENT / 1845 in two lines and is identical to the late Allen & Thurber dragoons except for the name. Number 26.

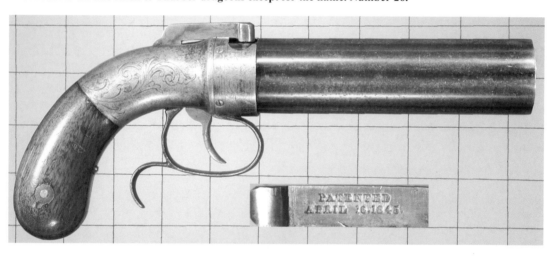

This intermediate dragoon is slightly later than the example at the top of the page. It has the late-type markings on the flat top hammer that now read PATENTED / APRIL 16, 1845. Number 39.

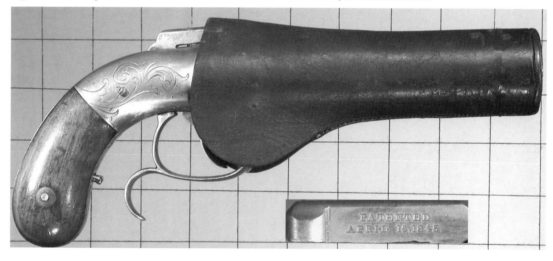

This late Dragoon has a round top hammer with in a rare barrel holster. This is the only type of holster that will accommodate a dragoon with the spur trigger guard. Number 65.

Chapter 12
THE SIX SHOT STANDARD PEPPERBOX AND ACCESSORIES

The man shown above is holding an Allen six shot Worcester standard pepperbox with fluted barrels.

As with the dragoons, the six shot standard pepperbox was carried-over virtually unchanged from the Allen & Thurber / Allen, Thurber & Co. period. Hammer and barrel markings remain the same as the dragoons. Occasionally, the April 16, 1845 patent date will be seen stamped in one of the barrel flutes.

There will be slight differences in the nipple shield etching but the later rose vine pattern is standard. The most common barrel length is four inches, but five inch barrels are not unusual. The standard caliber is 32, but a few 34 calibers will also be seen. The barrel and frame are blued, the hammer and trigger are casehardened, and varnished walnut grips are standard. Ivory, silver and pewter grips were optional.

From the early days of Grafton and Norwich, and through the Worcester period, the six shot standard was the most popular Allen pepperbox.

Allen & Wheelock six shot and five shot pepperboxes have the 1845 patent date and fluted barrels, but only early examples have the typical Allen-type frame engraving.

As the demand for pepperbox revolvers started to diminish, Allen cut his production costs by 12 cents per pepperbox by doing away with the modest frame engraving that had adorned his pepperboxes for over 25 years.

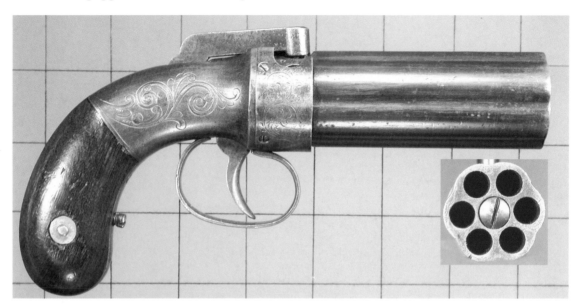

This early first model six shot Worcester standard with engraved frame and four inch barrel group is a carry over from the Allen, Thurber & Co. period and remained basically unchanged throughout production. The rose vine engraving on the nipple shield is standard. Number 204.

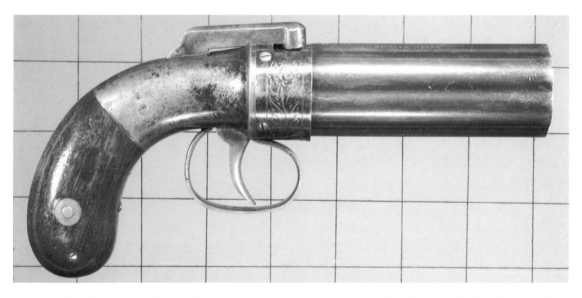

As competition increased, Allen was forced to cut corners wherever he could without sacrificing the integrity of the arm by eliminating the modest frame engraving. Allen's pepperboxes, like the single-shot bar-hammer self-cocking pistols without frame engraving, have round top hammers. Number 451.

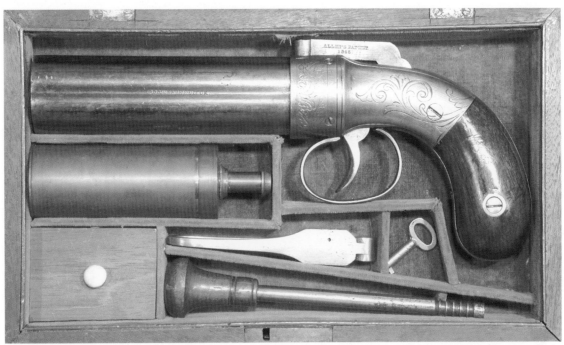

Pictured above is an engraved Allen & Wheelock 32 caliber six shot pepperbox with a five inch barrel group that is cased with accessories. The plunger-type powder flask is typical of the ones found in cased Allen pepperboxes. Number 426.

This four inch engraved pepperbox is also cased with accessories. The rather cheap looking little bullet mold is typical of those found in most original Allen cased sets. The combination cleaning rod / ramrod is also typical although no two seem to be alike. Number 42.

Mediterranean briar burl, grows at base of briar bush.

KAYWOODIE BRIAR

FLAME-GRAIN
KAYWOODIE

$10, Shape No. 07

Kaywoodie remembers when . . .

Mark Twain told the story about being run up a tree by a buffalo, and carrying a gun like the one shown here. It is an Allen and Wheelock Pepper Box made in the 1850's, and was a favorite gun during gold rush days. The pipe is a Flame-Grain Kaywoodie, coaxed from age-old Mediterranean briar by pipe-makers who learned from their fathers of Mark Twain's generation how a pipe should feel. The natural Flame-Grain is very rare. Your investment of $10. in the Flame-Grain Kaywoodie will pay rich rewards, it will yield years of pleasurable and manly smoking and its worth to you will increase—for where else can you find a pipe with such beauty and workmanship? Kaywoodie Company, New York and London, makers of fine pipes since 1851. Tr. 10-49

Send for literature picturing 49 Kaywoodie Pipes in colors, 630 Fifth Ave., N. Y. 20

POSSESSIONS TO CHERISH

This rather unusual 1940s ad for Kawoodie pipes features an Allen & Wheelock six shot Worcester pepperbox.

Chapter 13
THE FIVE SHOT PEPPERBOX

The early five shot Allen & Wheelock pepperbox is another arm that was carried over from the Allen, Thurber & Co. period. The markings are the same as on the six shots, and the dragoons.

This great little firearm, that provided five quick shots with a considerable amount of power, could be carried in a man's pocket or a lady's purse. It was not necessary to go through the formality of cocking the pistol as it was always ready to protect its owner.

However, it must have been a time consuming and expensive process to cast and machine the integral nipple shield on these little guns and soon, a new frame without the shield was put into production. The new design no doubt saved Allen a considerable amount of manufacturing expense without sacrificing the integrity of the revolver. Not only was the new frame cheaper to produce, the modest frame engraving was eliminated along with the six shot, thus saving the company 8 to12 cents per gun.

It is apparent that more barrels were made with the milled rebate on the barrels to allow for the nipple shield than frames to accommodate them. Regardless, these milled barrels were mated to the new shieldless frame. A few non-engraved shields were hand made and attached to the new frames.

Although these are some of the most generic guns in the Allen & Wheelock arsenal, they are also some of the most rare. The hammers on all shieldless non-engraved pepperboxes have a rounded top.

When the supply of cut barrels was exhausted, new barrels that were made without the rebate were utilized.

As with most Allen & Wheelock pepperboxes, blued barrel and frame, case hardened hammer and trigger were standard, as were the varnished walnut grips. The standard caliber is 32, the barrel length is three inches and occasionally, a specimen will be seen with ivory grips.

This early first model five shot has a nipple shield that is part of the frame casting and is a carry over from the Allen, Thurber & Co. period but marked Allen & Wheelock. The flat top hammer has the early 1845 patent date. All engraved five shots have a flat top hammer. (See inset.) Number 17.

64

This five shot second model pepperbox has a nipple shield that is separate from the frame. Although several have been observed over the years, it cannot be said for sure that they are actually a factory installation. Number 7.

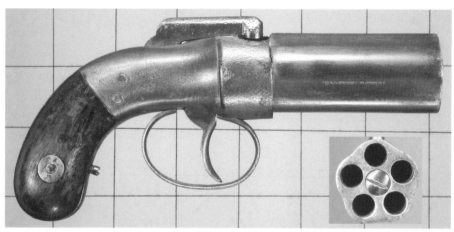

It is obvious that it was very costly to cast and machine the nipple shield as part of the frame. As a result, a limited number of five shot pepperboxes will have cut or rebated barrels that are attached to the shieldless frame. Number 5.

This third and final variation is the most common of the five shot series. It has the same frame as the gun pictured above but has the new barrel group that is not cut for a shield. All five shot models made without engraving have hammers that are round on top (see inset). Number 482.

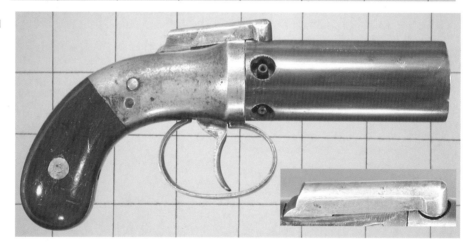

The third model shown above is the most commonly seen of the Allen & Wheelock five shot series.

It is easy to see how Allen was able to cut production cost without sacrificing the performance of the revolvers. As with Allen's other pepperboxes, at this point their days were numbered.

Chapter 14
THE FOUR SHOT PEPPERBOX AND ACCESSORIES

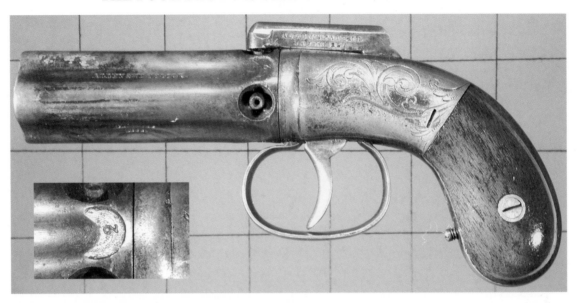

This first model four shot pepperbox has a casehardened barrel and a blued frame. It is marked ALLEN & WHEELOCK / PATENTED 1845 on two of the barrel flutes. It is also marked ALLEN'S PATENT / JAN 13, 1857 in two lines on the hammer. It has a hammer rest that has the number 2 on it. (See insert.) Number 300.

Most Allen pepperboxes were carried over from the Allen, Thurber & Co. era with little more than the name changed. Although the five shot went through several changes during the Allen & Wheelock period, the four shot is the only pepperbox that was totally designed, patented, and made exclusively by Allen & Wheelock. Although the basic action is the same as all other Allen & Wheelock pepperboxes, the main difference is the method of attaching the barrel group to the frame.

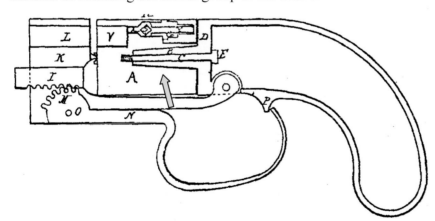

Part of patent number 16,368 dated January 13, 1857, covers the method of attaching the barrel group to the frame. The barrels rotate on the cone (see arrow) and are held in place by a free turning screw that enters from inside of the frame.

Allen's patent number 16,367 dated January 13, 1857 actually covers three different improvements, but the part pertaining to the four shot is the method of attaching the barrel to the frame by using a free turning screw that entered from inside the frame. This eliminates the shaft or center pin which the barrel group rotated and was used on all other Allen pepperboxes. A cone that was part of the frame casting not only acted as a bearing surface, but helped to support the barrels when the gun was fired. By eliminating the barrel stem or shaft that all other pepperboxes have, the gun could be made much smaller and compact by enabling the barrels to be made in a smaller cluster. This made it much easier to carry in a person's purse or pocket and gave the owner four quick shots with a considerable amount of power as fast as the trigger could be pulled.

The hammer markings read ALLEN'S PATENT / JAN 13, 1857, in two lines. This is the only Allen pepperbox to bear this patent date.

The standard is 34 caliber and the barrel length is three inches. Varnished walnut grips are standard but ivory was available.

There will be slight differences found, but as a rule, all 4 shots are basically the same. While some late examples have non-engraved frames, examples with engraved frames are the most common.

Some will have hammer rests and some will not. For some unknown reason, a bird's head will occasionally be stamped next to the serial number on the barrel.

Most barrels are blued but some are casehardened, which is rare. Casehardened frames are also occasionally seen but are equally as rare.

As these little guns are not seen in any great numbers, it is obvious that they were introduced at the end of the pepperbox era and production was limited.

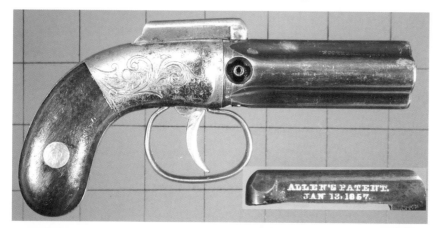

Although not seen in any large numbers, the engraved four shot with blued barrel and frame is considered the standard model. It is interesting to note that these little guns were 34 caliber and must have been a real handful when fired. Number 12.

This four shot is made without engraving but has a hammer rest. (See inset) Although the gun is in fine condition and does not appear to have been altered in any way, it is unmarked except for the patent date on the hammer and the number 409 on the barrel.

Although hammer rests are common on the larger frame bar hammer transitional revolvers and occasionally seen on the Navy side hammer percussion revolvers, the only Allen pepperboxes that have hammer rests are the four shots. It is not known if this was a special order or if they were installed at random.

This is the cone that the four barrel group rotates on. It is attached to the frame by a free turning screw that enters from the inside of the frame.

To make the barrel group smaller, the barrel stops were cut into the rotation teeth. The four barrel is the only pepperbox made this way.

By attaching the barrel group at the rear, the barrel group could be made much smaller.

There has been a considerable amount of discussion about the origin of the four shot pictured below. Although it does have some Allen features, it has as many non-Allen features. The barrel group is attached to the frame by a screw that enters from the side of the frame and fits into a groove in the rear of the barrel group. The nipples are the same as those used by Allen on the double barreled single trigger pistols. The number 00 is stamped on the frame. Other Allen firearms have been seen with the 00 mark as well.

The origin of this four barreled shotgun hammer pepperbox is not known but it does have some of the Allen characteristics. It has a hand turned barrel group with removable nipples. It is possible that it might have been Allen's last effort to keep a pepperbox on the market. Number 00 is marked on the frame and trigger guard. (See inset.)

The front part of the frame where the barrel attaches is different from other Allen pepperboxes.

The barrel group is held in place by a long screw that fits into a groove in the stem (see arrow).

The muzzle is similar but slightly thicker than other four-barrel pepperboxes.

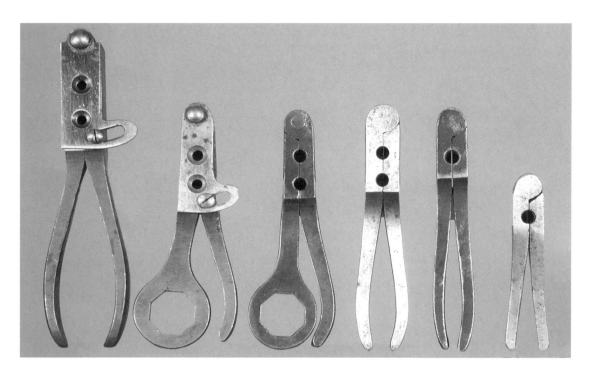

Pictured above are some of the different types of molds for Allen & Wheelock pistols. On the far left is a mold from a cased Navy side hammer. The next two are combination barrel wrench / bullet molds used on bar hammer single shot pistols and the last three are molds commonly found in cased pepperboxes.

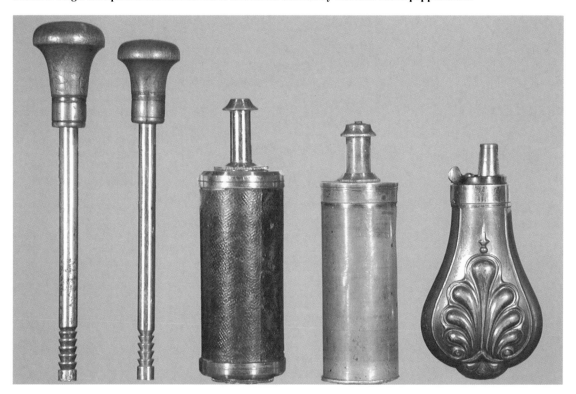

On the left are two different types of pepperbox cleaning rods. No two seem to be alike. The two plunger-type flasks both have storage in the bottom for percussion caps and are seen in cased Allen pepperboxes. Not all plunger flasks are wrapped with leather. The flask on the far right is typical of those seen in smaller cased Allen & Wheelock percussion pistols and revolvers.

Chapter 15
PERCUSSION REVOLVERS

Two Civil War soldiers are each armed with muskets and Allen & Wheelock belt model side hammer revolvers. Photo is credited to the Massachusetts Commandery, Military Order of the Loyal Legion and the U. S. Army Military History Institute.

70

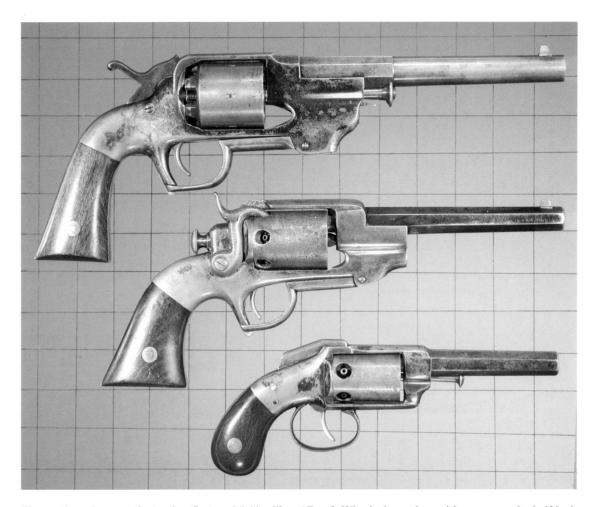

The revolver shown at the top is a first model 44 caliber Allen & Wheelock revolver with a seven and a half inch octagon and round barrel. Number 409. The second revolver is a late 36 caliber side hammer with a six inch octagon barrel. Number 213 from the Nick Peters collection. The revolver at the bottom of the picture is a late bar hammer that is referred to as the transitional model and was the first true revolver made by Allen & Wheelock. It has a four inch 32 caliber octagon barrel. Number 318.

The following chapters will cover the three different types of percussion revolvers that were manufactured by Allen & Wheelock.

The company's first true revolver was the transitional bar hammer pistol that was little more than a pepperbox with one barrel. It is covered by the same 1845 patent as all Allen & Wheelock pepperboxes and was made in three different frame sizes.

Second in production was the side hammer series that was a vast improvement over the bar hammer series and were made in calibers 36, 32, and 28 and in three different frame sizes. The large frame 36 caliber models are considered by most collectors as secondary military.

Third in the sequence of production was the center hammer model that was made in 44 and 36 caliber sizes. The large 44 caliber Army center hammer is probably the most recognized firearm of the Allen & Wheelock Company and is occasionally seen with military marks.

Chapter 16
BAR HAMMER REVOLVERS

The revolver on the top is a large frame, 32 caliber second model with a four inch barrel. Number 318. The middle pistol is also a second model, 32 caliber, but has the mid size frame with a three inch barrel. Number 202. The pistol on the bottom is a small frame 30 caliber with a two and a half inch barrel. Number 270.

The bar hammer percussion revolver, sometimes called the transitional revolver, was Allen & Wheelock's first venture into the revolver market and is covered by Allen's patent number 3,998 that was granted on April 16, 1845. This same patent also covers all of the Allen & Wheelock pepperboxes with the exception of the four shot.

As shown above, there are three distinctive frame and cylinder sizes and an early and late variation in each size. Early specimens were marked Allen & Wheelock either on the top flat of the barrel or on the top frame strap, and the patent information on the left side of the hammer. Later variations have the maker's name and patent information on the left barrel flat.

All variations have five shot cylinders that are engraved with scenes of animals in a forest. Some cylinders have different types of hammer rests, while others will have none. All models are standard with blued frame, barrel and trigger guard with casehardened cylinders, hammers and triggers. Varnished walnut grips are standard but ivory was an option. Examples with frame engraving exist but are very rare.

This first model 32 caliber large frame, long cylinder model has a screw-off barrel that had to be removed to gain access to the cylinder pin (see details below). It is easy to see why very few first models have survived. Number 302.

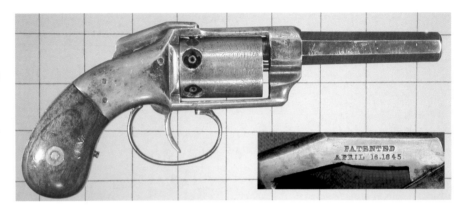

Below is an early transitional revolver that has been fitted with a cap shield. It is not known if this was a factory installation but the shield is mated to the frame perfectly.

The pistol on the right is a first model with a screw-off barrel that has been fitted with a cap shield. Unfortunately, the removable shield from the left side is missing. At this time, this is the only one like it that has been reported. Number 65.

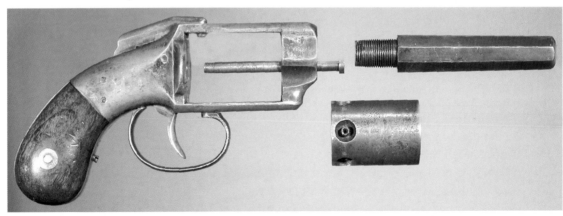

The barrel of the first model bar hammer revolvers had to removed to have access to the cylinder pin, which had to be removed with a screwdriver. It is easy to see why very few have survived.

The early revolver on the left shows how the barrel covers the screw head that is actually the cylinder pin. (See arrow.) It was necessary to remove the barrel to gain access to the cylinder pin. After the barrel was removed, a screwdriver had to be used to unscrew the threaded cylinder pin. The revolver on the right has the late-type cylinder pin that is held in place by a spring loaded ball that is inside of the front part of the frame. This was obviously a much better system and was used on all subsequent models.

Shown above is a cased first model long cylinder bar hammer percussion revolver that has the screw-off barrel. The set contains a combination bullet mold / barrel wrench, a combination bullet rammer / cleaning rod and a plunger-type powder flask that has a cap storage compartment in the bottom. Number 302.

All bar hammer transitional revolvers had nicely engraved cylinders. The large and medium size models share the same engraving as the belt size side hammer revolvers. The small frame has the same engraving as the 28 caliber side hammer pocket model.

Engraving on small frame revolvers is the same as on the 28 caliber side hammer pocket model revolvers.

The engraving on the large and medium size bar hammers is the same as the side hammer belt models.

This large frame second model bar hammer has the new improved second type cylinder pin. Markings on the top of the frame are ALLEN & WHEELOCK. The left side of the hammer is marked PATENTED / APRIL 16, 1845 in two lines. Number 199.

The medium size bar hammer revolver shown below is the most common. The length of the cylinder is one and a half inches, which is one eighth of an inch shorter than the long cylinder models. It is still 32 caliber and has both early and late markings.

This medium size third model has a short cylinder and frame (see arrow). The maker's name and patent marks are now on the left side of the barrel. Number 290.

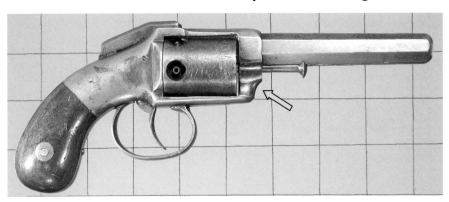

The frame area in front of the cylinder has been shortened from eleven sixteenth (see arrow in photo of ivory griped revolver) of an inch to one half of an inch (see arrow in photo above).

The small frame 30 caliber bar hammer revolver is a rather standard gun that has both early and late markings. All have two and a half inch full octagon barrels and a cylinder length of one and a half inches.

It appears that Allen did a little experimenting with the triggerguard and the placement of the markings, but other than that, all small frame models are the same, indicating that they were of later production.

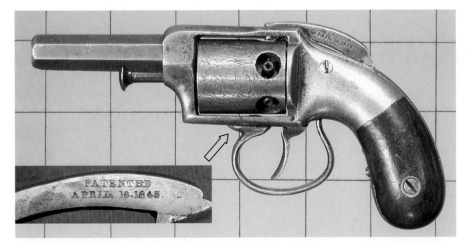

This early 30 caliber small frame model is marked on the top barrel flat ALLEN & WHEELOCK in one line and PATENTED / APRIL 16, 1845 on the hammer in two lines. It also has a different type trigger guard. (See arrow.) Number 3.

This small frame revolver is adorned with ivory grips. The barrel markings are the same as the gun above and the patent date remains on the left side of the hammer. Number 46.

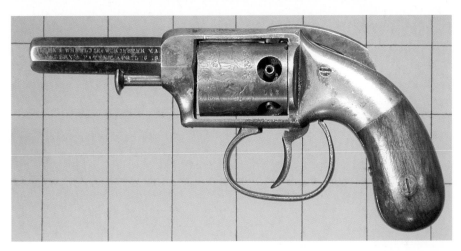

Late small frame models have the makers name and patent information marked on the left side of the barrel. There are no marks on the hammer. This is the most common of the small frame series. Number 270.

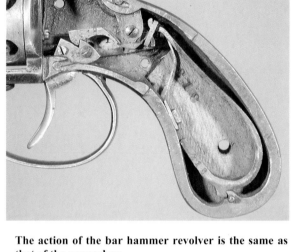

Above are the three sizes of cylinders used in transitional revolvers. On the left is a long cylinder from a long frame model that is one and five eighth inches long. The cylinder in the middle is from a medium size revolver and is one and a half inches long. The short cylinder on the right is from a small frame model and is one and one fourth inches long. All cylinders are engraved with scenes of animals in a forest. See pages 73 and 74 for details of engraving.

The action of the bar hammer revolver is the same as that of the pepperbox.

Shown above is the notch in the rear of the cylinder (see arrow) that should line up with the detent pin before reinstalling the cylinder. Note the hammer rest.

The method of rotating and locking the cylinder is the same as the pepperbox. Although there is a positive cylinder lock that is controlled by the trigger, it is necessary to have a spring loaded detent pin to keep the cylinder from free wheeling as the lock is only engaged when the trigger is pulled. Reinstalling the barrels on a pepperbox consists of simply sliding the barrel group onto the barrel stem but it is a little more difficult to reinstall the cylinder in the bar hammer revolvers. As shown in the photo on the left, it is necessary to make sure that the notch in the rear of the cylinder lines up with the detent pin located in the recoil shield.

Pictured below is a photo of the Allen & Wheelock bar hammer revolver that Rollin White used as the model for his patent number 19,671 that was originally issued on April 13, 1858. This is not to be confused with the revolver that White used for his 1855 patent for bored through cylinders.

This is the Allen & Wheelock transitional revolver that was used by Rollin White as the model that was presented to the patent office. Patent number 19,671 was issued to White on April 19, 1858. The photo is from the Smithsonian Institute.

Chapter 17
SIDE HAMMER PERCUSSION REVOLVERS

Members of the first battery, Massachusetts Light Artillery, are shown with their 36 caliber Allen and Wheelock side hammer percussion revolvers in August, 1861, at Camp Cameron. Photo is from the Massachusetts Commandry, Military Order of the Loyal Legion and the U.S. Army Military History Institute.

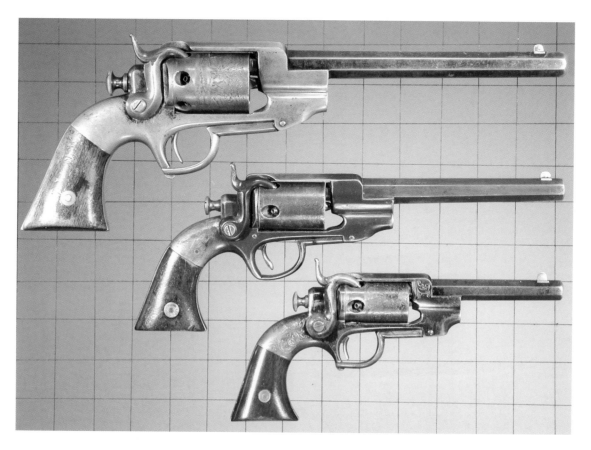

Pictured above are the three frame sizes of the percussion side hammer series. All have octagon barrels. On top is a late variation of the 36 caliber Navy percussion side hammer revolver with a six shot cylinder and an eight inch barrel. Number 441. The second pistol is an early 32 caliber with a six inch barrel and a friction latch trigger guard. Number 6. The third gun is an engraved late 28 caliber with a four inch barrel. Number 337.

The side hammer percussion revolver was a major improvement over the transitional bar hammer. It is a much advanced weapon that had several unique features described in Allen's patent number 16,367 dated January 13, 1857, which covers the combination trigger guard bullet rammer that is used on all Allen & Wheelock side hammer and center hammer percussion revolvers with the exception of the Providence Police Model. The second patent, number 18,836 dated December 15, 1857, describes a rotation disk to turn the cylinder, the locking device for the rotating disk and the hammer tumbler with a half cock position. The third patent, number 21,400, dated September 7, 1858, covers the modification of the front part of the cylinder pin to prevent fouling by squaring off the portion of the pin that extends between the cylinder and the point of entry into the frame. It is obvious that this improvement was in use before the patent date, as most specimens will be found with square pins.

The side hammer percussion revolvers were made in three distinctive sizes and the information in this chapter pertains to all three models. The 36 caliber six shot revolver is referred to as the Navy, the 32 caliber five shot as the belt pistol and the 28 caliber five shot as the pocket pistol.

Made with blued barrel and frame, casehardened hammer, cylinder, trigger and trigger guard and varnished walnut grips, although ivory is not uncommon.

Since the December 15, 1857 patent drawing shows a five shot revolver, it is the consensus that the belt model was the first produced. The new pistol was often referred to as Allen's Colt due to the resemblance of the Colt Root revolver, which also had a rear entry cylinder pin. In any event, the 36 caliber Navy was not far behind in production and may have been experimented with about the same time. The 28 caliber pocket models were considerably later.

Early side hammer percussion revolvers had a rather simple system of locking the trigger guard in place. Half of the latch was on the trigger stud part of the frame and the other half was on the guard itself. This system is referred to as the friction latch. All early side hammer revolvers with this type latch have multiple screw side plates. This system worked satisfactorily when the arm was new, but after some use the latch would not hold properly and soon a new spring latch locking system was introduced. This improvement consisted of a spring loaded catch that was installed in the trigger stud and simply latched onto the trigger guard when it was in the closed position. This same type latch is used on all later center hammer percussion and lipfire revolvers as well as the dropping block and revolving rifles.

The early friction latch system left a lot to be desired but was used on all three of the side hammer models. Production was limited. This system was not used on any other Allen firearms.

The spring latch system was a major improvement over the early friction latch. This type of latch was also used on the center hammer series as well as the dropping block rifle.

Allen was always making changes in his arms in an effort to cut costs and improve his products wherever he could. Many changes were made in the approximately two years of side hammer production. Although no factory records are known to exist, it is estimated that about 750 units of each were produced before being replaced by the much stronger center hammer series. This cannot be confirmed but appears to be a reasonable estimate.

Production of the side hammer series started sometime in 1857 and continued for two or three years. However, it was at this time that Allen & Wheelock was also entering into the cartridge era and there can be no doubt that he had a revolver with cylinders bored clear through in production as well.

At the time in history when these guns were being produced, Allen still had a rather strong hold on the multi-shot market with his pepperbox revolvers and his popular single shot pistols, which were still selling well.

80

One of the most distinctive characteristics of all Allen & Wheelock side hammer percussion revolvers is the nicely engraved cylinder of various animals and birds in a forest that adorned all three revolvers in the side hammer series. Each model has a different scene, as illustrated below.

Above is the cylinder engraving of animals in a forest that was used exclusively on 36 caliber six shot Navy side hammer percussion revolvers.

The cylinder engraving of the five shot belt model is considerably different than the 36 caliber Navy side hammer but is the same as the large and medium frame bar hammer revolvers.

Shown above is the cylinder engraving used on the 28 caliber five shot pocket models of ducks and feeding deer. This is the same engraving that is also used on the small frame bar hammer revolvers.

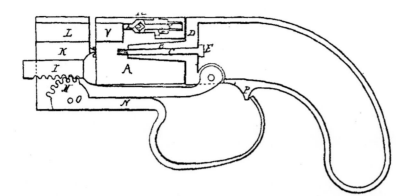

Patent number 16,367, of January 13, 1857 covers three different improvements. This included the method of attaching the barrel of the four shot pepperbox to the frame, a nipple with a gas check valve and the rack and pinion type bullet rammer that is activated by the trigger guard. This system is used on all side hammer and center hammer percussion revolvers.

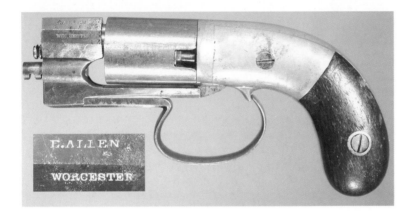

This is the actual brass frame patent model that Allen submited to the U.S. Patent office in 1856 and received patent number 16,367 on January 13, 1857. It is simply marked on two of the barrel flats, E. ALLEN / WORCESTER. (See inset.) The same principle of using the trigger guard to activate the cartridge extractor is used on the 44 and 36 caliber lipfire revolvers as well as percussion revolvers.

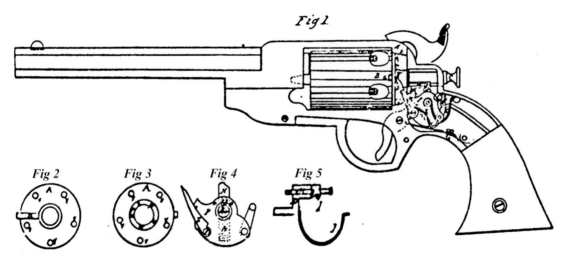

Shown above is Allen's patent number 18,836, dated December 15, 1857, which illustrates the basic construction of all side hammer revolvers. Since this is a five shot design, it is obviously a belt model.

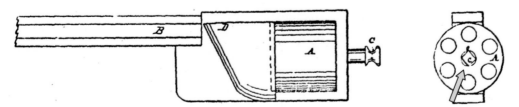

This excerpt from patent number 21,400 dated September 7, 1858, resembles the snout that is characteristic on only the revolving rifles. Regardless, it is still the basis of the anti-fowling cylinder pin that Allen used on all but the earliest side hammer revolvers. (See arrow.)

Patent information on early side hammer revolvers is on one of the flats of the barrel and on the frame under the trigger guard. For some unknown reason, these dates will be reversed on some of the early belt models. It is interesting that the patent date shown in the lower right picture is stamped Jan 12, but should be Jan 13.

The name and the Dec. 15, 1857 patent date is stamped on the top two barrel flats on the early belt models. These dates are reversed on some models.

The Jan. 12 1857 patent date that is under the trigger guard on this early friction latch revolver should be Jan. 13, 1857. (See arrow.)

Later markings are on the side of the barrel, where they will remain through the balance of production. Late friction latch models as well as early spring latch models have the two 1857 patent dates, but later models will have the addition of the December 7, 1858 date.

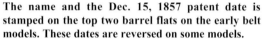

Intermediate barrel markings only have two 1857 patent dates on the barrel.

Late model side hammers have both of the 1857 patent dates plus the additional Sept. 7, 1858 date.

There are four different standard types of cylinders used in the side hammer percussion series as shown below. One other design exists but it is not considered a standard design and will be covered in the next chapter.

Type one cylinder   Type two cylinder   Type three cylinder   Type four cylinder

The 36 caliber Navy uses the type one and type four cylinder only. The 32 belt models use type two, three and four cylinders but the 28 pocket models only use type four cylinders. As cost conscious as Allen was, one has to wonder why he did not use the simpler type four as it required much less machining and accomplishes the same thing.

Two different types of hammer knurling are used on all side hammer models as illustrated in the photos on the right. There is no consistency and are used at random in early and late models as well.

Saddle knurling is on the left and tear drop on the right.

Above are the three different size cylinders that are used on Allen & Wheelock side hammer percussion revolvers. On the left is a six shot cylinder from a 36 caliber Navy that is one and seven eighths inches long. The cylinder in the middle is from a 32 caliber belt model and is one and eleven sixteenth inches long. The cylinder on the right is from a 28 caliber pocket model and is one and nine sixteenth inches long. All are nicely engraved with scenes of deer and other animals in the woods. (See page 80 for details.)

All Allen & Wheelock side hammer percussion revolvers have the same action.

There are six different types of side plates used on the various side hammer models. All but the type one will be seen on the belt models but only type one and type six are used on the 36 caliber Navies and the 28 caliber pocket models.

Type one side plate.

Type two side plate.

Type three side plate.

Type four side plate.

Type five side plate.

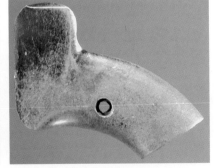

Type six side plate.

Four different types of cylinder pins are used on 36 caliber Navy revolvers and two different types on the 32 caliber belt and the 28 caliber pocket models.

The first type cylinder pin with the grease grooves was only used on early first model Navies.

The second type cylinder pin without grease grooves was used only on late first model Navies.

This third type Navy cylinder pin was the first to use the squared front end (see arrow) that was described in the September 7, 1858 patent. It was used on early second models.

The convex pinhead on the fourth type is the only difference from the third type. It is used on the late second model Navies for the remainder of production.

This first type belt or pocket cylinder pin has a round front end and will only be seen on early revolvers. Both early and late models all have round heads.

The second type belt or pocket cylinder pin with the square front end is found on most side hammer revolvers.

To remove the cylinder of a percussion side hammer revolver, it is necessary to put the revolver on half cock and rotate the cylinder until the notch on the rear of the cylinder is at the center of the left side of the gun. The cylinder can then slide out to the right after the cylinder pin has been removed.

Before removing the cylinder from any side hammer percussion revolver, the notch at the rear of the cylinder must be facing the left. (See arrow.)

Before reinstalling the cylinder, the lug on the rotating plate must be lined up horizontally with the slot on the cylinder. (See arrow.)

Chapter 18
36 CALIBER NAVY SIDE HAMMER REVOLVERS

This is Second Lt. William S. Rhodes of Co. B. 8th Regt., Infantry, Mass. Vol. Militia. He is armed with a sword and a 36 caliber Navy side hammer percussion revolver with a six inch barrel. The photo is from the Massachusetts Commandery, Military Order of the Loyal Legion and the U. S. Army Military History Institute.

Although not as popular as many other early Civil War percussion revolvers, the Allen & Wheelock 36 caliber side hammer did see limited military use and is considered a secondary military pistol. No known government contracts were obtained by Allen, but in the early days of the Civil War, the Army Ordinance purchased 338 Allen & Wheelock 36 caliber side hammer percussion revolvers on the open market for $14.13 each.[1]

One unit that carried the 36 caliber side-hammer revolvers was the 1st Massachusetts Battery Light Artillery. They were organized in August 1861 at Camp Cameron, Massachusetts and served with the Army of the Potomac during their three years of service. (See page 77.)

Although there are many small variations of the Navy series, in general, all 36 caliber side hammer percussion revolvers are basically the same. A threaded, rear entry cylinder pin holds the cylinder in place and can be removed either by hand or with a screwdriver. Six and eight inch barrel lengths are standard and only the 36 caliber has a six shot cylinder. The cylinder engraving is a scene of animals in a forest.

The side plate on early revolvers was attached to the frame by three screws, but after some frame modification, a much smaller side plate that required only one screw to hold it in place was introduced. Less significant changes were made in the cylinder pin as well as the machining process on the rear of the cylinder. The early example shown below was made without the rotating plate that is standard on all other side hammer percussion revolvers. The rotation teeth and the cylinder stops were cut into the rear of the cylinder, very similar to the pepperbox and the transitional revolvers. At this time, no other side hammer percussion revolvers have been observed with this feature but that does not mean that others might not exist.

This exceptionally fine cased 36 caliber Navy side hammer is marked ALLEN & WHEELOCK / ALLEN'S PATENT, JAN 13, 1857 on two of the barrel flats. The cylinder rotation teeth and stops are cut into the rear of the cylinder similar to the pepperbox or bar hammer revolvers but does not have the cylinder rotation plate that is standard on all other Allen and Wheelock side hammer percussion revolvers. It has a friction latch trigger guard, a type one three screw side plate and a type two round cylinder pin. It has an eight-inch octagon barrel and could possibly be an experimental model. Number 20 is on the frame and 13 on the barrel.

---

1. John D. McAulay, *CIVIL WAR PISTOLS,* Lincoln, Rhode Island, Andrew Mowbray Inc, p.18.

This is the cased early Navy side hammer that is shown on the preceding page. It has a distinctive sharp angle at the top rear of the frame. Unlike other side hammers, this specimen does not have the cylinder rotation disk. As shown in the inset above, the rear of the cylinder is made somewhat like the cylinder of the pepperbox or transitional revolver. Note the hammer rest on the cylinder.

Early first models have a set screw that enters the frame just behind the recoil shield and is partially hidden by the hammer when it is resting on the cylinder. Its purpose is to keep the collar that retains the rotating disk from turning as the cylinder is indexed. (See inset in photo below.) This screw was eliminated by changing the threads on the collar from right hand to left hand and will be standard on all side hammer percussion models.

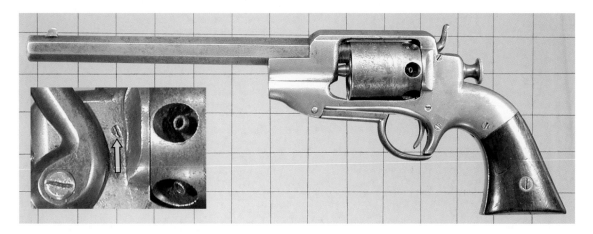

This early first model shown above has the early Allen & Wheelock marking as illustrated on page 82. It has a three screw side plate, friction latch and early type one cylinder pin with grease rings. This revolver also has the tumbler adjusting screw that is explained below. The set screw that locks the rotation collar in place is shown in the inset above. (See Arrow.) Number 44. The set screw was also used on early belt models as well.

Under the side plate of early first model 36 caliber side hammer revolvers is a small screw in the end of the hammer tumbler. On the end of this screw is a finely machined tip about three eighths of an inch long. (See arrow.) The head of the screw acts as a bearing surface and fits into the side plate to help bear the load of the tumbler when the hammer is cocked. When the revolver was being fitted, the end of the screw could be trimmed to the correct length to assure a tight fit and eliminate any end play in the tumbler. This feature has only been observed on early first model Navies and belt revolvers.

This late first model has the name and patent dates on the side of the barrel for the first time. The threads on the rotating disk retainer are now left hand and eliminates the need for a set screw. Number 23.

Early second models retain the three screw type one side plate but has the new snap latch trigger guard. This is the first model to have the type three square cylinder pin that is covered in Allen's September 7, 1858, patent number 21,400. The barrel length is eight inches. Number 46.

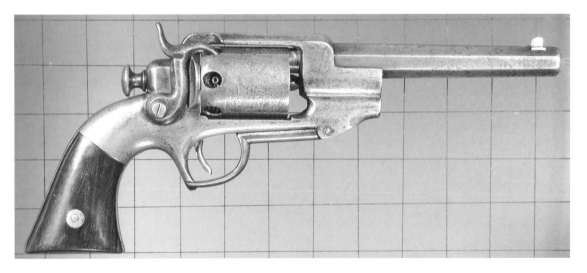

This late second model with a six-inch barrel is the same as the preceding revolver shown above but has the new type four cylinder pin that has a convex head. Number 70. From the Pete Kiefert collection.

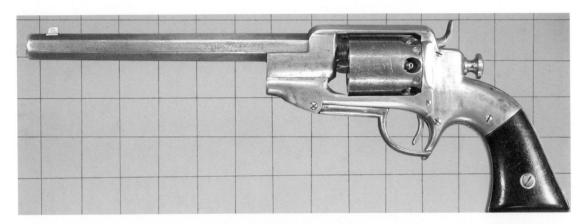

This late second model has hammer rests on the cylinder and differs from the early second model by the use of a new type four convex head cylinder pin. The convex head pin replaces the old concave pinhead that was used on all preceding models. This type was much easier to machine thus cutting production cost and would remain standard. The barrel length is eight inches. Number 117.

This eight inch barreled third model is the most common 36 caliber side hammer. The new one screw type six side plate was used and would remain standard for the remainder of production. Number 441.

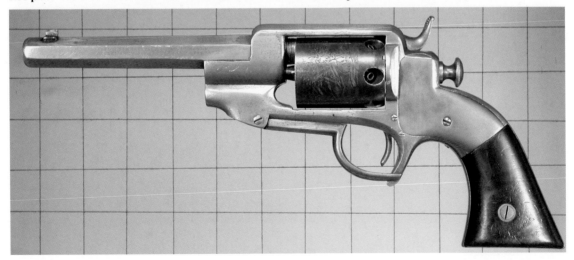

This late 36 caliber Navy side hammer has a six inch barrel, a snap latch trigger guard and a one screw side plate. Number 184. From the Doug Stack collection.

This unidentified soldier has a musket with a bayonet and an Allen & Wheelock belt model side hammer percussion revolver.

Chapter 19
32 CALIBER SIDE HAMMER BELT MODEL REVOLVERS

Private James W. Thompson of Co. G., 18th Reg., Ind. Vol, Inf., with his musket and long barrel Allen & Wheelock belt model revolver. Photo from the Wm. Van Velzer collection at U.S. Army Military History Institute.

The belt size side hammer series is little more than a downsized version of the 36 caliber Navy revolver, the major difference being that the 36 has a six shot cylinder and the belt models are five shot. Cylinders are engraved with scenes of animals in a forest.

Although the belt models can be found in 31, 32 and 34 caliber, the 32 is the most common. All have octagon barrel lengths of four, five, six and seven and one half inches.

Like all other side hammer percussion revolvers, belt models have a rear entry cylinder pin, are single action and have a combination trigger guard that also serves as the bullet rammer. Frame and barrels are blued, the hammer, trigger and trigger guard are case hardened and the standard grips are varnished walnut but ivory is not uncommon.

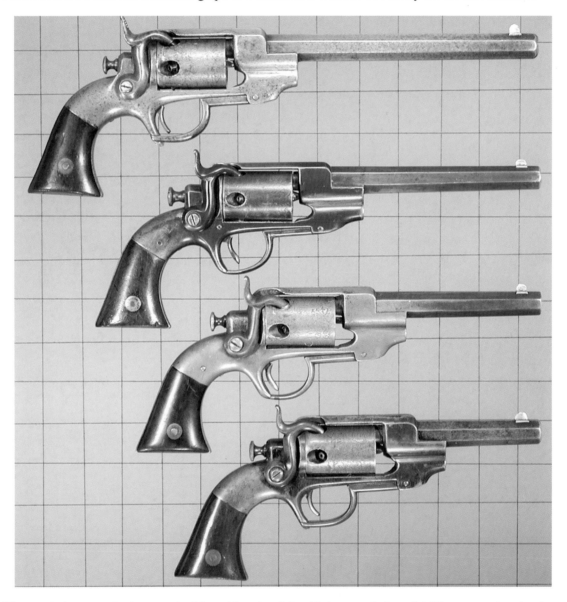

Illustrated above are the four standard barrel lengths of the side hammer belt model. The top revolver is a late third model with a seven and a half inch barrel, a one screw side plate and a spring latch trigger guard. Number 484. The second revolver is an early friction latch first model with six inch barrel and a three screw side plate. Number 6. The third is also a three screw first model friction latch with a five inch barrel. Number 29. The revolver on the bottom is a later friction latch model with a two screw side plate with a four inch barrel. This pistol has a slightly different frame opening at the front of the cylinder. This appears to have been due to a different machining process. Number 357.

The belt models are the most common of the side hammer series and are seen in more variations than either the 36 or the 28. They can generally be classified in three different models. First models have three screw side plates and a friction type trigger guard latch and normally have a type two cylinder. The exception is the pistol shown below that for some unexplained reason has a type three cylinder that is matching and correct. The side plate screw pattern on very early first models are the same as shown in patent number 18,936 dated December 15, 1857 that is illustrated on Page 81. Only the January 13, 1857 patent date is used on this early revolver.

This very early first model side hammer belt revolver has a 31 caliber six inch barrel that is marked ALLEN & WHEELOCK / PATENTED JAN. 13, 1857 on two of the top barrel flats. This early gun has a friction latch trigger guard, a type three cylinder, which is numbered to the gun, and an early cylinder pin that is round in the front. It also has an adjusting screw that enters into the exposed hammer tumbler that extends through the side plate (see inset). Only very early Navy and belt models have the adjusting screw. This early belt model had a set screw to lock the rotating collar in place the same as the early Navy models. This type two side plate has a sharp angle at the top rear of the frame like the Navy pictured in the top photo on page 87 (see arrow). The screw pattern on the side plate is identical to that of the patent drawing. Number 6.

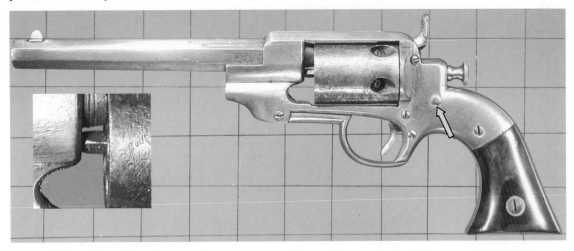

This standard first model belt revolver is marked ALLEN & WHEELOCK and ALLEN'S PATENT, DEC 15, 1857 on two of the barrel flats and JAN 13, 1857 on the frame under the trigger guard, as illustrated in the top photo on page 82. Also standard is the type two cylinder, late type square cylinder pin, (See inset) type 3 side plate and friction type trigger guard latch. The left end of the hammer tumbler extends through the side plate on early belt models. (See Arrow.) Number 38.

Later first models are more consistent and have the type three, three screw side plate with the hammer tumbler extending through it as shown on the revolver on the bottom of the preceding page.

Shown above is another standard first model belt pistol that has a four inch barrel. It is rare to see an early side hammer in this condition. Number 57.

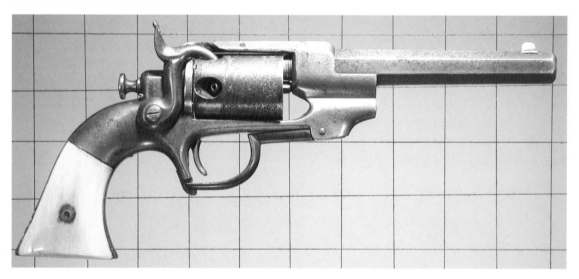

This is a rather unusual belt model that should be shown later in the chapter as it is a very early third model with a one screw side plate and a later spring latch trigger guard latch and a lovely set of ivory grips. It has the early two date barrel markings but has an early type three cylinder. Number 324.

There will always be things that do not fall in line with the normal sequence of production as indicated by the belt model shown above. It has all of the characteristics of an early third model, but has an early type three cylinder that is correctly numbered. In turn, the second model belt pistol with a friction latch trigger guard shown on the lower photo on page 95 has a type four cylinder when it should be a type three cylinder. These things are very confusing but that is a good example of why collecting Allens is never boring.

Changes on the early belt models came quickly in order to cut production costs. The first significant change was to remove the top screw from the side plate, which eliminated a tedious machining process. In order to accomplish this and at the same time keep the new type four side plate secured firmly to the frame, it was necessary to move the back screw about three eighths of an inch closer to the hammer tumbler.

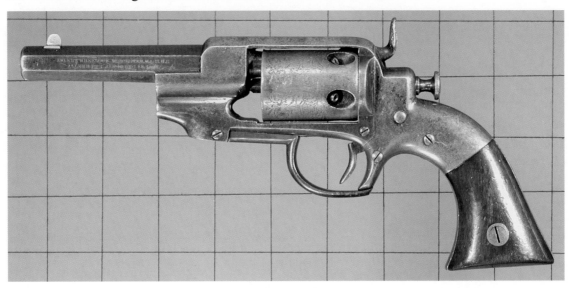

This early second model has the new type four side plate and is now held in place with two screws. The type three cylinder and the late type cylinder pin are used as well as the early friction style trigger guard latch. Note the late markings on the side of the barrel. Number 26.

The next improvement consisted of making the hammer tumbler slightly narrower to accommodate the new type five side plate that allows the tumbler to be inside of the frame.

This late second model two screw friction latch has the early markings as illustrated on page 82. A type four cylinder was used with the second type belt model square cylinder pin and the type five side plate. The hammer tumbler is enclosed in the frame on this and all subsequent models. Number 21.

The third variation had gone through a considerable number of changes from the earlier models. A one screw type six side plate replaced the multi-screw variations. A much more efficient spring latch replaced the friction type trigger guard latch. Both features are standard for the remainder of production.

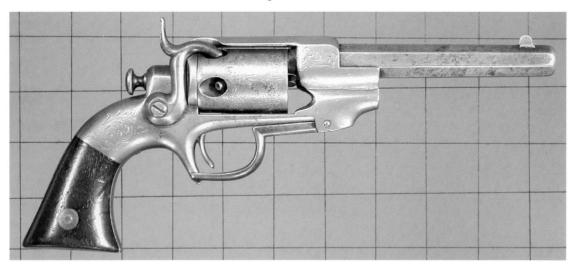

This is an early third model that is adorned with modest frame engraving. It is also equipped with a new type six one screw side plate, type four cylinder and the newly designed snap latch trigger guard. Although this is a late gun, the Sept 7, 1858 patent date pertaining to the squared off cylinder pin is still absent although the improvement is in use. Number 163.

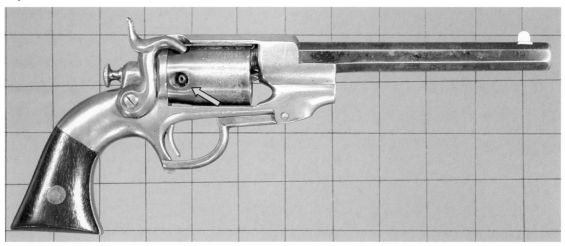

This final variation of the belt size side hammer has very small nipple openings in the cylinder (see arrow). By arranging the nipples so they enter the cylinder at a sharper angle, it gives room for about one eighths of an inch more powder in each chamber. Although the September 7, 1858 patent improvement for the squared cylinder pin had been in use for some time, this is the first time the date is used on a belt model. Number 118.

It is interesting to note that the nipple openings on the cylinder of the gun pictured above are much smaller than those seen on other side hammers. By changing the angle at the point of entry into the cylinder chamber, it is possible to get an additional one eighth of an inch of powder in the chamber without any other modifications. This small, but efficient, improvement was surely a late innovation, as it is the only one of its kind that has been accounted for to date.

Chapter 20
28 CALIBER SIDE HAMMER POCKET REVOLVERS

This Civil War soldier is armed with a Sharps carbine, a bowie knife, a cavalry saber and a 28 caliber Allen & Wheelock side hammer percussion revolver. Photo is from the Richard Carlile collection.

Other than size, the 28 caliber side hammer percussion pocket model is nearly identical in appearance to its two big brothers, the 36 Navy model and the 32 belt model revolvers.

Although not nearly as popular as the larger models, the 28 was produced in three different variations, representing early, intermediate and late production.

This early first model 28 caliber pocket model has a friction latch trigger guard, a type one side plate, early markings and a four inch octagon barrel. Although not visible, the front of the cylinder pin is square. Number 78.

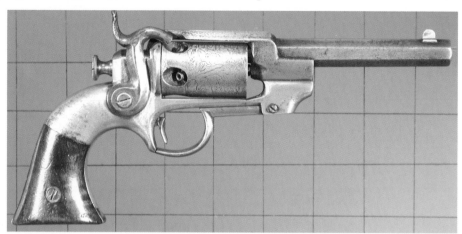

This is a little later than the pocket model shown above and has intermediate markings with the name and dates on the left side of the barrel flat (see inset). Only two dates are used. This pistol also has a square cylinder pin. Number 108.

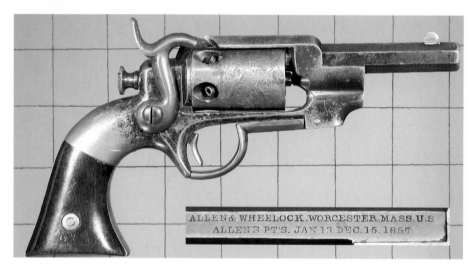

This second model has a two screw side plate. As the screw pattern is basically the same as the three screw models, it is more than likely the top screw was omitted due to an oversight rather than by design. It also has a square cylinder pin and the same markings as the revolver above. Number 224.

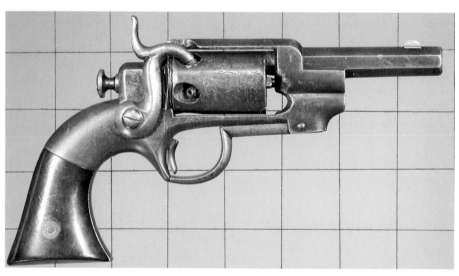

The left side view of the first model 28 caliber on the opposite page shows the type one three screw side plate that is used only on the first model 36 caliber Navy and 28 pocket side hammers. All 28s have the type four cylinder.

The left side view of this second model has a type one three screw side plate with a slightly different screw pattern. The only other difference from the first model is the intermediate markings that are now in two lines on the left side of the barrel.

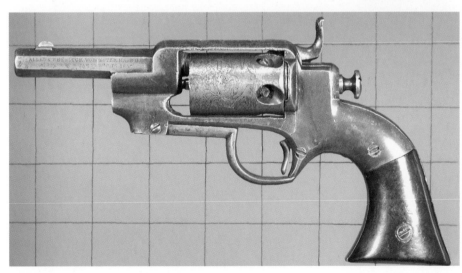

The left side view of this second model pocket model shows a two screw side plate. As this is the only pocket model that has been observed with this type of screw pattern, it is not considered a production model.

As with all of the other side hammer percussion series, blued frame and barrel, casehardened cylinder, trigger, and trigger guard with varnished walnut grips are standard. However, silver plated examples with ivory grips do exist as shown on the next page.

The standard octagon barrel lengths are three and four inches. Several different types of bullet molds can be seen in Allen's cased percussion revolvers but the shell type flask seems to be standard.

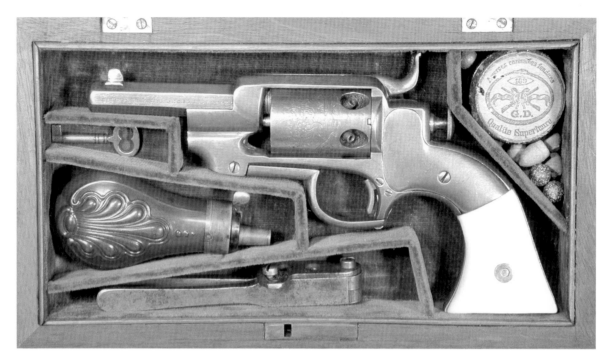

This final third model has a three-inch barrel, a one-screw type 6 side plate, the improved spring latch trigger guard and has the addition of the September 7, 1858 patent date. It is silver plated with ivory grips and is cased with accessories. For some reason, this late revolver has a round cylinder pin. Number 880.

This late third model has a four-inch octagon barrel with late markings. This is a nicely engraved little gun in unfired condition that is cased with accessories. Number 337.

Chapter 21
CENTER HAMMER REVOVLERS

Corporal Peter Morse, Co. F, 2nd Regt., Michigan Vol. Cav. is pictured with his 44 caliber Allen & Wheelock center hammer percussion Army revolver. The *Springfield Research Service* lists five 44 Allen & Wheelock revolvers that were issued to the 2nd Regiment of the Michigan Calvary. Photo is courtesy of the U.S. Army Military History Institute and the Alfred K. Abbott Collection.

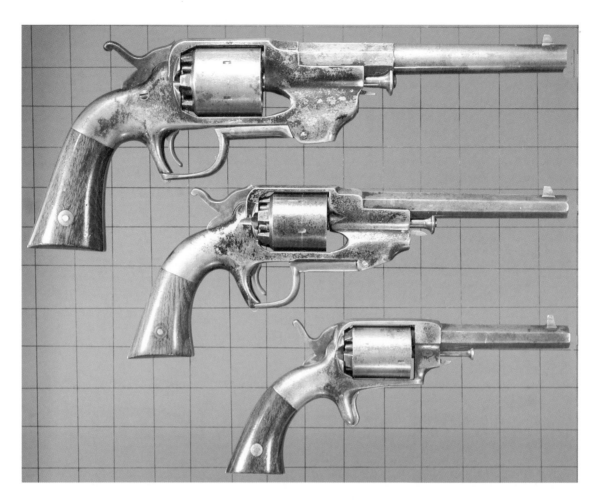

The top gun is an early variation of the 44 Army with a standard seven and a half inch octagon and round barrel. Number 409. The second revolver is a 36 caliber Navy with a six inch octagon barrel. Number 82. The bottom gun is a 36 caliber Providence Police pistol with a four inch octagon barrel. Number 58.

The following chapters cover the three different revolvers in the center hammer percussion series. The most popular was the six shot, 44 caliber Army revolver. This was followed at some distance by the six shot, 36 caliber Navy revolver and much further back is the five shot, 36 caliber spur trigger revolver usually referred to as the Providence Police model.

After the pepperbox, the center hammer Allen & Wheelock 44 Army and 36 Navy revolvers were Allen's most recognizable arms and were undoubtedly designed with military use in mind. Introduced at the beginning of the Civil War, these were the right revolvers at the right time. A much sturdier gun than the side hammer, the production was limited only by the capacity of Allen's factory. The barrel markings on both guns are ALLEN & WHEELOCK. WORCESTER. MASS. U. S. / PT'S. JAN. 13. DEC. 15. 1857. SEPT. 7. 1858, in two lines, on the left side of the barrel. The January 13, 1857, patent for the combination trigger guard and bullet rammer is the only patent that applies to the revolver. The December 15, 1857, and September 7, 1858, patents are for the earlier side hammer series and have nothing to do with the center hammer revolvers.

The die stamp that Allen used to put his name and patent dates on the barrel of the 44 Armies appears to have been slightly longer than the octagonal part of the barrel where the stamp is placed. The result is that several characters in the second line are missing. At first, this was thought to be just a miscalculation, but after examining many of these revolvers, this stamping remains consistent.

The photo on the left shows the typical omission of the A in the word Allen's and the 58 part of the 1858 date on the second line.

Two different types of actions are found in both the 44 and 36 percussion center hammers Army and Navy revolvers but the action of the Providence Police model is similar to that of the later cartridge pistols. The later action is rare on the 44 but is more common on the 36, indicating that production started after the 44 Army. Production of both revolvers continued into the E. Allen & Co era for a short period of time. More than likely, production ended when the Providence Police model was introduced.

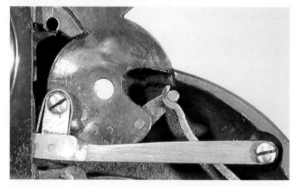

Above is the so-called hinge pawl type action that is used on early 44 and 36 caliber center hammer percussion revolvers (excluding the Providence Police model). The operating hand is not visible, but is located directly under the cylinder and has a favorable angle of attack on the rotation teeth of the cylinder.

Above is the late simplified action, where the operating hand is connected directly to the hammer. This action was not as smooth at the early action but was much easier and cheaper to manufacture. This action is used on most 36 center hammers percussion but is only seen on late 44s.

This is another case where Allen was using an improvement long before the patent was granted. The early action was not shown in a patent until April, 1862, at least a year and a half after Allen started using it on both the center hammer lipfire as well as the percussion revolvers. Since this is not an isolated case, the possibility exists that his patent may have been pending or tied up in court before it was granted.

The early, hinged pawl type action gives a smooth operation, as the operating hand is located directly under the rear of the cylinder and has a very good angle of attack on the rotation teeth. Although not quite as smooth, the later type action was much cheaper and easier to manufacture, thus trimming costs. Since the 44 and 36 lipfires shared the same early type actions and their production ended in September of 1863, it would be safe to assume that the actions on the 44 and 36 percussion revolvers did not change until after November, 1863.

There is no patent data directly related to the center hammer percussion revolvers, but three very important features covered in patents pertaining to other Allen firearms were used on the center hammer percussion series. The cylinder pin and its retainer are part of

Allen's patent number 33,328 dated September 24, 1861 for the 44 caliber lipfire revolver. The early action is part of patent number 35,067 dated April 29, 1862 and is from the revolving rifle patent. The cylinder locking system that is controlled by the trigger is part of patent 33,509 dated October 22, 1861 and is for the action used on late cartridge revolvers. As important as these three improvements are, it remains a mystery why none of the Allen & Wheelock-made guns bear any of these patent dates.

It has been estimated that only about 750 of the Army and 500 of the Navy revolvers were produced during the Allen & Wheelock era, which was roughly the same period of time as the Civil War. Most early studies of firearms were based on serial numbers but as early Allen & Wheelock firearms were not serial numbered, the question arises as to what were these production figures based on? Although the numbers of the guns will appear on all major parts, they provide no purpose other than identification during fitting and assembly. On two different occasions, two identical 44 Army revolvers with the same numbers were observed. It would not be until later in E. Allen production that four digit numbers can be seen stamped on the heel of the grip frame. If these numbers were consecutive serial numbers, later guns would have larger numbers but this is not the case, as two and three digit numbers can also be seen on late revolvers and long arms as well.

It has long been thought that Allen did not start production of the center hammer percussion series until the courts had ordered him to end the manufacturing and selling of cartridge revolvers in November, 1863. This cannot be accurate, as it is known that the U.S. Army Ordinance Department bought 198 Allen & Wheelock 44 caliber center hammer revolvers from William Read & Sons of Boston on December 31, 1861, almost 2 years earlier, for $22.00 each.[1] Although it isn't stated whether these guns were percussion or lipfire, there is very little chance they were lipfire. The Army preferred the tried and true percussion system to the unproven and often unreliable lipfire cartridges.

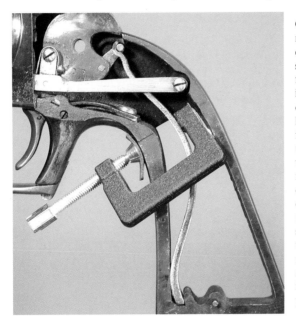

On the left is an early 44 caliber center hammer Army revolver with the grips and side plate removed. On early 44 percussion and early lipfire revolvers with the side plate screw that enters from the right side of the frame, it is important to follow the procedure that is illustrated on the left. On the early revolvers, the right entry side plate screw also doubles as the axle that the hammer rotates on and is constantly under pressure from the main spring. By removing the grips and using a small "C" clamp to relieve the tension from the main spring, the side plate screw can easily be removed. Place a small piece of leather between the clamp and the frame to protect the finish. Later 44 caliber percussion and 44 caliber lipfire revolvers were modified and the side plate screw moved to the left side of the frame. On those models, it is not necessary to relieve the pressure of the main spring before removing the side plate as the hammer rotates on an axle shaft that is cast to the inside of the frame as illustrated in the upper right photo on the preceding page.

---

1. John D. McAulay, *CIVIL WAR PISTOLS,* Lincoln, Rhode Island, Andrew Mowbray Inc, p.16.

Chapter 22
THE 44 CALIBER CENTER HAMMER ARMY REVOLVERS

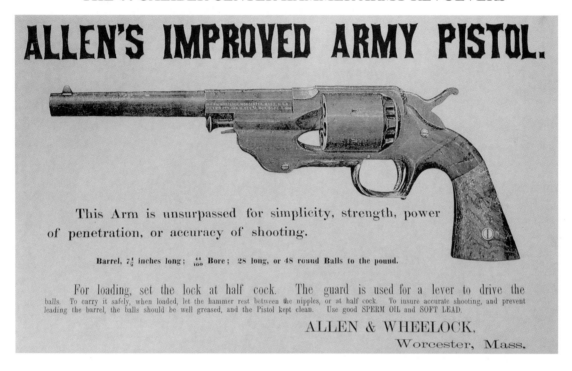

ALLEN'S IMPROVED ARMY PISTOL.

This Arm is unsurpassed for simplicity, strength, power of penetration, or accuracy of shooting.

Barrel, 7½ inches long; 44/100 Bore; 28 long, or 48 round Balls to the pound.

For loading, set the lock at half cock. The guard is used for a lever to drive the balls. To carry it safely, when loaded, let the hammer rest between the nipples, or at half cock. To insure accurate shooting, and prevent leading the barrel, the balls should be well greased, and the Pistol kept clean. Use good SPERM OIL and SOFT LEAD.

ALLEN & WHEELOCK,
Worcester, Mass.

In this advertising brochure for ALLEN'S IMPROVED ARMY PISTOL, Allen claims: *"This arm is unsurpassed for simplicity, strength, power of penetration, or accuracy of shooting. Barrel, seven and a half inches long, 44/100 bore; 28 long, or 48 round balls to the pound. For loading, set the lock at half cock. The guard is used for a lever to drive the balls. To carry it safely, when loaded, let the hammer rest between the nipples, or at half cock. To insure accurate shooting, and prevent leading the barrel, the balls should be well greased and the pistol kept clean. Use good SPERM OIL and SOFT LEAD.* **ALLEN & WHEELOCK, Worcester, Mass.**

The cylinder on the far left is the early variation with the nipples that enter from the inside of the chambers. This type of cylinder is distinguishable by the dished out area at each nipple opening. (See arrow.)

On the near left is the late and most common type cylinder with the nipples entering from the outside. This type of cylinder is used on later 44 Army and all 36 caliber center hammer percussion revolvers including the Providence Police pistol. (See arrow.)

Although no known government contracts were issued to Allen, a considerable number of 44 center hammer revolvers were in the government inventory.

In 1861, Benjamin Hannis carried the title of Armory Sub Inspector. Part of his job was to inspect Allen & Wheelock pistols. Several martially marked 44 Armies with the *BH* inspector's cartouche have been observed. A correctly cartouched 44 Army, from the

Billy Puckett collection, (number 284) also has an *H* sub inspector's mark on all major parts. Another 44 from the Doug Stack collection, (number 454) is not cartouched but has the *DD* sub inspector's mark of Daniel Dunsmore, USN gunner, 1861 to 1868. Sub inspector marks are very small and are often overlooked.

In the 1995 edition of the *Springfield Research Service*[1] on serial numbers, volume four lists the usage of 14 Allen & Wheelock revolvers and serial numbers, nine by Co. I, 3rd Michigan Volunteer Cavalry and five by Co. A, 2nd Michigan Volunteer Calvary.

Another slightly conflicting report titled, *44 Caliber Allen & Wheelock Revolvers in Federal service As Of June, 30, 1863,* lists 59 guns issued to the 2nd Michigan Cavalry, six issued to the 3rd Michigan Cavalry, Company I, and 33 issued to the Pennsylvania Cavalry, Company A.[2]

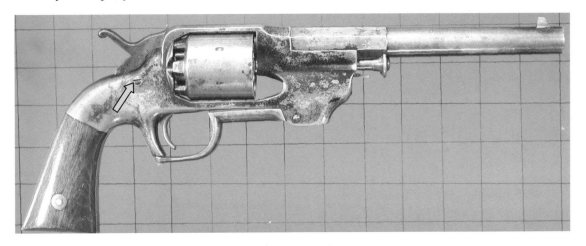

This first model is the most commonly seen 44. It has the first type cylinder with the inside nipples and the early type action. The side plate screw is located on the right side of the frame (see arrow). Number 409.

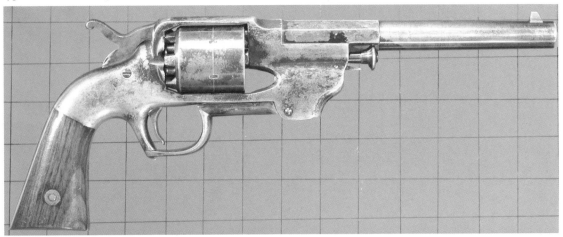

This second model 44 Army is identical to the first model except it has a new type cylinder with conventional nipples that enter the cylinder from the outside. The first type action is still used. Number 323.

In 1901, Francis Bannerman bought 38 Allen & Wheelock 44 revolvers for $26.27 each. This might explain why it is not uncommon to see a 44 in near mint condition.

---

1. Springfield Research Service, *SERIAL NUMBERS OF U. S. ARMS*, volume 4, 1995 edition, p. 304.
2. John D. McAulay, *CIVIL WAR PISTOLS*, Lincoln, Rhode Island, Andrew Mowbray Inc, p. 18.

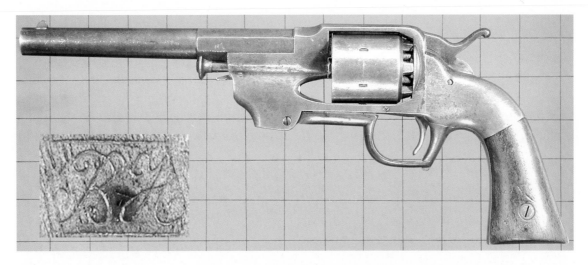

This second model has the cylinder with the conventional rear entry nipples and is martially marked with the proper *BH* inspector's cartouche on both sides of the grips (see inset). This is the mark of Benjamin Hannis, who was an Armory Sub Inspector in 1861. Number 148. From the Norm Szymonik collection.

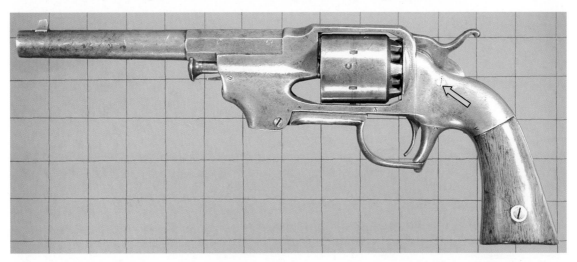

Although it is hard to see in the photo above, the side plate screw on this third model enters from the left side of the frame (see arrow). Models with left entry screws will have late actions. Like all later variations made during the E. Allen & Co. era, it is not marked with the maker's name. The number on all parts is 318, but 2318 is stamped on the heel of the grip frame. It is not unusual to see late 44 Armies with numbers well above the 2,000 range.

On the first and second models with the early action, the side plate screw enters the frame from the right side and doubles as the axle that the hammer rotates on. The tension of the main spring should be relieved before the side plate screw is removed. (See photo on the bottom of page 104.)

With third models, where the side plate screw is on the left side, it is not necessary to relieve the tension of the main spring before removing the screw. These models have a stud that is cast into the frame for the hammer to rotate on and the screw attaches to it.

Since there are no patents directly related to the percussion center hammer revolvers, it is evident that Allen simply borrowed selected features from the 44 lipfire and other revolvers that had already been patented.

One of the finest firearms made by any of Allen's companies is this late 44 caliber Army center hammer revolver. It is thought to be Ethan Allen's personal pistol. The markings on the left grip date the gun to late-1864 or 1865, sometime after the death of Thomas Wheelock in May of 1864 and before the formation of E. Allen & Co., probably early in 1865. The timing of a series of events had to be just right for this pistol to exist today. The revolver is engraved by Gustave Young, the best gun engraver of that, and probably any other, period. Young had been working exclusively for Samuel Colt but due

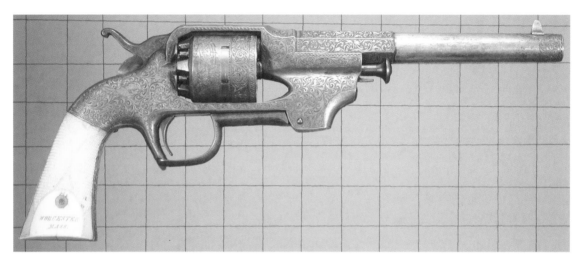

This fine ivory stocked 44 caliber Army center hammer revolver is profusely engraved and has hand-carved grips. This is said to be Allen's personal pistol. An eagle is engraved on the right side of the frame and WORCESTER MASS. engraved on the right grip. Number 2322. From the Perry Hansen collection.

A close up of the right side shows some of the detailed engraving that adorns this fine Allen revolver.

An eagle with its wings spread is engraved on the right side of the frame just below the rear part of the engraved hammer.

to the fire that burned down the Colt factory, Young found himself out of work in early 1865.

This revolver is profusely engraved with more coverage than any other known Allen. The frame, lever, hammer, cylinder and octagonal section of the barrel are completely covered with scroll engraving. Among the inhabitants is the Roman Centurion on the top strap; dogs, rabbits, deer and men are engraved on the cylinder and an eagle on both sides of the frame. The entire revolver has been silver plated with a gold wash applied to the cylinder and gold plating to the brass front sight. The checkered ivory grips have a flattened panel at the bottom that are engraved "E. Allen & Co / MAKERS" on the left side and "WORCESTER / MASS." on the right side. The coat of arms on the top strap has not been identified.

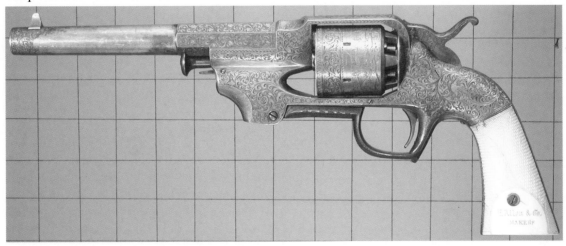

The side plate screw is located on the left side of the frame of this late Army and the number of the pistol is on the heal of the butt. That is not a serial number.

This close up of the left side reveals the magnificence of this revolver. As pictured on the top of the following page, the eagle that is engraved on the left side is different from the one on the right side.

The cylinder engraving is in two parts. The top part is a scroll-type engraving with a border on top and the bottom is a modified version of the cylinder engraving found on the 32 caliber rimfire revolvers.

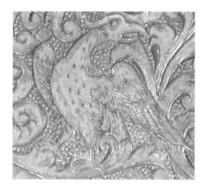

The eagle engraved on the left side is different from the right side.

The engraving on the hammer matches the engraving on the frame.

A Roman Centurion and various weapons are engraved on the top strap.

The trigger guard / loading lever is also nicely engraved to match the rest of the gun.

This face of a gargoyle is engraved on the back strap.

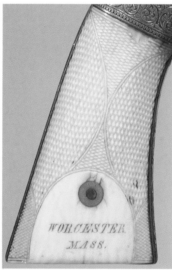

"WORCESTER / MASS." is carved on right of the grip.

"E Allen & Co. / MAKERS" is carved on the left grip.

The number of the gun is on the bottom of the butt strap and is surrounded with engraving. All late 44 percussion Army revolvers are marked in the same place.

The engraving wraps around the gold-plated brass front sight. The revolver is totally covered with engraving with the exception of about three inches of the round part of the barrel.

This Ethan Allen letterhead shows that the 44 Army percussion revolver was still part of the company's line of products as late as August 4, 1866. (See arrow.)

To see an Allen & Wheelock lipfire revolver that has been converted to rimfire is not unusual. However, it is very rare to see a percussion revolver that has been converted to rimfire. The pistol shown below is one such gun. A newly fashioned ejector tube has been attached to the right side of the barrel similar to that of a Colt or Remington cartridge revolver. The bullet rammer has been removed from the gun, and the trigger guard has no other function.

Although this appears to be a professional alteration, no other such conversions of this type have been seen on an Allen & Wheelock percussion Army 44. However, this is not to say that others like it do not exist.

The revolver is of late manufacture, with the side plate screw located on the left side of the frame, and has a late action. The gun is not marked, but it was made during the E. Allen & Company era and could possibly be a factory conversion. It is reasonable to assume that Allen as well as other gun manufacturers were continually experimenting with ways of converting their percussion revolvers to accept metallic cartridges when the Smith & Wesson patent expired.

All major parts have the same number with the exception of the cylinder, which has none. As the number is marked on the rear of the cylinder, it was machined off during the conversion process.

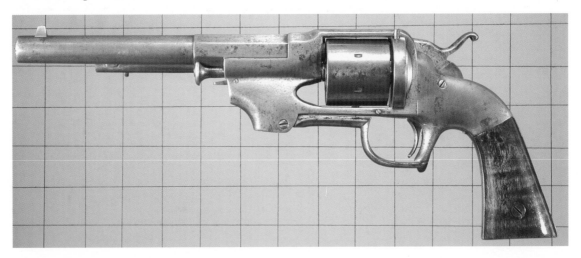

This late 44 percussion Army revolver has been converted to use 44 rimfire cartridges, and is unmarked except for the numbers. Number 476.

The right side view of the 44 conversion shows the ejector tube that has been attached to the side of the barrel. A groove was cut in the front side of the frame for the tube to fit into so it would line up with the chambers.

The conversion ring is held in place by a small screw located at the top of the ring (see arrow). When the screw is removed, the plate can be tipped forward for removal. Note that the hammer has been modified by removing the striker.

The rear of the percussion cylinder has been cut approximately 3/8 of an inch, leaving only the rotation teeth. The loading gate is held in the closed position by a "J"-shaped spring as shown in the following photos.

The rear of the conversion ring shows the "J"-shaped spring that doubles as the firing pin and loading gatekeeper.

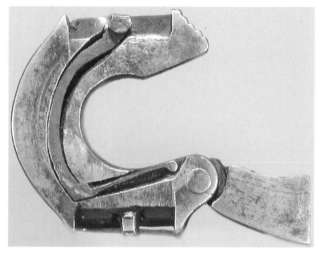

The loading gate must be open for removal of the cylinder. The small projection at the bottom center of the conversion plate fits into a notch in the frame to help hold it in place.

Chapter 23
36 CALIBER CENTER HAMMER NAVY REVOLVERS

As with the 44 caliber center hammer percussion revolvers, there is no patent that is directly related to the 36. The barrel is marked on the left side ALLEN & WHEELOCK, WORCESTER MASS, U.S. / ALLEN'S PATENT JAN 13, DEC 15 1857, DEC.7, 1858, in two lines.

Designed and made along the same lines as its big brother the 44, the 36 center hammer Navy was made in both an early and a late variation. While all of the 44s were made with a seven and a half inch octagon and round barrel, all Navies have full octagon barrels that are standard in lengths of seven and a half, six and five inches.

The 36 is a good looking, well built revolver with blued barrel and frame, and case hardened hammer, trigger and combination loading lever trigger guard. The same rack and pinion type bullet rammer that was used on the earlier side hammer series is also used on the center hammer 36.

The early models have the first type hinged pawl action, as shown on page 103. This action was smoother and more reliable, but the later action was easier to make, requiring a lot less machining, and consisted of fewer parts.

The 36 caliber Navy was put into production well after the 44 Army, as some of the different features that were used on the early 44s have not been seen on the 36.

As with the 44 Army, there is sufficient evidence to support the fact that the 36 was made well after the Allen & Wheelock era.

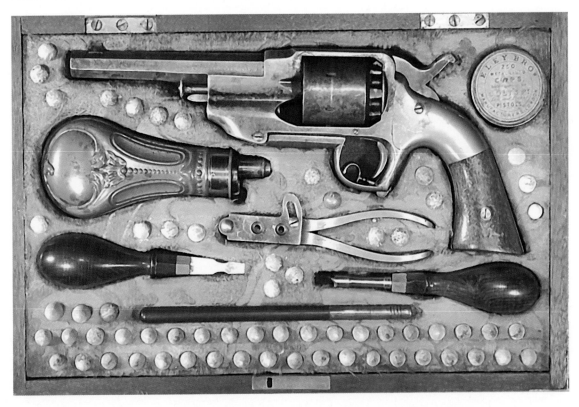

This late five inch barrel 36 caliber center hammer is in an unusual type of casing. Number 106.

114

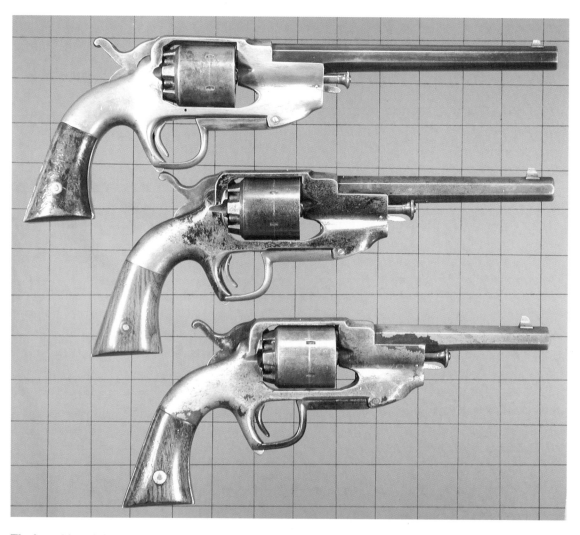

The barrel length is the only viable difference of the center hammer Navy revolvers. The top pistol has a full octagon seven and a half inch barrel. Number 133. The middle pistol has a six inch barrel. Number 82. The pistol on the bottom has a five inch barrel and is number 199.

This is a very unusual 36 caliber Navy center hammer that has finely checkered ivory grips and the remains of silver plate. This is a late gun and is absent of any barrel markings. Number 251.

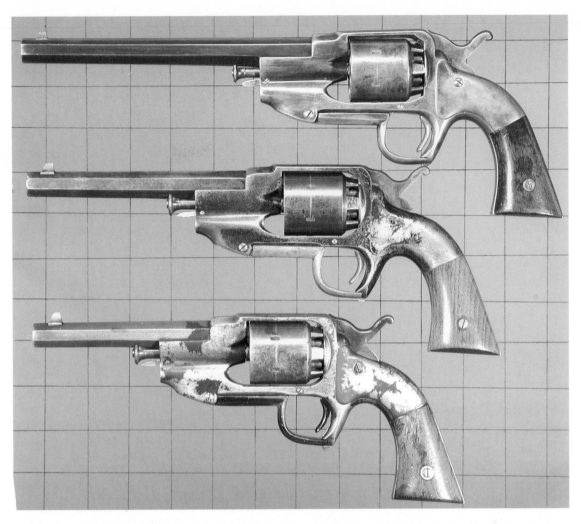

Shown above is the left side view of the three 36 caliber center hammer Navy revolvers that are shown on the preceding page. The revolver on the top with the seven and a half inch barrel is not marked and probably never was. It has the characteristics of a late model and was probably made after the Allen & Wheelock era.

The left side view shows that there are no barrel markings indicating that the pistol was probably made during or before the E. Allen & Co. era. The cylinder has the roll engraving from the 22 revolvers. (See p. 134 to see the cylinder engraving.) To do this, the second and third panels were repeated. This is quite possibly an exposition gun and is of the same period as the 44 from the Hanson collection that is pictured in the preceding chapter.

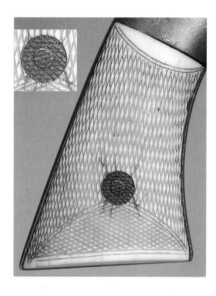

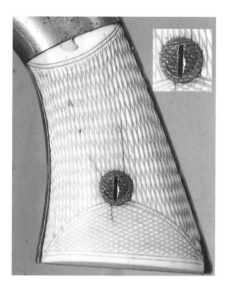

This is a close up of the nicely checkered ivory grips from the center hammer Navy revolver that is illustrated on the preceding page. The grip escutcheons and the grip screw are also checkered. (See insert on each grip.)

All center hammer Navies have a six shot cylinder that has a chamber depth of one and three eighth inches. There seems to be no variation in the cylinder except for the size of the hole in the cylinder for the cylinder pin.

Early models had a larger cylinder pin that measured .224 leaving a small frame area between the spring loaded cylinder pin latch and the bullet rammer. Consequently, the latch lever had to be made very thin and after the hole was drilled for the screw, there was very little metal left and any excessive pressure would cause it to break off.

This was partially corrected by reducing the diameter of the cylinder pin to .215, which allowed the latch to be made slightly thicker thus eliminating most, but not all, of the breakage problem.

There is no size difference in the diameter of the bullet rammers between the early and late models but it seem like a slightly smaller rammer would have given more room to make the latch lever stronger.

It is interesting to note that early revolvers with the larger cylinder pin have the early type action and revolvers with the smaller cylinder pin have the late type action. This has been consistent with all center hammer Navy revolvers that have been observed.

The early cylinder pin has a larger head and the latch is very thin and comes to a point.

The late cylinder pinhead is considerably smaller and the latch is thicker with a rounded end.

Chapter 24
PROVIDENCE POLICE REVOLVERS

The so-called 36 caliber Providence Police model was the last percussion revolver to be made by Allen, and is in a class all its own. Unmarked and made without loading lever or trigger guard, it is obvious that Allen wanted to put an inexpensive revolver with a considerable amount of firepower on the market.

Although these revolvers are commonly referred to as an Allen & Wheelock product, in all probability, they were actually made later, during the E. Allen & Co. era. However, there is no doubt that they came from the Allen shop, as the cylinder pin latch, the cylinder locking device, and the action are all covered in one or more of Allen's patents.

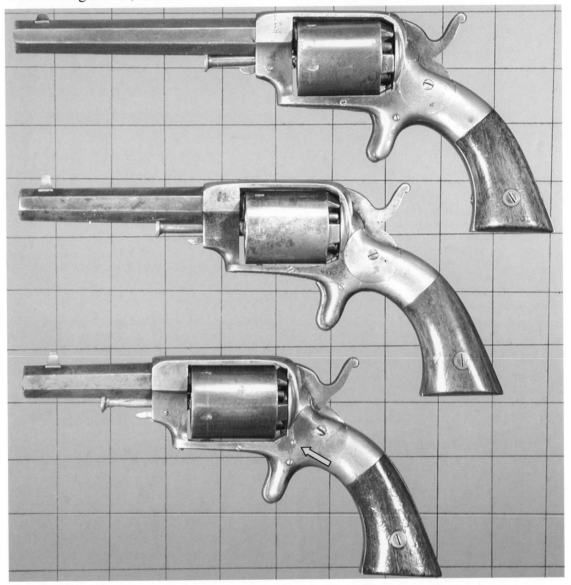

The Providence Police model is standard in the three barrel lengths shown above. The top pistol has a five inch octagon barrel. Number 467. The middle pistol has a four inch barrel. Number 58. The pistol on the bottom has a three inch barrel and has an additional screw (see arrow) to keep the side plate from rotating. It is generally agreed that this is the early variation and the other two are late. Number 79.

Students of Allens have wondered for years why these pistols were not marked. There is no way of knowing for sure but a good guess would be that Allen knew production would be limited and was simply too cheap to have the correct die stamp made. Since it is known that the 44 Army and the 36 Navy center hammer percussion revolvers were made during the E. Allen & Co. period and were also unmarked, this is not such a far-fetched theory. If they had been made during the Allen & Wheelock era, Allen had plenty of those stamps and surely would have marked them.

As there are no records to indicate that the Providence, R.I. Police Department ever used these pistols, it is a mystery how it became known as the Providence Police pistol.

The only variation that has been noted is the addition of a little screw between the side plate and the frame. Numbers do not indicate which is early or late, but it is generally agreed that the one screw variation is later, as it would have eliminated the drilling, threading and installation of a very small screw, whereas a small internal pin accomplished the same task.

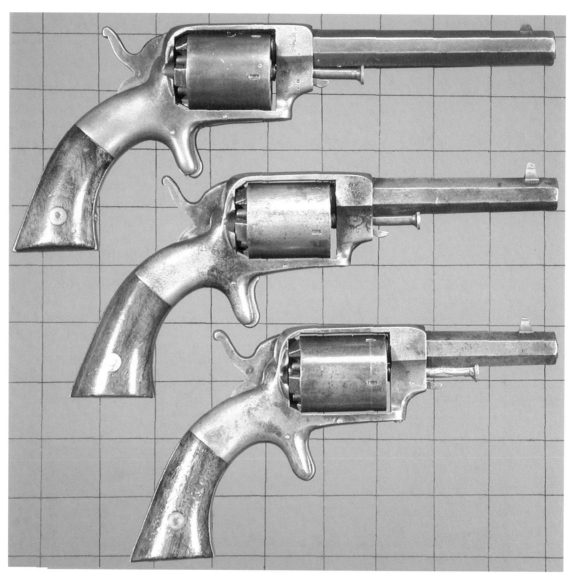

This picture of the three pistols above is the right side view of the same pistols pictured on the previous page.

Chapter 25
CARTRIDGE PISTOLS AND REVOLVERS

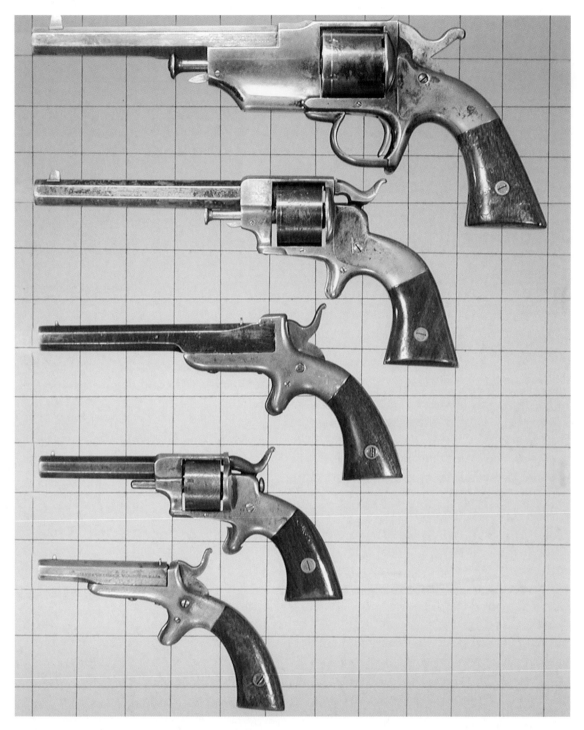

The pistol on top is a 36 caliber lipfire revolver with six inch barrel. Number 110. Second pistol is an early 32 caliber rimfire with a five inch barrel. Number 308. The third pistol is a 32 caliber single shot side swing with a five inch barrel. Number 234. The fourth pistol is a button head 22 caliber rimfire seven shot revolver with a three inch barrel. Number 625. The pistol on the bottom is a single shot 22 rimfire side swing with a two and three quarter inch barrel. Number 975.

Although the company of Allen & Wheelock was a pioneer in the manufacture of cartridge revolvers, it is not known exactly when the company actually started their production. During the trial of White vs. Allen & Wheelock, White's attorneys claimed that Allen & Wheelock had illegally produced and sold 25,000 revolvers with bored through cylinders starting in 1857. It is entirely possible that Allen started production before that, as neither he nor his attorneys challenged either the date or the numbers.

All cartridge revolvers are based on two of Allen's patents, one of which had very little to do with any cartridge revolver.

The two patent dates marked on the barrels of all Allen & Wheelock rimfire and lipfire revolvers are September 7 and November 9, 1858. The September 7 patent is number 21,400, and is actually for the anti-fowling cylinder pin for the side hammer percussion revolvers and the gas deflector or snout for the revolving rifle. There is no mention in the text of the patent for anything that pertains to the cylinder pin of a cartridge revolver. The head of the pin does have somewhat of a resemblance to the hourglass shaped cylinder pin used on first model 22s, and it does enter from the rear, so possibly that was part of Allen's reasoning for using that patent date.

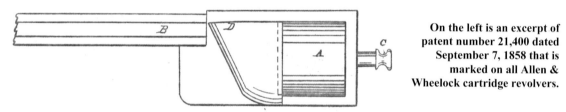

On the left is an excerpt of patent number 21,400 dated September 7, 1858 that is marked on all Allen & Wheelock cartridge revolvers.

The second patent is number 22,005 dated November 9, 1858 and covers that method of attaching the hammer on the outside of the case. It also described *"a cylinder with its chambers or barrels passing clear through it."*

In this brief description of the two patents that all Allen & Wheelock cartridge revolvers are based on, the November 1858 patent covering the chambers bored clear through is the only item from both patents that actually applies to all Allen & Wheelock cartridge revolvers. This patent is illustrated on page 126 of the 22 caliber revolver chapter.

The patent that is applicable to most Allen & Wheelock revolvers is patent number 33,507, dated October 22, 1861, that describes the internal action used on all but the very early 22 and 32 rimfire revolvers. This patent describes a new action that incorporates the cylinder stop to the trigger and is fully described and illustrated in the rimfire review chapter on page 121. This was not only a major improvement for Allen & Wheelock cartridge revolvers but it was also used in all center hammer percussion revolvers as well. It not only makes the action smoother and more reliable, but it eliminates several machined parts and a spring that were time consuming to make and install.

It would be reasonable to estimate that approximately 95% of all Allen & Wheelock revolvers incorporated the feature of controlling the cylinder locking mechanism with the trigger, which in turn was controlled by the position of the hammer. As important as this feature was, that patent date was not used on an Allen revolver until the E. Allen & Co. era around 1865.

All Allen & Wheelock cartridge revolvers were infringements of the Rollin White patent and production was halted in November of 1863.

Chapter 26
INTRODUCTION TO THE 22 AND 32 RIMFIRE REVOLVERS AND PISTOLS

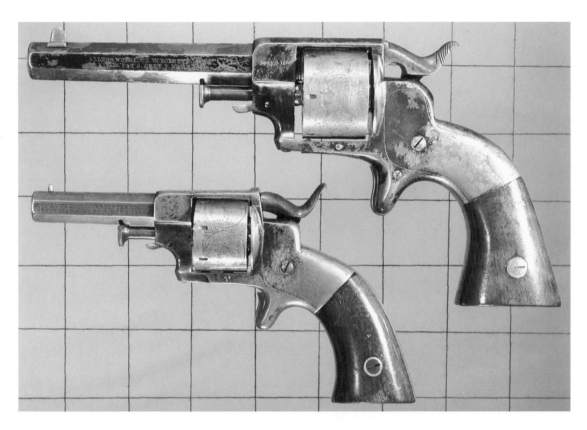

Shown above for size comparison is a late second model 32 caliber rimfire, six shot revolver with a four inch octagon barrel. Number 621. The second pistol is a fourth model 22 caliber, seven shot rimfire revolver that has a two and a half inch octagon barrel. Number 127.

Although not as popular with today's collectors as some other gun makers of the period, Allen was nevertheless a pioneer in mass producing and manufacturing small, practical single and multi-shot firearms that would fire a fixed cartridge. His 22 and 32 caliber rimfire pistols and revolvers were some of the finest small arms that were available at that time and were not only reliable but also affordable.

He was also an early inventor of cartridge making machinery that was superior to any other equipment of the day. The principals that Allen patented would greatly improve the quality of rimfire and later lipfire cartridges.

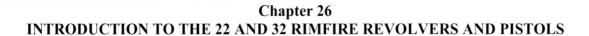

Barrel markings are the same on all Allen & Wheelock cartridge revolvers.

Production of the 22s was into the second model when the 32s came on line. Almost identical except for size, the first model 32 had all of the features of its little brother with the exception of a much stronger hammer and a six shot cylinder, compared to the seven shot cylinder of the 22s.

About midway through production, the frame was changed to give the grips a gentler angle. Revolvers with the late grips also have the late action as shown on the next page.

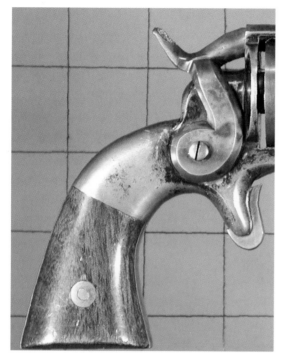 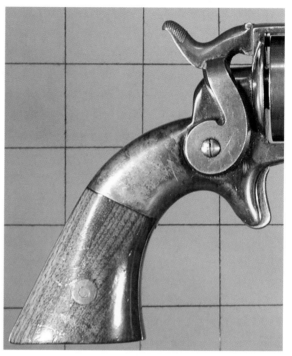

Both early 22 and 32 caliber rimfire revolvers had quick drop grips and a thick recoil shield. Steel grip escutcheons were used on all early pistols.

The new streamlined grips are referred to as the Smith & Wesson or slow drop style. Note the thin recoil shield and the change to brass grip escutcheons.

On October 22, 1861, Allen was granted patent number 33,509, which described a new type of action that used the trigger to activate the cylinder stop. This improvement was not only used on later 22 and 32 caliber rimfire revolvers but on all lipfire as well as all center hammer percussion revolvers.

As it will be pointed out on the following page, it was a much simpler design that eliminated several moving parts and made the revolvers more reliable without sacrificing the performance or integrity of the pistol.

The following excerpt is from Allen's patent that covers the new type action; "*The nature of my invention consists in construction of the stop, cock and the trigger of revolving guns or pistols of such shape that the trigger operates the stop.*"

Although the 22 preceded the 32 by only a short period of time, it had gone through several changes before production of the 32 started. The major improvement on the 32s was the heavy construction of the hammers. Unlike the flimsy hammers on the early 22s, the 32 hammers were made strong enough to withstand average use without breaking.

It is obvious that Allen was infringing on the Rollin White patent for a pistol with a bored through cylinder, but with the help of his lawyers and many continuances, production would continue for over four years. Although Allen was surely aware that it would only be a matter of time until he had to cease production, he would continue to make changes to improve his cartridge pistols right up to the bitter end.

It is very doubtful that production of his line of percussion pistols and revolvers had ever stopped, so the court injunction would not have put him totally out of business.

Illustrated below are two 32 caliber rim fire revolvers with the left grip and side plate removed to show the difference between the early and late actions. The operating hand and spring have also been removed to show the actions. All cartridge and center hammer percussion revolvers use the same principle of integrating the cylinder lock with the trigger. Only early 22 and 32 revolvers have the early type action.

The cylinder lock on revolvers with an early action is controlled by a catch on the hammer tumbler. See drawing below.

The cylinder lock is controlled by the trigger on later revolvers. This eliminates several moving parts and gives a smother operation. See drawing below.

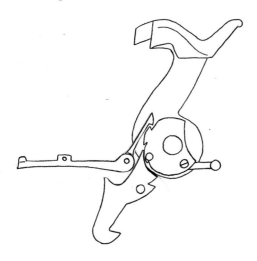 

The catch in the top of the hammer tumbler catches the link on the cylinder lock to release the cylinder.

On the late action, the cylinder lock is released when the trigger moves forward as the revolver is cocked.

Production of revolving cartridge pistols would not resume until after White's patent expired in 1869 and Allen had incorporated with his two sons-in-law, Sullivan Forehand and Henry Wadsworth. Some time after Wheelock's death on May 21, 1864, the name of the firm became E. Allen & Co. Many early cartridge revolvers marked with that name were made from left-over Allen & Wheelock parts that were assembled after White's patent expired, before changing over to their new line of revolvers with birds head grips.

The injunction had no effect on the single shot, side swing 22 and 32 pistols and production continued. Although Allen did not obtain his patent for his ejector system until March 7, 1865, the improvement was in use long before. All but the very early Allen & Wheelock marked 32s have ejectors, but the 22s do not. It would not be until the E. Allen & Co. era before 22 single shot pistols would be equipped with ejectors.

The following 1871 price guide from the Great Western Gun Works listed the following Allen 22 and 32 caliber rimfire pistols for sale:

- 22 caliber seven shot revolver with rosewood stock and rifled barrel...... $7.00
  Full nickel or silver plating, extra...1.50
- 32 Caliber six shot revolver with three inch barrel.............................9.00
  With four inch barrel...9.25
  With five inch barrel...9.50
  Full nickel or silver plating, extra...1.75
- Single shot 22 with rifled three inch barrel.....................................3.25
- Single shot 32 with four inch barrel...3.75

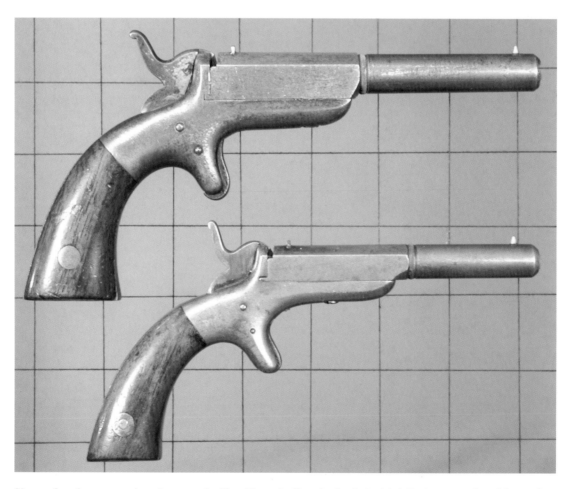

Shown for size comparison is an early 32 caliber rimfire single shot pistol that was made without ejector. Number 455. The pistol on the bottom is an early 22 caliber rimfire single shot pistol. Allen & Wheelock 22s did not have ejectors. Number 215.

Chapter 27
22 CALIBER RIMFIRE REVOVLERS

The soldier above is holding a late model Allen & Wheelock 22 caliber seven shot revolver.

The seven shot 22 caliber rimfire was not only the first Allen & Wheelock cartridge revolver; it was one of the first American cartridge pistols to be mass produced. Although it would later be judged to be an infringement of the Rollin White patent, on September 7, 1858, Allen was issued patent number 21,400. A brief description of his patent is as follows: *"Forming the stud or pin to support the tumbler and hammer solid with the case or frame when the hammer is placed outside of the case, and constructed and operated substantially as described."* This describes the method of attaching the hammer on the outside of the frame and also states that: *"The cylinder is made with barrels passing through it as seen in fig. 5, the cartridges being made with a projecting rim and primed, etc".*

Although there are many variations of the Allen & Wheelock 22 revolver, all models are basically the same. Standard features were blued barrel and frame, casehardened cylinder and hammer with varnished walnut grips. The cylinder pin is used to punch out spent shells from the cylinder. All earlier guns had nicely engraved, seven shot cylinders, with five different panels that consisted of two crossed rifles with a pistol on each side, a horse with a rider, cannons and guns, an Indian with a bow, and a ship with a castle in the background. Later variations have un-engraved cylinders. These revolvers have two different actions and a variety of hammer designs. About midway through production, the grips were changed from the quick drop to the so-called Smith & Wesson slow drop style grips. Soon thereafter, the internal action was changed to the simplified configuration as detailed on page 123.

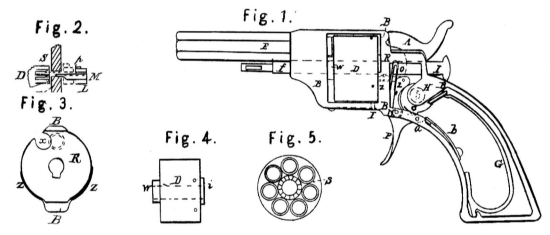

Patent number 22,005 dated November 9, 1858, covers the method of attaching the hammer on the outside of the case but also describes *"a cylinder with its chambers or barrels passing clear through it."*

The photo on the right is the pistol that Allen presented to the U.S. patent office to obtain his patent number 22,005. It is hard to imagine how much difference there is between the patent model and the actual pro-duction model. The hammer and the location of the rear entry cylinder pin appear to be the only thing that the prototype has in common with the first model 22. Photo is courtesy of Smithsonian Institute.

ALLEN'S
PATENT
SEVEN SHOOTER,

THE LIGHTEST AND BEST REVOLVER IN THE WORLD,
WEIGHT ONLY 7 OUNCES.

The advantages of this Arm over all others, consists in the superiority of its workmanship, the rapidity of loading and discharging, the accuracy and GREAT FORCE with which it shoots, the convenience and safety with which the Arm and Ammunition may be carried. The Cartridges are waterproof, and the pistol may remain charged for any length of time, in any climate, with certainty of fire at all times.

FOR SALE BY THE TRADE GENERALLY.

ONION & WHEELOCK,

Manufacturers, Importers and Jobbers of

GUNS, REVOLVERS, RIFLES, PISTOLS,
GUN MATERIAL AND SPORTING ARTICLES
OF EVERY DESCRIPTION,
No. 99 Maiden Lane,
NEW YORK.

This early full page ad is for ALLEN'S PATENT SEVEN SHOOTER. William Onion was Allen's nephew and was in partnership with Thomas Wheelock during the 1850s and early 60s.

There are six different frame designs on the 22 caliber revolver. First models were made with a sighting groove that ran the entire length of the top strap. The entry point for the hammer was offset to the right and had a very small, weak looking hammer.

The second type frame retained the full length-sighting groove but has a much larger hammer that enters the frame at the center.

The third type has a smooth top strap with a wide rear-sighting notch. Fourth, fifth and sixth type frames have a flat top with a smaller raised sighting lug located at the rear of the top strap. Fifth and sixth type have a thinner recoil shield. The sixth type also has the new type Smith & Wesson grips and a slightly slanted breech. This is the most common frame variation and is used on the majority of 22 revolvers.

First type frame has an offset hammer entry.

Second type frame has a center hammer entry.

Third type frame with a wide rear sighting lug.

Fourth type frame has standard size rear sighting lug.

Fifth type frame has a thin recoil shield and a slanted breech.

Sixth type frame has the later Smith & Wesson type slow drop grips.

Hammer breakage on early models was a major problem. Allen soon devised a sort of bumper that was cast into the frame to form a shoulder between the hammer and the recoil shield to absorb some of the shock when the hammer fell. (See photo on bottom of page 131.) The addition of the shoulder was one of the early improvements of the first model and was soon abandoned in favor of the second type hammer that was thicker and much stronger.

Shown below are the different types of hammers used on the 22 caliber revolvers.

First type right side.   Second type right side.   Third type right side.   Fourth type right side.

First type left side.   Second type left side.   Third type left side.   Fourth type left side.

First type has a very thin hammer face with saddle-type knurling, and a striker that enters the frame to the right of center.

Second type hammer was nearly doubled in width and had teardrop knurling, and a striker that enters the frame to the right of center.

The third type hammer is much larger, has a round hammer face and a striker that enters the frame in the center. This hammer was used on all second, third and very early fourth models.

Fifth type right side.

The fourth type hammer now has a half round top and square bottom face that is used only in conjunction with the fifth type frame. Early examples have engraved cylinders and the first type action but later ones have the second type action. This change obviously had nothing to do with improving the operation of the revolver and was probably nothing more than a style change. It was at this point that the new type frame with a slanted breech and thinner recoil shield would be introduced.

Fifth type left side.

The fifth and final type hammer shown on the left has a square face. This type will be standard throughout the remainder of 22 production including the E Allen & Co. variations. The saddle-type hammer knurling would also remain standard.

(On the left.) Two different types of hammer knurling used on 22 caliber revolvers. Very early first models have a saddle-type knurling but later first models have teardrop knurling, which is used up to and including the third model. For some unknown reason, the saddle knurling will be brought back starting with the fourth model and would remain standard.

As shown on the right, the cylinders on early 22s measured .663 inches long compared to later standard cylinders that measure .725. The shorter cylinder is only seen on a few very early first models.

Pictured below are the four types of cylinder pins used on Allen & Wheelock 22 revolvers.

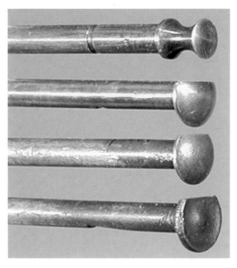

The cylinder pin shown at the top is the first type hourglass pin and is used on first models only. It is held in place by a ball type detent that is activated by the same spring that controls the cylinder lock. (See inset on next page.)

The second type round head and pin enters the frame from the front and is used only on second models. It is held in place by a setscrew located under the front of the frame.

Although similar in appearance to the second type pin, the third type is a rear entry pin that is used on the fourth button head models. It has a different detent notch that is held in place by the same system that is used on the first model pin.

The fourth type pin is the most common, and is used in conjunction with the spring latch retainer that is used on early fourth models to the end of 22 production.

IDENTIFYING THE MODELS OF THE 22 CALIBER REVOLVERS

- First models have first type frame and either first or second type hammers with a rear entry hourglass cylinder pin.

- Second models have a setscrew located under the front of the frame to retain the second type front entry cylinder pin. Both second or third type hammers and frames are used.

- Third models have a similar type button head cylinder pin that enters the frame from the rear. It is most common with the third type frame, but occasionally will be seen with the second type frame.

- Fourth models have a spring latch cylinder pin retainer and are the last of the quick drop grips. The third type hammer is used with the third type frame and fourth type cylinder pin. This combination remains standard throughout the remainder of production.

- Fifth models have a newly designed frame with more graceful, slow drop type grips that are generally referred to as the Smith & Wesson type. This model has a half round and half square, type four hammers, a much thinner recoil shield and a slanted breech. Early variations have engraved cylinders and the early type action. Later variations have un-engraved cylinders and late type action. For the first time, the trigger screw that has been hidden under the side plate will now be on the outside of the frame.

- The sixth models all have the late frame with the type five square hammer face and the late action. This is the most common Allen & Wheelock 22 revolver and is seldom seen with an engraved cylinder.

As illustrated in the following pictures, there were a considerable amount of changes that took place during the days of 22 production.

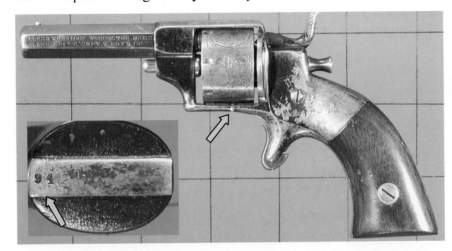

This early first model 22 revolver is distinguished from other first models by the very thin strap under the cylinder and by the pin rather than a screw that holds the cylinder stop in place. (See arrow in main photo.) The cylinder is shorter on early first models and measures .663. The number 94 is stamped on the heel of the frame. (See inset.)

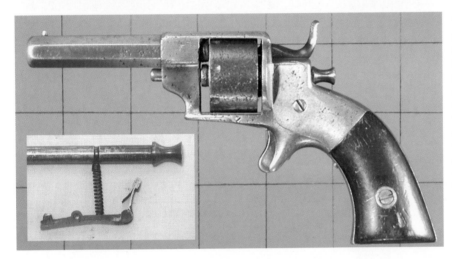

This is a little later first model and is unmarked. It has a slightly thicker frame strap under the cylinder and a screw that holds the cylinder stop. Shown in the insert is the method of securing the rear entry cylinder pin. A spring loaded ball fits into a groove in the pin. The same spring also activates the cylinder lock. This system is used only on early 22s and 32s. Number 226.

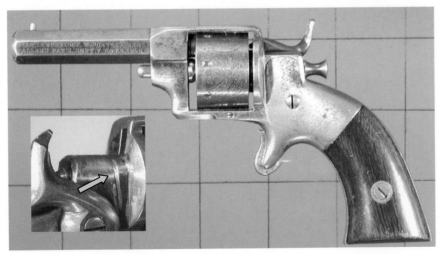

The light-weight hammer was obviously a weak point, and to compensate for this, a shoulder was cast into the recoil shield to absorb some of the shock when the hammer fell. (See arrow in inset.) The number was moved to the frame under the left grip and the length of the cylinder has been increased to .725 inches. The length remained standard. Number 812.

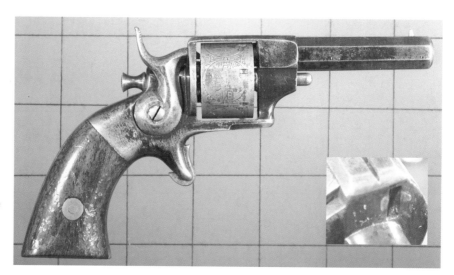

This is the standard first model 22 that has the type two hammer face that is about twice the thickness of the first type hammers. This eliminated the process of casting and machining the shoulder, but the hammer still enters the frame to the right of center. (See insert.) Number 801.

Second models have a setscrew for a cylinder pin retainer. It is questionable if this was much of an improvement but regardless, they were made in first, second, third and fourth type frames. The revolver pictured below is possibly a one-of-a-kind as the frame was originally made for a first model with a rear entry cylinder pin but the hole was plugged as shown in the inset photo. It also has the second type hammer.

This very early second model uses the early offset hammer and the first model frame. This is a transitional piece, as the rear of the frame was originally drilled out to accept the rear entry first model cylinder pin, but was later plugged. (See arrow in inset.) It is possibly one-of-a-kind. Number 874.

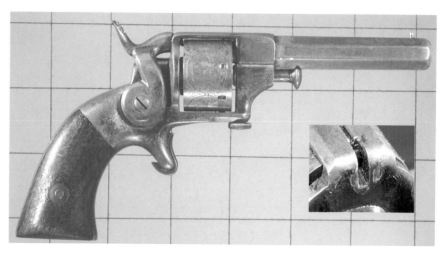

This second model has the second type frame, which is similar to the first type, having the long sighting groove on the top strap. The new and much stronger third type hammer enters in the center of the frame, as do all of the remaining 22 models. Number 452.

This is the first model to use the third type frame that has a rather wide raised rear sight located at the breech end of the top strap. (See inset.) Unlike the first and second frame, the new frame has a smooth top and was probably a little easier to machine, thus cutting production costs slightly. Number 81.

This is actually the same model revolver as the one shown above but has a standard size rear sighting notch. Although all variations with the setscrew cylinder pin retainer are rare, this is considered the standard model. Number 44.

Third model button head 22s were also made with second and third type frames, but the third frame models are the most popular. The same system of a spring loaded detent ball to retain the cylinder pin used on first models is used on all rear entry cylinder pins.

The third model 22 is commonly refered to as the button head model and will be seen with both the second and third type frame. It is not known why Allen would revert back to the rear entry cylinder pin, unless they were cheaper to produce. The revolver on the left has the second type frame and the third type cylinder pin. Number 844.

This late third model has the third type frame with a flat top strap. The cylinder pin is retained by a spring loaded detent that goes through a hole in the frame directly above the cylinder stop. This is the same spring that is also used to lock the cylinder stop. This is the last model to have the tear drop hammer knurling and steel grip escutcheons. Number 312.

The fourth model shown below was the first to have brass grip escutcheons and the spring latch cylinder pin retainer that would be used on all subsequent models. Note the thinner recoil shield and the slightly slanted breech.

Fourth models are the first to have a front entry cylinder pin that is retained by a spring loaded latch, as covered in Allen's patent 33,328 dated September 24, 1861. The saddle-type hammer knurling that had not been used since the early first model is now standard. This is also the first model with brass grip escutcheons. Number 127.

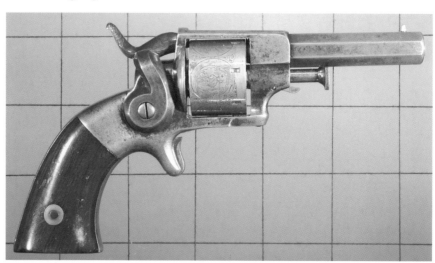

All fifth models have the Smith & Wesson slow drop grips and will remain standard.

This early fifth model still has the third type hammer, but the new fifth type frame referred to as the Smith & Wesson type grips, are now standard throughout the remainder of production. As a result of the new design, the trigger screw is now located on the outside of the frame. (See arrow in inset.) Number 45.

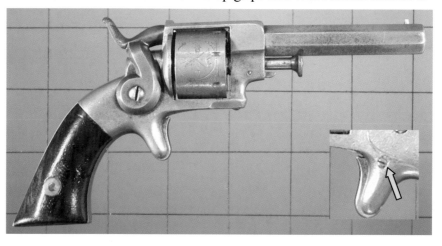

The fifth model is very similar to the preceding revolver but has the fourth type hammer face that is round on the top and square on the bottom. This was the last model with the early type action that is described on page 123. Number 625.

This late fifth model is the first 22 caliber Allen & Wheelock revolver without cylinder engraving. This is also the first model to use the simplified, late action that is described on page 123. (See inset.) Number 225.

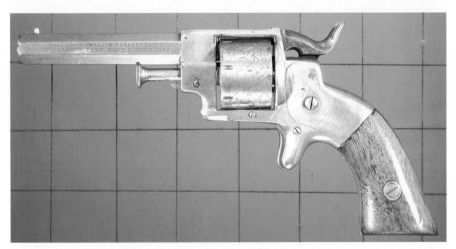

The sixth and final model of the Allen & Wheelock 22 caliber revolvers is the most common. The only difference between this and the fifth model is the new type five hammer face. this is one of the very few sixth models that have cylinder engraving. Number 25.

When production of Allen & Wheelock 22 revolvers halted, there were many parts and revolvers in various stages of assembly. As Allen was not a wasteful man, the parts and pistols were stored until the White's patent had expired in 1869. By that time, Thomas Wheelock had passed away and Allen had incorporated with his two sons-in-law, Sullivan Forehand and Henry Wadsworth, thus forming the company of E. Allen & Co. The 22s that were assembled from these parts were identical to the Allen and

Wheelock 22s except they now had a blade front sight and the grip escutcheons were smaller. They are marked either E. Allen & Co. or Ethan Allen & Co.

This early ETHAN ALLEN & CO. 22 caliber revolver has the additional Sept 2, 1861 patent date. It has the remains of gold plating and is nicely engraved. Early Ethan Allen 22 and 32 revolvers with the square butt design will have two slash marks under the hammer knurling. (See inset.) Number 1732.

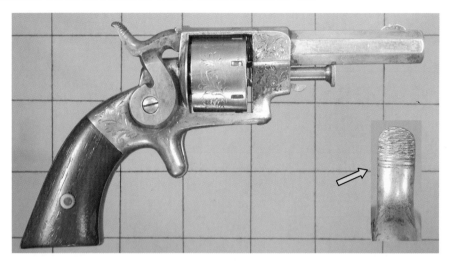

The change to bird's head grips was the final design change on the Allen 22 caliber revol-vers. This style remain-ed standard for the remainder of the E. Allen & Co. period and through the Forehand & Wadsworth era until production ended some time in the 1890s. Number 6427.

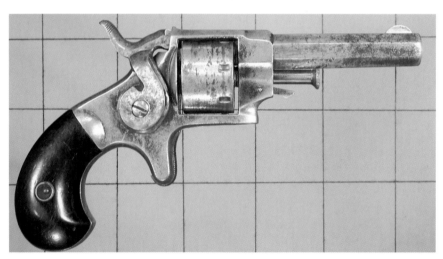

Most Allen & Wheelock 22 revolvers have cylinder engraving as shown below. Only late fifth and sixth models have un-engraved cylinders.

Shown above are the five different panels that are engraved on the cylinders of 22 caliber revolvers. The first panel on the left has two crossed rifles with a pistol on each side, the second a horse and rider, the third is military articles, the fourth an Indian with a bow (the seal of Massachusetts), and the fifth is a sailing ship with a castle in the background.

Allen & Wheelock 22 caliber revolvers came in both wood and Gutta-purcha cases. The following are some cased 22s from the author's collection.

This typical wood case was made for Allen & Wheelock 22 caliber revolvers. The varnished and lined walnut box was made in several different sizes, to accommodate the later revolvers with Smith & Wesson type grips, which are longer than early models.

This early first model 22 revolver is in a typical wood case, with a cleaning rod, key and 46 22 caliber rimfire cartridges that have raised A & W head stamps. (See page 186 for close up.) Number 94.

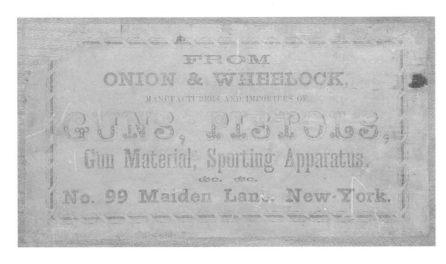

FROM
ONION & WHEELOCK,
MANUFACTURERS AND IMPORTERS OF
GUNS, PISTOLS,
Gun Material, Sporting Apparatus.
&c. &c.
No. 99 Maiden Lane, New-York.

The Onion and Wheelock label is glued to the bottom of the case shown on the left. William Onion was Allen's nephew and was in the importing business in New York City with Thomas Wheelock.

138

Occasionally an Allen & Wheelock 22 revolver is seen in a Gutta-percha case. They were available in either black or a dark shade of maroon and were also made in several different lengths. Some cases were slightly longer, and some had a small notched out area to accommodate the setscrew on second models .

The lovely gold and silver plated, late first model 22 revolver is in a Gutta-percha case. This is an early case, and will only accept a 22 revolver with the early type grips. Number 149.

Ivory stocked and engraved 22 caliber Allen & Wheelock revolvers are rare. This late second model with a setscrew cylinder pin retainer is one of three like it that have been observed with consecutive numbers. Number 19.

This early third model button head 22 revolver has an early second model frame, and is in a wooden case. Note the cut out in the top of the case to allow for the hammer spur. The case is slightly narrower than most wood cases. Number 844.

This cased, late third model button head 22 revolver is silver plated and has ivory grips. Note that the top of the case is also notched out to allow for the hammer spur. Number 498.

Although unmarked, this late fifth model is nicely engraved and stocked with mother-of-pearl grips. Pearl grips are rare on any Allen handgun. Number 34.

This silver-plated, sixth model 22 has ivory grips and cylinder engraving, which is rare on late model 22s. The Gutta-percha case is slightly longer than normal to allow for the longer Smith & Wesson type grips. Number 755.

This double cased set of fourth model 22 revolvers have ivory grips that are monogrammed with the initials L J P. This set was formerly in the H.H. Thomas collection and are featured on the front cover of his book *The Story of Allen and Wheelock Firearms.* An Onion & Wheelock label is attached to the inside of the case. Numbers 197 and 203.

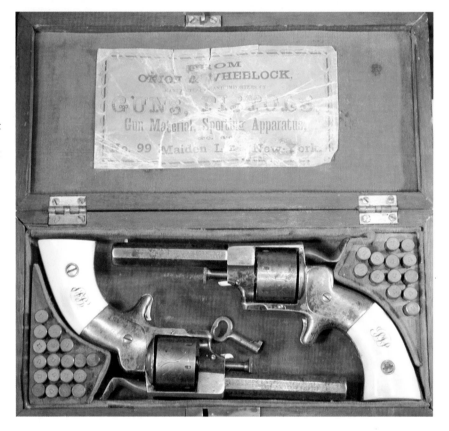

The set of 22 revolvers in the above photo is the only double cased set of Allen & Wheelock revolvers that has been accounted for at this time. Although the label is on the inside of the lid, it would normally be attached to the outside bottom of the box, like the one on page 137.

A few early E. Allen & Co. square-butt 22 revolvers were put in wood cases, but later E. Allen & Co. and Forehand & Wadsworth 22 revolvers with birds head grips that are cased are usually in Gutta-percha boxes.

Chapter 28
22 CALIBER RIMFIRE SINGLE SHOT PISTOLS

Commonly referred to as the side swing, these simple little guns were made without Allen's patented ejector system. It appears that production started about the same time as the 32 rimfire single shots, as both pistols have the same characteristics. Both the very early 22 and 32 pistols have a crowned muzzle and steel grip escutcheons.

Most specimens are simply marked ALLEN & WHEELOCK but some will have the addition of WORCESTER, MASS. in one line on the left side of the barrel flat.

All that have been observed have blued barrel and frames, casehardened trigger and hammer with varnished walnut grips. Barrel lengths range from two and three quarter to four inches and were made in both full octagon and octagon and round barrels.

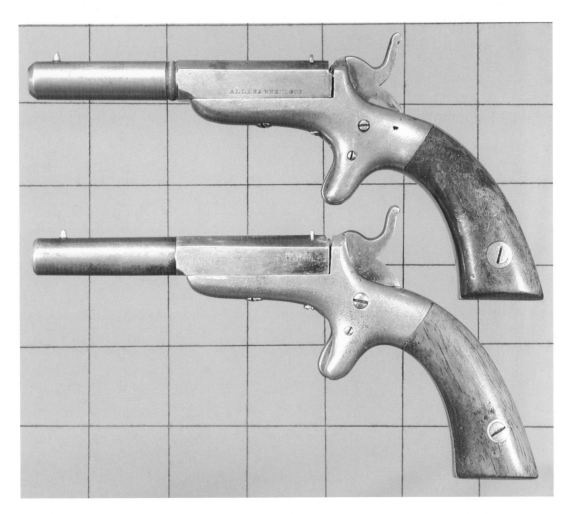

The pistol on the top is a seldom seen first model with a three and a half inch octagon and round barrel that has a knurling ring in the center of the barrel, steel grip escutcheons and a crowned muzzle. Number 215. The pistol on the bottom is a standard later model and also has an octagon and round three and a half inch barrel. Number 390.

Another feature that is consistent with the 32 single shot is that early 22s also have a much thinner locking lug. Later 32 and 22s have a much thicker lug and those differences are illustrated in on page 159.

142

Although all of the standard size E. Allen & Co. 22 caliber side swing pistols have cartridge ejectors, none of the Allen & Wheelock made 22 caliber side swing pistols have been noted with this system.

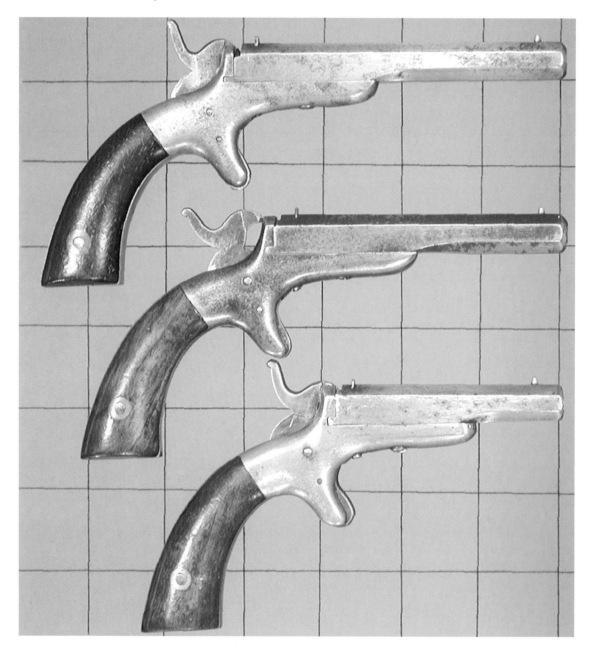

The three 22 caliber, rimfire single shot side swing pistols pictured above with octagon barrels are basically identical with the exception of the barrel length. The pistol on the top has a four inch barrel. Number 268. The second pistol has a three and a half inch barrel. Number 782. The pistol on the bottom has a two and three quarter inch barrel with a slightly different frame. Number 382.

Since these pistols were not equipped with ejectors, it was surely a problem removing the spent shell as the early cartridges tended to swell after being fired. It is doubtful that over a few thousand were made and are seldom seen today.

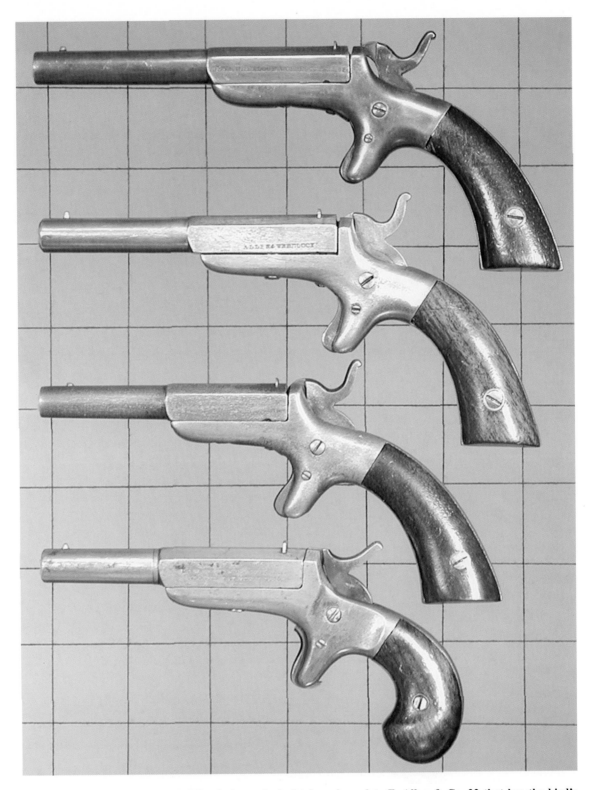

Shown above are three Allen & Wheelock-marked pistols and one late E. Allen & Co. 22 that has the bird's head grips. The pistol on top has a four-inch barrel. Number 55. The second pistol has a three and five eighths of an inch barrel. Number 530. The third pistol has a three inch barrel. Number 975. The E. Allen & Co. single shot on the bottom has a three inch barrel and is equipped with Allen's patented ejector system. Number 8551. Note the very high number on the E. Allen & Co. pistol.

This young Civil War soldier is holding an early third model button head Allen & Wheelock 22 caliber revolver.

Chapter 29
32 CALIBER RIMFIRE REVOLVERS

This soldier from a heavy artillery regiment is armed with a banjo and a first model Allen & Wheelock 32 caliber rimfire revolver is protruding from his jacket. It is interesting to note that the setscrew that retains the cylinder pin is very loose. This might explain why so many Allen revolvers will be seen with a nail in place of the original cylinder pin. Photo is from the Herb Peck Jr. collection and provided by Doug Stack.

Production of the 32 caliber rimfire revolvers started shortly after the 22s. Allen had strengthened the fragile hammer and the weak frame that had been a problem on the early 22s. Needless to say, the 32s were a much stronger and more powerful pistol and Allen claimed that it would shoot through a three inch board at 25 feet. This was quite a claim as the era of practical cartridge pistols was only a few years old.

The first patent that applied directly to the 32 caliber revolver was number 28,951 issued to Allen on July 3, 1860. This patent covered a raised area on the recoil shield behind the cylinder that was in line with the barrel, reinforcing the head of the cartridge that was in the firing chamber. This eliminated some of the drag when the cylinder was turned. Allen referred to this improvement as the inclined plane. The patent drawing clearly shows a first model 32 rimfire revolver with a setscrew cylinder pin retainer. The 1860 patent date does not appear on the very early first models, but does on later ones. Other markings are the same.

Although this improvement was used on all 32, 36 and 44 lipfire revolvers, only the 32 lipfire and the 32 rimfire revolvers carry the additional July 3, 1860 patent date. Allen thought enough of his inclined plane patent that he applied for a reissue, which was granted February 4, 1862. The reissue added a slightly better explanation to make the original patent more understandable. The improvement was such an efficient innovation that it was used on all large caliber Allen cartridge revolvers.

The second patent that applied to the 32 revolver was patent number 33,509, which was issued on October 22, 1861. This patent covered Allen's new improved and simplified action that also applied to the 22 as well as several other Allen revolvers. This improvement eliminated the delicate cylinder stop linkage, referred to as a hinged pawl that was activated by the hammer tumbler and replaced it with a simple connection that was controlled by the trigger. This not only eliminated several moving parts, it made for a much smoother, more reliable operation that was easier to manufacture.

Standard features of the 32 are a blued frame with an octagon barrel that was available in lengths of three, four and five inches. The six shot cylinder, hammer and trigger was case hardened and the walnut grips varnished. The cylinder length of early first models was .905 of an inch, but was soon lengthened to .940, and would remain the standard length of all short cylinder models throughout the remainder of production.

Cylinder engraving consists of a country scene with dogs chasing a rabbit. Later models with long and short cylinders were not engraved, for the most part. Changes in the frame, hammer faces and the internal action coincide with the 22 revolvers.

Production continued until November 1863, when the courts ordered Allen & Wheelock to cease production on all revolvers with bored through cylinders. The injunction did not affect the manufacture of percussion pistols and revolvers, single shot cartridge pistols, or the cartridge making part of the Allen & Wheelock operation.

In 1871, the Great Western gun catalog listed Allen's 32 revolvers with a 4 inch barrel for $9.25. Ivory grips were available for $2.00 extra and nickel or silver plating was an extra $1.75.

The abbreviated patent excerpts shown on the following page apply to 32 revolvers, but the improvements are used on other Allen cartridge pistols. Although the patent for the inclined plane appears to be insignificant, it was a major improvement as one of the problems with early cartridges was that they would tend to blow out when the pistol was fired. Allen's improvement may not have totally solved this problem, but it certainly was a step in the right direction.

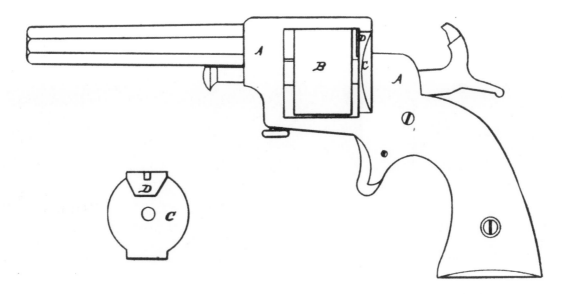

Patent number 28,951 dated July 3, 1860, is the first patent that applies to the 32 caliber rimfire revolver. Allen describes his patent as follows: ***"The nature of my invention consists in constructing the recoil-plate of a revolving cartridge-pistol with a projection in the form of an inclined plane in the rear of the cylinder, so as to relieve the pressure from the end of the cartridge and allow the cylinder to revolve with freedom."*** This innovation will also be seen on all 36, 32 and 44 caliber lipfire revolvers. NOTE: This patent was reissued on February 4, 1862.

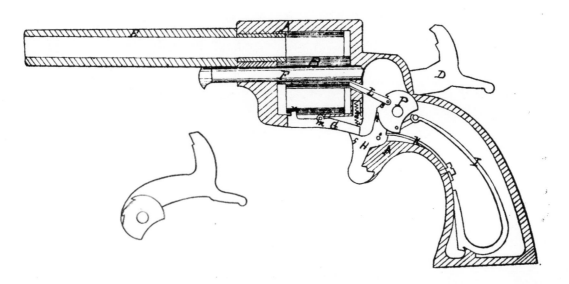

This is Allen's patent number 33,509 dated October 22, 1861. This patent refers to the late or simplified action that was also used on the later 22 revolvers, as well as other Allen revolvers. In his patent application, Allen makes the following claim: ***"The nature of my invention consists in constructing the stop, cock, and trigger of revolving guns or pistols of such shape that the stop is operated by the trigger."***

There are three basic models of the 32 rimfire revolvers with differences in each model that consist of variations of the frames, hammers, cylinder pins and retainers.

Three different types of top straps were used on eight slightly different frame variations. The top strap shown below at left is from a very early model and is seldom seen. The top strap in the middle photo is the most common and is used on later first models, all second models and early third models. The third type on the right is used only on later third models and will be seen in brass as well as steel and in long cylinder models with 1.20 inch long cylinders as well as short .940 inch long cylinder models.

This top strap that is beveled where the hammer enters the frame is seldom seen.

This top strap that is squared where the hammer enters the frame is the most common.

The third type top strap is thinner and slightly rounded. The front is dished out for style.

Shown below are the different frame variations that were used on 32 rimfire revolvers. Note that the late third model frame has a flat side lower frame strap exactly like the late first models. This is consistent with the brass frame series as well.

Early first model frame with .905 cylinder and beveled top strap.

Intermediate first model with .905 cylinder and square top strap.

Late first model with .940 cylinder, flat lower frame and 1860 date.

Second and early third model with spring latch cylinder pin retainer.

Late third model frame with thinner and sculptured top strap.

Late third model long cylinder steel frame with flat sided lower frame.

On the left is a short cylinder brass frame model that is identical in size to the steel frame model. This is one of the few late 32 revolvers to have an engraved cylinder.

On the right is a brass frame 32 long 1.20 inch cylinder revolver. It also is identical to the steel frame model.

The three different styles of hammers used on the 32s is shown below. The first type hammer has a round face and used in conjunction with the early type action only.

The second type hammer is round on top and square on the bottom. It is used only on intermediate second models but with both early and late actions.

The third type hammer has a square face and is the most common. It is used on later second and on all third models with the late type action.

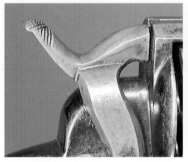

First type has a round hammer face.

Second type has a half round and half square hammer face.

Third type has a square hammer face and is the most common.

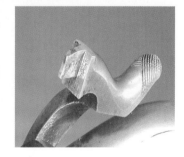

First type is round.

Second type is round and square.

Third type is square.

The early cylinder shown on the far left is .025 of an inch shorter than the standard short cylinder shown in the middle. Late in the production of the third model, a long cylinder model that was approximately one quarter of an inch longer than the standard short cylinder models was introduced.

The cylinder on the far left measures .905 and is from an early 32. The cylinder in the middle measures .940 and is the length of all standard short cylinder models. The cylinder on the near left is from a long cylinder model and measures 1.20 in length. All have a six shot capacity.

On the left is the first type cylinder pin that is used only on first model 32s with the setscrew cylinder pin retainer.

This cylinder pin is used on all models that have the spring lever cylinder pin retainer that is common on all 32s that were made after the first model. Long cylinder pins are the same length.

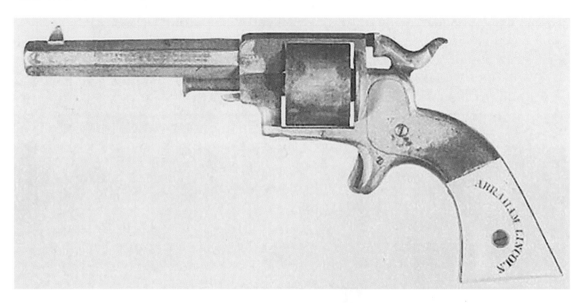

Abraham Lincoln was the owner of this early third model 32 that is gold plated with inscribed ivory grips. Mr. Lincoln Isham, great grandson of President Lincoln, presented this pistol to the Smithsonian Institute in 1958. Photo is courtesy of the Smithsonian Institute.

A QUICK REFERANCE TO IDENTIFY 32 RIMFIRE REVOLVERS

- First model: The most distinguishing feature of the first model is the setscrew cylinder pin retainer and quick drop grips. Early examples have a beveled top strap and lower frame strap. Later examples have a square top strap and flat sided lower frame strap.

- Second model: All examples have a spring latch cylinder pin retainer and early quick drop grips. All three types of hammers and both early and late type actions are used. All second models have the standard short cylinder that is .940 inches long.

- Third model: All third models have the Smith & Wesson type slow drop grips as illustrated on page 122. This model comes with short and long cylinders in both steel and brass.

This early first model 32 is adorned with ivory grips that have the head of a Buccaneer carved on the left side. It is silver plated with a 3 inch barrel and is in a typical wood case with a key and cartridges. Number 230.

This second model 32 has an engraved cylinder and a four inch barrel. It is in a wooden case with 20 cartridges that have the raised A &W head stamp on them. Number 621. A close up of the A &W head stamp can be seen on page 186 in the boxes and bullets chapter.

This late second model 32 revolver has a five inch barrel with ivory grips. There is a cleaning rod in the wood case along with a key and a box of Allen & Wheelock No. 32 cartridges. Number 432.

The following three first model 32 caliber revolvers represent early, intermediate and late variations. Production of the 22 revolvers preceded the 32 but not by much.

This early first model has the first type frame, (see inset) and ivory grips with silver plating. Although the incline plane is used, the 1860 patent date is not used on early first models. Tear drop hammer knurling is used. The cylinder is .905 inches long. Number 230.

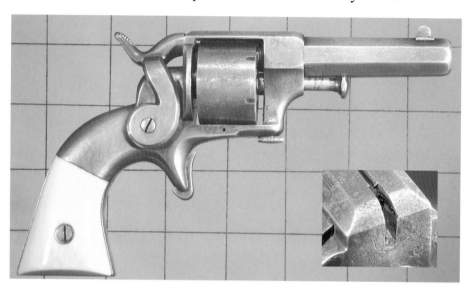

This intermediate variation of the first model has a second type frame with the squared off top strap (see inset). This style will remain standard on all remaining models. The 1860 patent date is still not used. Number 549.

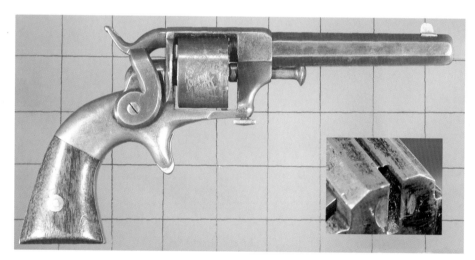

This late first model has a standard length cylinder that is .940 inches long. The 1860 patent date is now stamped on the left side of the frame (see inset). Note the flat frame side below the cylinder where it is beveled on other models. (See arrow.) Number 429.

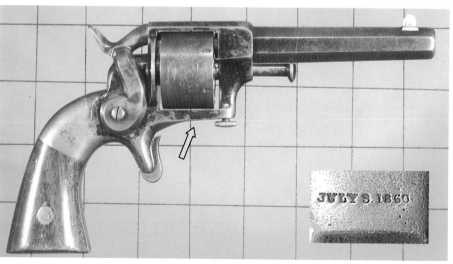

Although all 32 rimfire revolvers have the inclined plane, the July 3, 1860 patent date was not used on early models. It is possible that the patent had not been granted when production started or the proper die stamp was not yet available. All remaining variations of the 32 caliber revolvers are equipped with a spring latch cylinder pin retainer that is part of Allen's patent 33,328, issued September 24, 1861.

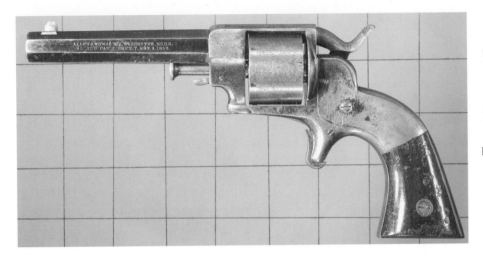

This early second model retains the first type hammer, and is the first model to have the spring latch cylinder pin retainer. This improvement is part of Allen's patent number 33,328, dated September 24, 1861. The 1860 date is there but very lightly stamped. Number 260.

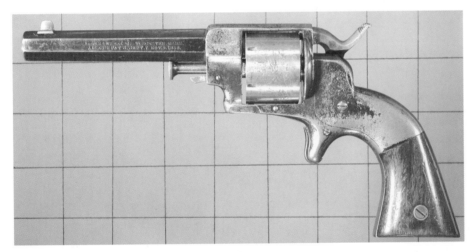

This intermediate variation of the second model has a second type hammer face that is half round and half square. This is the first model to have brass grip escutcheons that are standard on all remaining models. Number 707.

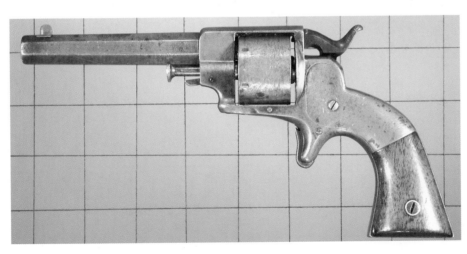

This second model has a square hammer face, which is standard on all remaining models. This is the last model to have the the early type action. Number 249.

154

The revolver shown below is the last model to have the rolled cylinder engraving that has been standard on 32 revolvers since their inception. Only a few individual revolvers have engraved cylinders from this point on. This is also the first model to have the simplified late action that is described on page 123.

This late variation of the second model has a five inch barrel and is the first 32 revolver to have the late type action. This was the last model to have an engraved cylinder as standard. Number 308.

This late second model with an unengraved cylinder is the last variation to have the early type quick drop grips. It is silver plated and has a five inch barrel. This is the most often seen Allen & Wheelock 32 caliber rimfire model. Number 10.

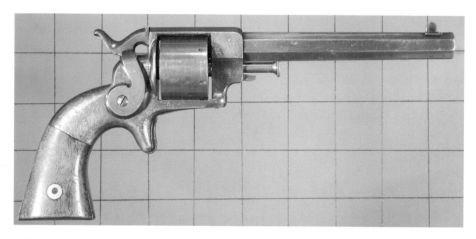

The revolver shown below is the first model to have the newly designed Smith & Wesson type slow drop grips. This style change remains standard for the remainder of Allen & Wheelock and E. Allen & Co. production.

This early third model is the first to have the new Smith and Wesson or slow drop type grips. It is nickel plated with a four inch barrel. This was the last variation with a straight top strap. Number 263.

Starting with the revolver shown below, all following models have the new sculptured frame. It was at this point that Allen brought out his new long cylinder model that accommodated the 32 caliber long rimfire cartridge.

All long cylinder models have the late sculptured top strap and the slow drop grips.

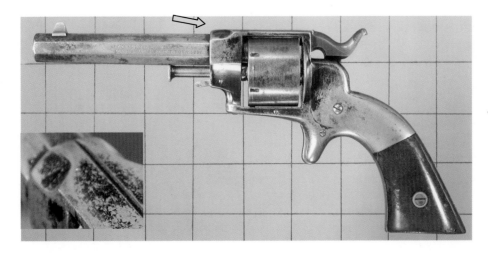

This is the first model to have the newly sculptured top strap. (See arrow and inset.) This style of frame is used on all remaining 32 rimfire models. Number 327.

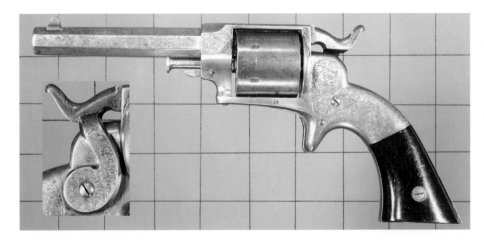

This third model is the first with the long cylinder. The frame and hammer has scroll engraving in Gustave Young style. The grips are made of rosewood. Number 838.

This is the same variation as the engraved revolver shown above but retains most of the original blue. It is unusual to see an Allen & Wheelock in this condition. Note the slightly different contour of the frame (see arrow). Number 659.

156

Brass frame 32 revolvers are rare but were made in short as well as long cylinder versions. All are of late production and made with the third type frame. It is possible that other models may have been made with brass frames but none have been reported at this time. Remember, an Allen collector never says never.

This brass frame short cylinder 32 revolver has traces of the original silver plate. Most brass frame 32s were silver plated, but to see one with more than a trace remaining is rare. Number 24.

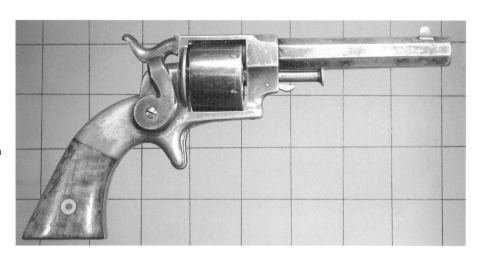

Brass framed 32s were also made in the long cylinder variation and are about as common as the short cylinder version. Number 230.

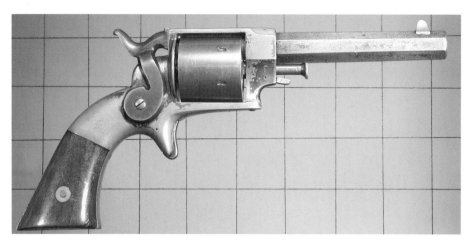

Although not seen in great numbers, early and a few late 32 caliber rimfire revolvers were made with engraved cylinders. The engraving on most 32 Allen & Wheelock revolvers is so light that it is difficult to see what is actually engraved on the cylinder.

Cylinder engraving on the 32 caliber revolvers is normally found only on early models with early type grips. The only exception is that occasionally, a short cylinder brass frame revolver will be seen with an engraved cylinder but only a few have ever been observed. Only short cylinder models have engraving.

Chapter 30
32 CALIBER RIMFIRE SINGLE SHOT PISTOLS

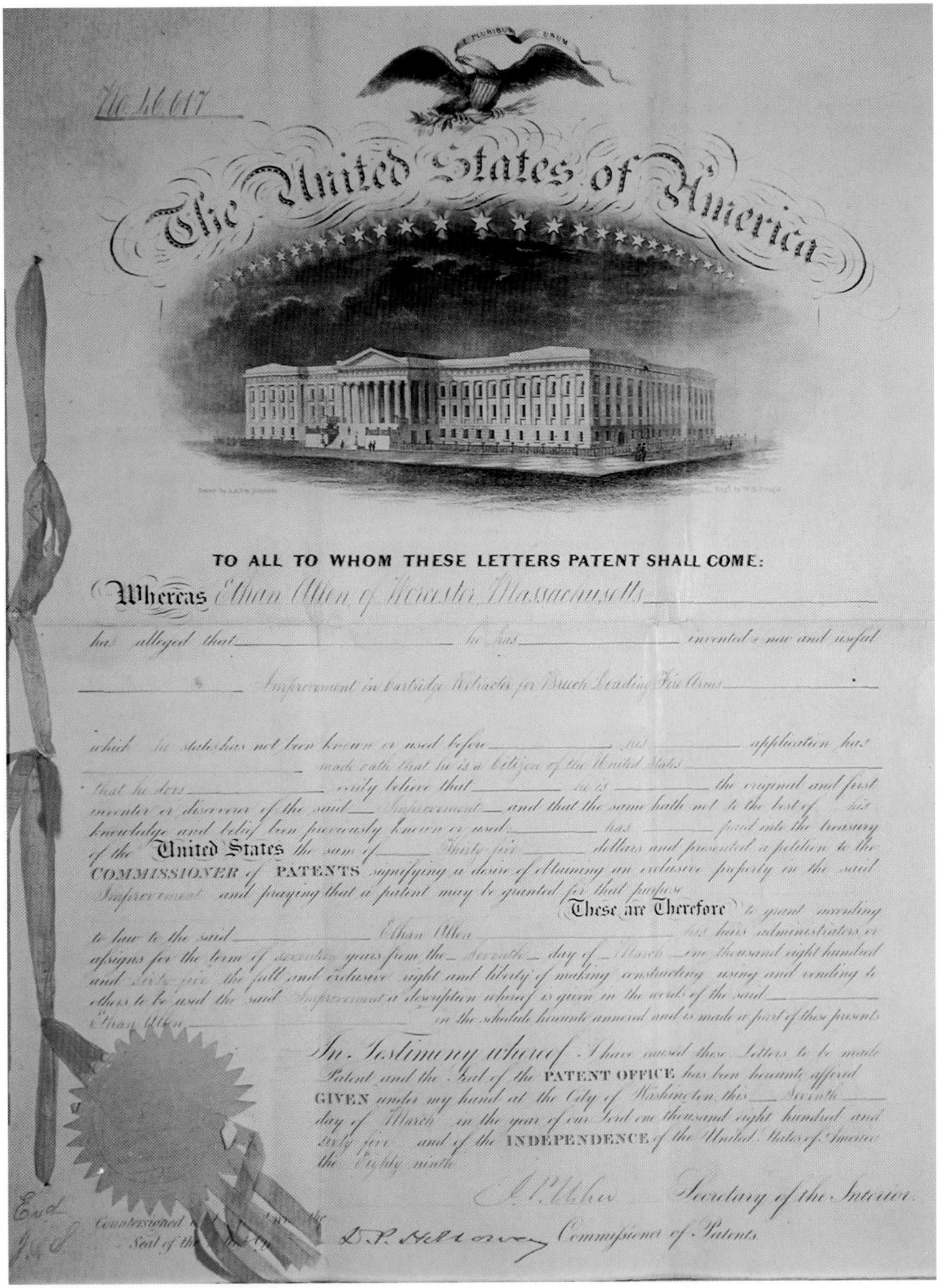

Shown above is the cover page of the original patent number 46,617 that was granted to Ethan Allen on March 7, 1865, that covers the side swing ejector system of the 32 caliber rimfire single shot pistol.

158

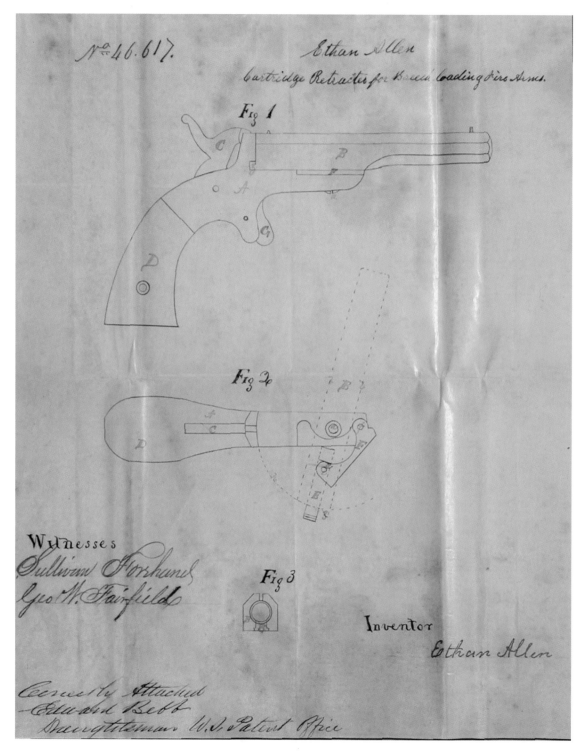

This is the original drawing that Allen presented to the U.S. Patent office for a cartridge retractor for breech loading firearms. It is signed by Ethan Allen and witnessed by Sullivan Forehand and George W. Fairfield. The date that the patent was applied for is unknown.

More commonly known as the 32 side swing, this is another example of Allen using an improvement long before the patent was issued. Patent number 46,617 that covers the ejector system was issued March 7, 1865, ten months after the death of Thomas

Wheelock and at the beginning of E. Allen & Co. This was more than likely due to a patent dispute with J.P. Lee who had an identical patent, but at any rate, Allen's patent stood up and it was eventually awarded to him. Allen must have been very sure that he would win his battle with Lee as he had been using his ejector system on the 32 caliber rimfire single shot pistols for years.

Since the cartridge single shot pistols were not affected by the court's November, 1863 decree, production of these popular little guns continued through the E. Allen & Co. period and into the Forehand & Wadsworth period with only a few changes.

In typical Allen fashion, his description on the patent application rambles on for the better part of a full page. Although not in his exact words, a simple translation is as follows: *Put the pistol on half cock, turn the barrel to the left and the spent cartridge will automatically be ejected.*

Very early 32 side swing pistols were made without ejectors and a few will be seen with steel grip escutcheons, dating the start of production sometime before October 1861.

Very early single shot 32 pistols that were made without ejectors had a small aligning lug. (See arrow.)

All later models made with the ejector system had a thicker aligning lug. (See arrow.)

The simple but efficient ejector pushed the spent cartridge out when the barrel was turned. (See arrow.)

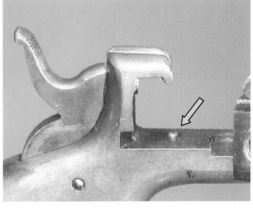

The barrel is locked in the closed position by a small spring loaded pin. (See arrow.)

Trying to determine the sequence of production has proven to be difficult. It is certain that the models without ejectors and with the small aligning lug are the first models. After that, it becomes a matter of just illustrating the differences in the variations.

160

Some will have a long overlap, some will have short overlaps and some will have no overlap at all. One variation will have no overlap with a square breech. But rather than attempting to determine which came first, the chicken or the egg, the following descriptions will simply explain the differences in the variations.

It can be assumed with a reasonable amount of certainly that the pistol on the top right is the first model 32. It is made without the ejector system, has steel grip escutcheons and a small locking lug on the barrel. This is the only single shot 32 to have a knurling ring on the barrel between the octagon and round part of its four inch barrel. Number 455. The pistol on the bottom right has a four inch octagon barrel, brass grip escutcheons and does not have an ejector. Number 215.

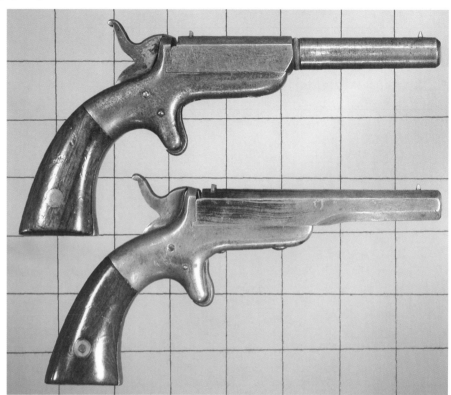

Although the pistols on the right are the same basic design as the two above, these and all subsequent 32 rimfire single shot pistols were made with ejectors. The pistol on the top has a rather rare five inch full octagon barrel. Number 83. The pistol on the lower right has a four inch, octagon and round barrel and is rarely seen with Allen & Wheelock marks. Number 888.

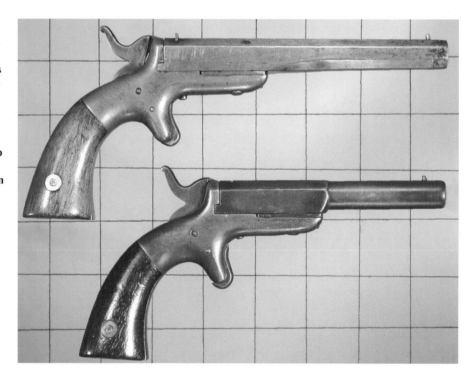

As there were many other single shot cartridge pistols on the market at that time, it cannot be said for sure that Allen invented anything other than his ejector system.

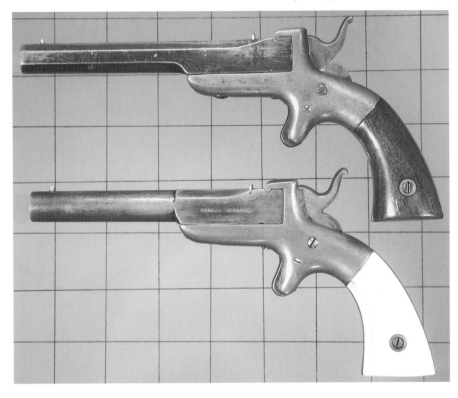

The two 32 single shot pistols on the left both have short frame overlap and ejectors. The top pistol has a five inch octagon barrel, and is absent of any marks. Number 234. The pistol on the bottom left has a four inch octagon and round barrel with ivory grips. It is simply marked Allen & Wheelock. Number 576

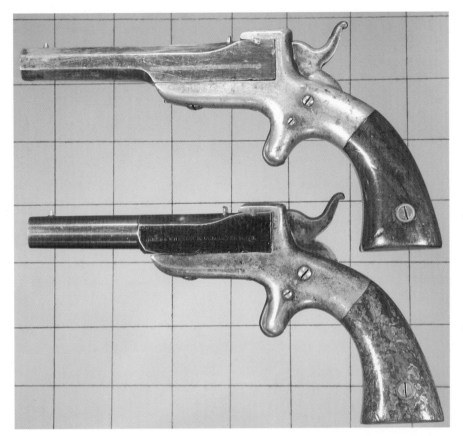

The two single shot pistols on the left both have long frames that overlap the barrel. The pistol on the top has a four inch full octagon barrel and both have ejectors. Both are marked ALLEN & WHEELOCK, WORCESTER, MASS on the left side of the barrel. The number on the top pistol is 92. The pistol on the bottom has a four inch octagon and round barrel and looks to be unfired. It is marked the same as the above pistol. Number 247.

162

The three pistols on the right are identical except for the barrel length. These are the square breech variation and it is not known if they are early or late in production. The pistol on the top has a six inch barrel. Number 433. The pistol in the center has a five inch barrel. Number 56. The pistol on the bottom has a four inch barrel. Number 648. All are marked ALLEN & WHEELOCK, WORCESTER , MASS. in one line.

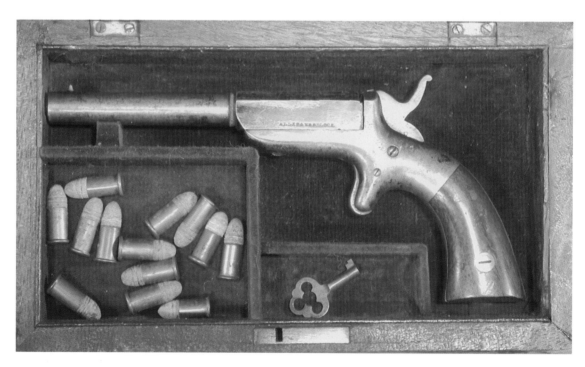

This early first model 32 single shot has a knurling ring in the center of its five inch barrel. It is made without Allen's patented ejector system and has steel grip escutcheons. Number 128.

Chapter 31
LIPFIRE REVOLVERS

The following chapters will cover the four different calibers of lipfire revolvers made by Allen & Wheelock. Although slightly different than the rimfire revolvers, they were also infringements on Rollin White's patent.

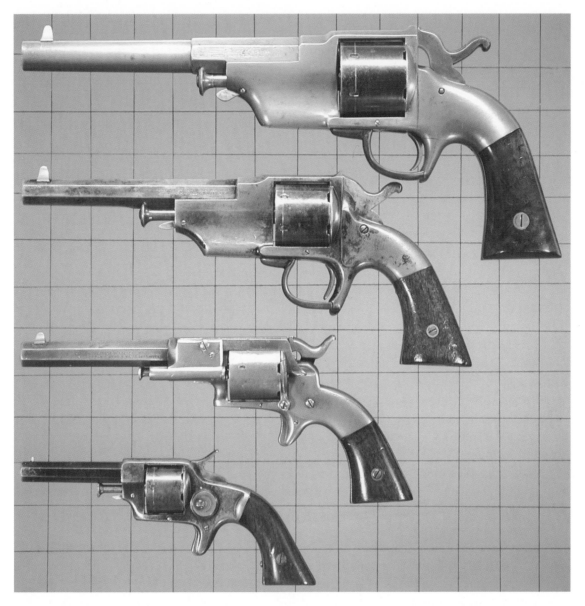

Illustrated above are the four different Allen & Wheelock lipfire revolvers. The top revolver is an early 44 caliber with narrow grips. Number 50. Second is a 36 caliber with a six inch barrel. Number 110. The third revolver is a 32 caliber with a five-inch barrel. Number 73. The revolver on the bottom is a 25 caliber with a three inch barrel that is unmarked. Number 616. All are 6 shot except the 25 and it is a seven shot.

At the time that Allen was developing his lipfire revolvers, Smith & Wesson was already suing Allen & Wheelock for patent infringement. It was only through the efforts of his attorneys, and the fact that the court was overloaded with similar cases, that allowed the proceedings to go on for nearly four years before coming to trial. Being an intelligent man, there could not have been any doubt that Allen was fully aware that all of his revolvers with bored through cylinders were a definite infringement of White's patent. It is unknown if Allen's motives were to make a better cartridge, or to try to find some small loophole to get around White's patent, but the principle of the lipfire system was nothing short of ingenious. Regardless, Allen was not only able to make a stronger cartridge that used only one eighth of the amount of expensive priming powder used in rimfire cartridges, but he also invented and manufactured the machinery to produce both the cartridges and the firearms that use them.

On April 29, 1862, Allen was granted patent number 35,067. This is the first firearm patent that mentions anything about being made to accept a metallic cartridge with a tongue or lip.

Although this patent is basically for the 44 caliber lipfire revolving carbine, there are several interesting improvements included in the patent that actually pertain to the 44 and 36 caliber percussion and the 22 and 32 rimfire revolvers as well.

Once again, from the patent: *"The nature of my invention consists in providing the latch of revolving firearms, which load with a metallic or other cartridge with a tongue or lip, which is received into a corresponding recess in the frame of the arm."*

The latch that Allen refers to in the above description is the new loading gate and it's latch that is now hinged at the bottom.

His explanation goes on and on, but that was the major point of that part of his patent. Later in the patent, Allen describes the new type of action as follows:

"Another part of my invention consists in so constructing the lever for revolving the cylinder that the part that comes next to the cylinder is lifted nearly perpendicular to the rear face of the cylinder, thereby turning it with greater ease than by the common method, where the turning lever is diagonal to the face of the cylinder."

What Allen is describing is the type of action shown in the drawing in page 174. This action was not only used on the 44 and 36 caliber lipfire revolvers, but also on the early 44 and 36 center hammer percussion revolvers as well. This would indicate that in typical Allen fashion, he had been using this improvement long before the patent was issued. As the patent does not have the date that it was filed, there is no way of knowing how long it took the patent office to grant the patent to Allen.

As with most Allen & Wheelock pistols, the frames and barrels are blued and the trigger guard and hammer are casehardened with varnished walnut grips as standard. Barrel markings are: ALLEN & WHEELOCK. WORCESTER. MS. U. S / ALLEN'S PAT'S SEPT 7. NOV 9.1858 in two lines.

It has long been debated which was produced first, the 44 caliber lipfire or the center hammer, 44 caliber percussion revolver. As no patents exist that directly apply to the 44 percussion pistol but have many features related directly to Allen's cartridge revolvers, it is reasonable to assume that the lipfire did indeed precede the percussion revolvers, but not by much. To further help confirm this, the internal action of the 44 and 36 lipfire revolvers were unchanged throughout production, while changes did occur in the center hammer percussion series, thus indicating that they were produced later and longer than the large caliber lipfire revolvers.

Records show that in 1861, Allen had more than 200 hands working in his factory contributing to the upcoming war effort. There can be little doubt that he was producing large caliber 44 and 36 caliber revolvers, along with a variety of cartridges, in an attempt to secure a government contract. In all probability, both the lipfire and percussion revolvers were being produced at the same time.

The 32 has often been referred to as the first model lipfire, but that cannot be accurate. The July 3, 1860 patent date that is on all 32 lipfire revolvers is for the inclined plane patent. (See patent number 28,951 on page 147.) It was originally designed for the first model 32 caliber rimfire revolver but is also used on 44, 36 and 32 lipfire revolvers. The 25 lipfire and the 22 rimfire are the only Allen & Wheelock cartridge revolvers that do not have this feature.

There has been much speculation over the years about why the 25 caliber lipfire revolvers are unmarked. Actually, at least two pistols are known at this time that are correct and properly marked. It should be kept in mind that the 25s were the last of the lip fire series and came out just before the November 1863 court decision banning Allen & Wheelock from making any revolvers with bored through cylinders. It cannot be confirmed but the general consensus is that Allen made these little revolvers to resemble the small frame Smith & Wesson pistols as an "in your face" gesture since Smith & Wesson were suing Allen at that time. The markings on the two pistols that have been observed are identical to all other Allen & Wheelock cartridge revolvers, so Allen would not have had to bear the expense of having a new die stamp made. A possible explanation is that the few marked 25s that are known were made before the court injunction and the remainder were made afterwards. Also, it is known that about as many were made during the E. Allen & Co. era as were made during the Allen & Wheelock era, so it is possible that the company had just received a supply of frame castings before production was halted and were finished later, after White's patent had expired.

Allen was the only producer of lipfire ammunition, and as the cartridges became harder to find, many revolvers were converted to accept rimfire and even centerfire cartridges. The conversion was done in two basic ways. The quickest and easiest way was simply to cut the rear of the cylinder down about one sixteenth of an inch as shown in the top right photo on the following page. This would allow the rim of the cartridge to clear the recoil shield. Another method was to ream the rear of the chambers out to allow the rim of the rimfire cartridge to fit properly into the rear of the chamber as shown in the top center photo on the following page.

The second method kept the original appearance and allowed the use of lipfire ammunition as well. In either case, it was necessary to enlarge the loading port, in order to allow the rim of the rimfire cartridge to clear the loading port and enter the cylinder without removing it from the pistol. A third type of conversion to centerfire uses an entirely different method, which will be explained in the 36 caliber chapter.

It cannot be ruled out that Allen did not convert some of his own lipfire revolvers at the factory. Being a smart businessman and the only maker of lipfire ammunition, he surely knew that the cartridges would not always be available everywhere and could very well have made cylinders that would accept rimfire cartridges as well as lipfire cartridges. A case in point is that a good share of 36 caliber Navy lipfire revolvers will be seen with converted cylinders and unaltered loading ports. As the lipfire cartridges do not have the rim that encircles the base of the cartridge when a lipfire revolver was converted to rim or centerfire, it was necessary to enlarge the loading port to allow for the extra width of the rim on the cartridge. After this was done, however, there would be a telltale gap between

166

the loading gate and the frame of the pistol. If there is no gap, it is quite possible the gun was made to accept either cartridge.

Shown below are the three most commonly seen lipfire cylinders. On the left is the original unaltered cylinder. In the center is the most often seen conversion that allows for either rimfire or lipfire cartridges to be used and the third is a cut down cylinder and altered hammer with which only centerfire cartridges can be used.

This original lipfire revolver with an unaltered cylinder lipfire cartridge inserted in one of the chambers

The chambers of this lipfire revolver have been reamed out to accept rim and lipfire cartridges as well.

The rear of this cylinder has been cut down and the hammer altered. Only center fire cartridges can be fired.

This original lipfire cylinder has not been altered.

This reamed out cylinder is for rimfire as well as lipfire cartridges.

This cut down cylinder is for rimfire or centerfire only.

Pictured above are the four different sizes of the lipfire cylinders. From left to right is the 44 that is one and nine sixteenth inches long. The 36 is one and five sixteenth inches long. The 32 is one and five eights inches long and the 25 caliber is seven eighth of an inch long.

On September 23, 1863, Allen & Wheelock ceased production of all revolving firearms with bored through cylinders. This included the lipfire as well as the rimfire revolvers, but not the single shot pistols.

In addition to making parts for his own firearms, Allen also made a limited number of lipfire cylinders for Tranter revolvers, which were converted from percussion to lipfire.

Chapter 32
44 CALIBER LIPFIRE REVOLVERS

Cocked and ready! Captain Augustine L. Hamilton of Co. 1, 6th Regt. Mass. Vol. Inf. has his first model top hinged Allen & Wheelock 44 caliber lipfire revolver ready for action. He enlisted in the military on August 17, 1860 and was one of the Minute Men of 1861. He was promoted to the rank of Captain on August 8, 1862 and mustered out of the 6th on June 3, 1863. On May 10, 1864, he was commissioned into the 8th Co. and mustered out on August 11, 1864. Photo is courtesy the U.S. Military History Institute and the Gil Barrett collection.

This photo appears to have been taken at the same time as the one on the preceding page but the revolver is in his sash. It appears to be a wide grip model. (See arrow.)

The rather fuzzy picture of Captain Hamilton on the left appears to have been taken at the same time as the photo on the preceding page. Of special significance is the butt of the revolver that is protruding from his belt. (see arrow). There is no doubt that the cocked pistol that he has in his hand on the first picture is a top hinged 44 caliber Allen & Wheelock lipfire revolver. Although there is only one fourth of an inch difference in width between the wide grip and the narrow gripped 44, the shape of the butt would appear to be that of a wide grip model such as the one belonging to Lt. Col. Melvin Beal that is shown below.

The first model 44 caliber lipfire revolver shown below is the rarest of all 44 lipfires and belonged to Lt. Col. Melvin Beal. The possibilities are that both officers either owned identical pistols or Hamilton was posing with Beal's gun. It is obvious that they were friends as both were from Lawrence, Massachusetts and served together. The photo on the left of Captain Hamilton with the revolver in his sash does appear to be a wide grip model. (See page 173.)

Carved in the right grip of this first model 44 Allen & Wheelock lipfire revolver is "M. Beal. Lt. Col. 6Th Mass." and was owned by Lt. Col. Melvin Beal. Number 164.

Lt. Col. Melvin Beal of Co F, 6ᵗʰ Regt. Mass. Vol. Inf. was the owner of the first model Allen & Wheelock lipfire revolver shown on the preceding page. He entered military service at the outbreak of war on April 15, 1861 and was also one of the Minute Men of 1861. The 6ᵗʰ Regt. Mass. Vol. Mil. was summoned to Boston by Special Order No. 14, issued on the afternoon of April 15, 1861, by the Adjutant General of Massachusetts. After being involved in a riot at Baltimore on the 17ᵗʰ of April that resulted in the death of four and the wounding of 36, they were the first regiment to arrive in Washington completely uniformed and equipped for service. After serving three enlistments, he was mustered out for the last time on October 27, 1864, at Reedville, Massachusetts. Photo is courtesy of the U.S. Military History Institute and the Gil Barrett collection.

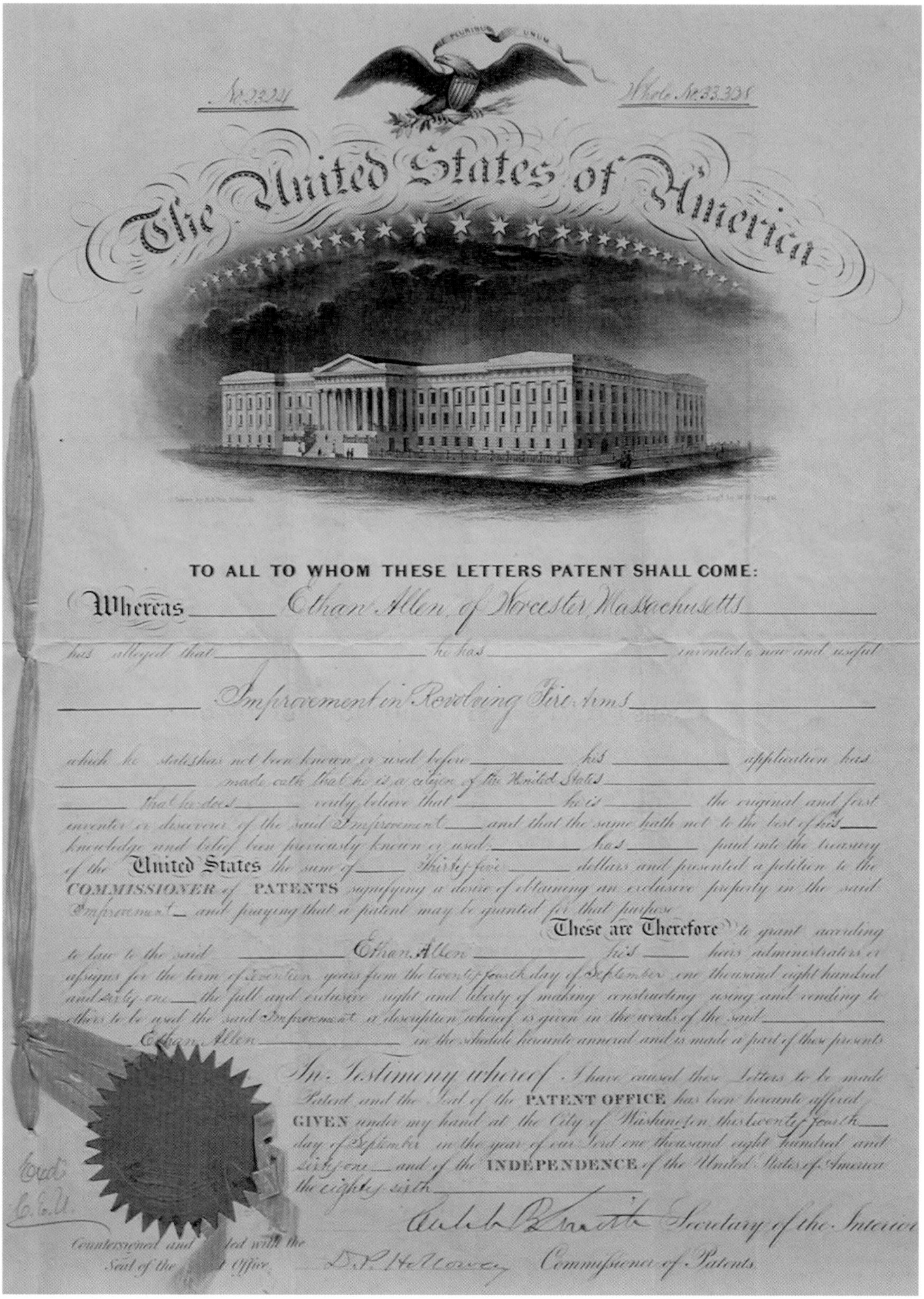

No. 2324 Whole No. 33,328

E Pluribus Unum

The United States of America

TO ALL TO WHOM THESE LETTERS PATENT SHALL COME:

Whereas Ethan Allen, of Worcester, Massachusetts has alleged that he has invented a new and useful Improvement in Revolving Fire-Arms which he states has not been known or used before his application has made oath that he is a citizen of the United States that he does verily believe that he is the original and first inventor or discoverer of the said Improvement and that the same hath not to the best of his knowledge and belief been previously known or used; has paid into the treasury of the United States the sum of Thirty-five dollars and presented a petition to the COMMISSIONER of PATENTS signifying a desire of obtaining an exclusive property in the said Improvement and praying that a patent may be granted for that purpose.

These are Therefore to grant according to law to the said Ethan Allen his heirs administrators or assigns for the term of seventeen years from the twenty-fourth day of September one thousand eight hundred and sixty-one the full and exclusive right and liberty of making, constructing, using and vending to others to be used the said Improvement a description whereof is given in the words of the said Ethan Allen in the schedule hereunto annexed and is made a part of these presents.

In Testimony whereof I have caused these Letters to be made Patent and the Seal of the PATENT OFFICE has been hereunto affixed. GIVEN under my hand at the City of Washington this twenty-fourth day of September in the year of our Lord one thousand eight hundred and sixty-one and of the INDEPENDENCE of the United States of America the eighty-sixth.

Caleb B. Smith Secretary of the Interior

Countersigned and sealed with the Seal of the Patent Office.

D. P. Holloway Commissioner of Patents.

Exd C. E. W.

Shown above is a photo of the original cover page from Allen's patent number 33,328 for the 44 caliber lipfire revolver that was issued on September 24, 1861.

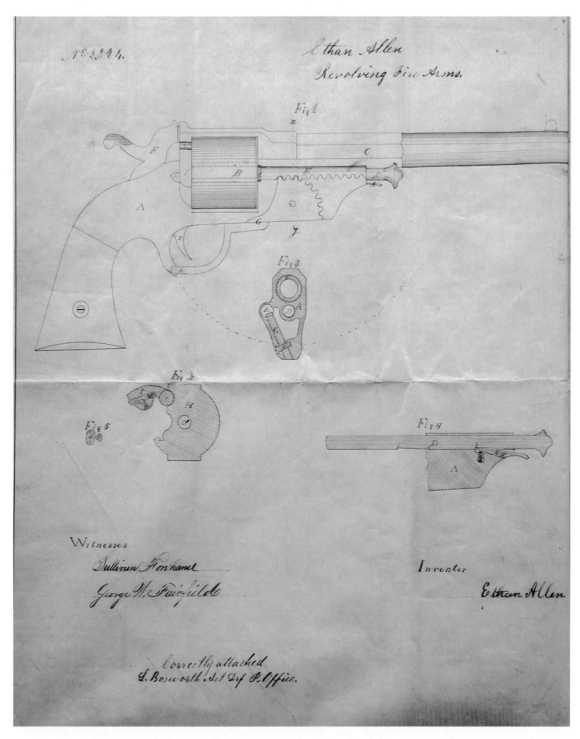

This is the original drawing of patent number 33,328 that Allen submitted to the U.S. Patent office. It is signed by Ethan Allen and witnessed by Sullivan Forehand and George W. Fairfield.

On September 24, 1861, Allen was granted patent number 33,328. It shows a drawing of what has come to be known as the Allen & Wheelock 44 caliber, first model lipfire revolver. The patent makes the following statement: *"The pistol is designed to shoot metallic cartridges and has six chambers within cylinder,"* but does not mention anything about it being a lipfire. It is entirely possible that it was Allen's intention for it to be a large caliber rimfire revolver in the first place.

As the patent on the lipfire cartridge predates the revolver by one full year, in all likelihood this is another case where Allen was using an improvement long before he had received his patent. It would not have made any sense for Allen to be making cartridges for a gun that did not exist, and no other manufacturer was making lipfire revolvers.

After a typical rambling description of what his improvement does, and with every part labeled with a letter, Allen describes the loading and unloading procedure of his new invention as follows: *"The latch "I" is raised and the cartridge is put into the cylinder "B" through the opening and the cylinder is turned by hand as each is filled until all the chambers are charged. The latch "I" is now closed and the cartridges discharged by the ordinary method. The latch "I" is again raised and the cylinder is turned by hand until one of the chambers comes in range with pin "E" when guard-lever "G" is unhooked at "p" and is carried around to "t', as indicated by dotted line, which carries the pin "E" through the cylinder and ejects the cartridge-shell and the operation is repeated until all the shells are expelled, when the cylinder is charged as before."*

The complicated loading instructions were surely written by a highly paid patent attorney as the procedure could have been summed up as follows:
"Open the loading gate, put a cartridge in each chamber, close the gate and shoot. After six shots, open the gate and eject the spent cartridges, using the trigger guard-lever. Repeat if necessary."

Allen and his patent attorneys always had a way of describing a very simple operation in a very complicated manner that was usually very confusing, but they had to be precise.

Although no U.S. government contracts are known, the 44 and 36 lipfire revolvers are considered as secondary military revolvers. However, noted author and authority, Clive M. Law, states on page 24 of his book titled, *Canadian Military Handguns, 1855–1985,* that the Allen & Wheelock 44 lipfire is considered a Canadian military pistol. In his article, he states that a unit in the Montreal area received 34 Allen and Wheelock lipfire revolvers that were made in 1868. It has long been unknown what happened to the 44 and 36 lipfire parts that Allen & Wheelock must have had in their inventory when their production was halted. As White's patent did not expire until 1869, there seems to be a slight conflict in dates but it could also mean that Allen may have assembled the guns and sold them illegally.

Although the action used on all 44 and 36 caliber lipfire revolvers had been in use for quite some time, it was not seen in a patent until April 29, 1862, when patent number 35,067 was granted. Also included in the same patent is the bottom hinged loading gate that was being used on all 36 and most 44 lipfire revolvers. (See page 174.)

This massive looking 44 was made in four different frame variations. All are basically the same and were designed to use Allen's number 58 lipfire cartridges. Although the action used in all 44 and 36 lipfire revolvers are the same, the side plate screw on early models enters from the right side of the frame. Like on the 44 percussion revolvers, that screw not only holds the side plate in place but is also the axle that the hammer rotates on. As with early 44 percussion revolvers, it is necessary to remove the grips and relieve the tension on the main spring before the side plate screw can be removed properly. This can be accomplished by using a small "C" clamp as illustrated on the bottom of page 104.

There are a number of similarities between the 44 lipfire and the 44 percussion to support the theory that they were both being made at the same time.

There are two different models of the 44 lipfire series and each model was made with wide grips as well as narrow grips. The first model is distinguished from the second model by the top hinged loading gate and the side plate screw that enters from the right side of the frame. The narrow gripped first model differs only slightly from the wide grip variation but both models have the inclined plane improvement.

Pictured above is a first model 44 caliber lipfire revolver as shown in the patent drawing. The loading gate is hinged at the top of the frame as shown on the patent drawing on page 171. The side plate screw enters from the right side of the frame and doubles as the bearing surface or axle shaft that the hammer rotates on. The wide bell or flair grips measure two and an eighth inches from front to back at the bottom. First models do not have a main spring tension adjusting screw. Number 161. From the Piet Broekzitter Collection.

The wide grips are two and one eighth inches wide at the longest point and the more common narrow grips are one and seven eighth inches wide.

The narrow grip measures one and seven eighth inches and the wide grip is two and one eighth inches at its widest point. A quarter of an inch difference.

One of the major improvements on the second model is the relocation of the side plate screw from the right side of the frame to the left side. At first this would appear to be only a minor change, but upon closer examination, it becomes obvious that it was a major improvement. This was accomplished by casting a five sixteenth inch round shaft to the inside of the frame for the hammer to rotate on. This gives the hammer a much better bearing surface and makes it much simpler and easier to remove the side plate for cleaning or to make adjustments to the action. This also eliminates the small screw that had to support the strong tension of the main spring. This was a huge improvement as the continual stress on the screw often caused it to bend and even break, which is one reason why it is common to see an early 44 percussion or lipfire that is missing the side plate because the screw broke under the constant pressure of the mainspring.

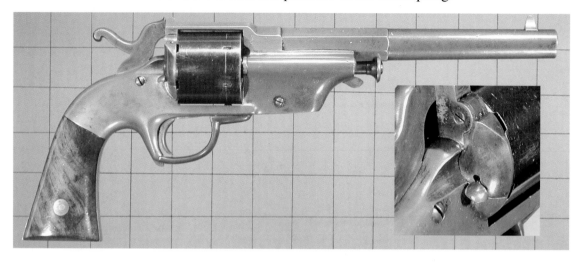

This late first model differs only in that it has narrow grips that measure one and seven eighth inches from front to back at the bottom. This and all later 44 lipfire revolvers will have the inclined plane. See inset for a close up of the top hinge loading gate. Number 50

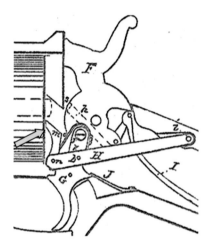

On the left is an excerpt from patent number 35,067 that shows the favorable angle of the operating hand where it makes contact with the rotation teeth on the cylinder. (see arrow). This action was used on all 44 and 36 lipfire and early 44 and 36 percussion revolvers.

On the right is another excerpt from the same patent that features the new bottom hinge loading gate.

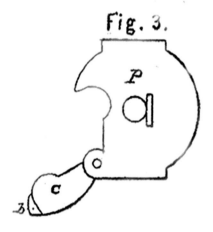

Another improvement that was made to the second model 44 was the new bottom hinge loading gate that is part of Allen's patent 35,067 dated April 29, 1862. This patent actually applied to the revolving carbine but there are many features that referred directly to the large frame 44 and 36 lipfire revolvers.

The earlier top hinge loading gates had a very weak locking system that consisted of a spring loaded pin with a rather flimsy releasing lever that could easily break. The bottom hinge gate had a much stronger lock and was much more reliable.

All 44 caliber lipfire revolvers have the inclined plane improvement (see arrow).

The action that is used on the 36 and 44 center hammer percussion and lipfire series was not included in a patent until April 29, 1862 in patent number 35,067 and was actually for the revolving rifle. As no changes have ever been noted in the lipfire series, it would be safe to assume that the early action was not changed to the late action on the percussion center hammer series until after the injunction in November 1863.

Second model 44 lipfire revolvers are distinguishable from the first models by the bottom hinge loading gate and the side plate screw that enters the frame from the left side. This coincides with the 44 caliber percussion as well.

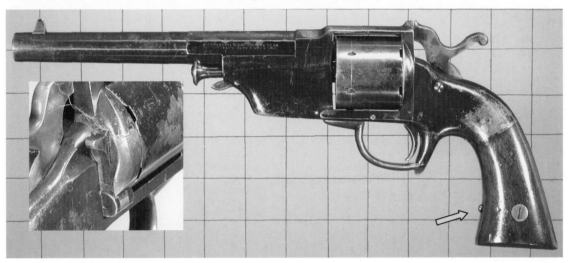

This is a second model with narrow grips and the top hinge loading gate. This was a more practical system. (See inset) Note that the second models have main spring tension adjustment screws. (See arrow.) Number 258.

The wide bell-shaped grips and the loading gate that is now hinged at the bottom of the frame distinguishes this second model from the first model. The side plate screw has been relocated to the left side of the frame and was a huge improvement. Number 204.

As illustrated in the previous chapter, many lipfire revolvers of all calibers were converted to rim or centerfire in several different ways. The early second model 44 that is pictured on the following page has been converted to centerfire by cutting the rear part of the cylinder down by about one sixteenth of an inch.

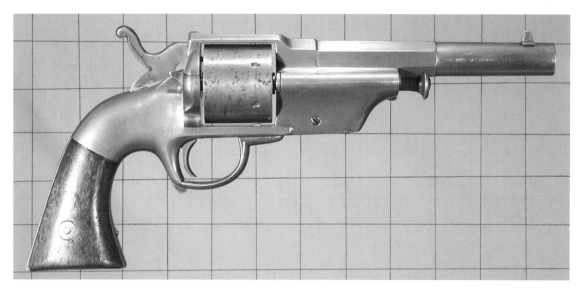

Above is an early second model 44 with wide grips and a shortened six inch barrel that has been converted to centerfire. The conversion was accomplished by cutting down the rear of the cylinder one sixteenth of an inch. The loading port has been enlarged and the hammer modified. Number 56.

All 44 and 36 caliber lipfire revolvers share the same unique rack and pinion type ejector system that incorporates the use of the trigger guard to eject spent cartridges. In his patent, Allen claimed that the head of the plunger is large enough to push out the spent casing without going all the way into the cylinder and would omit lost motion.

This system works on the same principal as the trigger guard / loading lever used on earlier percussion revolvers. The ejector system is part of Allen's patent number 33,328 dated September 24, 1861, and illustrated on page 163.

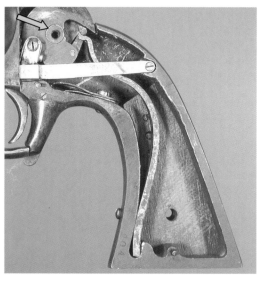

Above is a late 44 lipfire revolver with the side plate and left grips removed. It is a little hard to see, but the hammer is mounted on an axle shaft that is cast into the frame (see arrow). This was a major improvement over the early models and not only made it easier to gain access to service the action but it gave the hammer much more support than the earlier method.

On the left is a view of how the rack and pinion ejector system works. This is the same system the 36 lipfire uses and the same principal that the 32 lipfire uses.

Chapter 33
36 CALIBER LIPFIRE REVOLVERS

As there are no noted variations, it is obvious that the 36 caliber lipfire revolver was produced later than its big brother, the 44. All 36s have loading gates that are hinged at the bottom and the action is identical to the 44s.

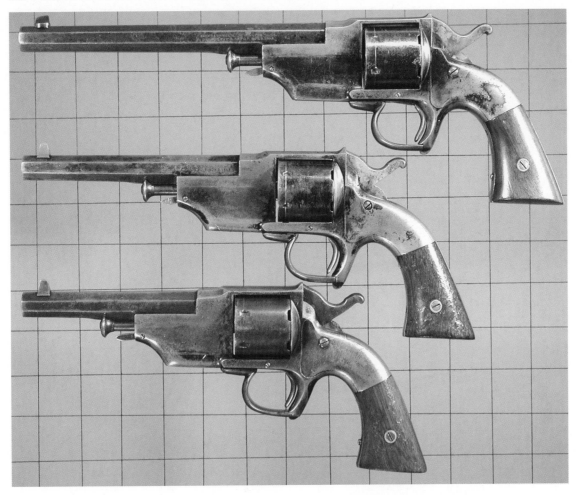

No major variations of the original 36 caliber lipfire revolvers have been noted. The three standard barrel lengths are shown above. The revolver on the top has an eight inch barrel and has been altered to chamber rimfire cartridges as well as lipfire. Number 337. The middle revolver has a six inch barrel and is an original lipfire. Number 110. The revolver on the bottom is also an original unaltered lipfire and has a 5 inch barrel. Number 274 from the collection of Piet Broekzitter, Alblasserdam, The Netherlands.

Barrel markings are the same as on all other Allen & Wheelock cartridge revolvers. All original 36 lipfire revolvers have full octagonal barrels, with standard lengths of five, six and eight inches. Occasionally one will be seen with correct nickel plating.

Made to chamber Allen's number 56 lipfire cartridge, many were converted to rim or center fire using the same methods as illustrated in the lip fire introduction chapter.

There appears to be as many conversions as there are unaltered 36 lipfires around, so it is entirely possible some left the factory with modified cylinders that would accept rim as well as lipfire cartridges.

Pictured below is the ultimate revolver. This 8 inch barreled, 36 caliber Allen & Wheelock Navy lipfire revolver has been converted to accept rimfire and centerfire as well as lipfire cartridges. As this is a masterful piece of gunsmithing, there is the possibility that this conversion could have been one of Allen's brainstorms and done at his factory.

Many 36 caliber lipfire revolvers seen today will accept either lip or rimfire cartridges and it has long been speculated but not confirmed that these guns could have been converted before they left the Allen factory. It would seem that Allen would have been smart enough to realize that lipfire cartridges would not always be available.

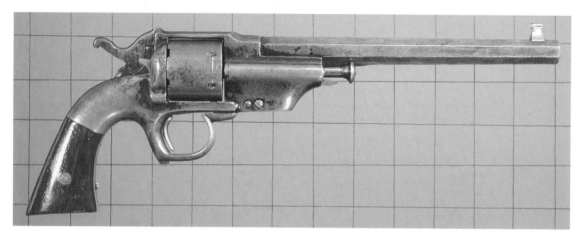

This 36 caliber lipfire has been converted to accept not only rimfire cartridges by boring out the rear of the cylinder, but by the addition of a cleverly placed firing pin and a slight modification to the original hammer, the pistol will now also shoot centerfire ammunition as well. Number 210.

The firing pin has been expertly placed in the recoil shield in order to line up with the center of the cartridge. Note the notch that has been cut into the hammer (see arrows).

The firing pin extends through the inclined plane on the inside of the recoil shield (see arrow). Note that the loading port has been altered to allow for rimfire or centerfire cartridges.

Several conversions of this type have been reported but this is the only one that could be considered as possibly being done in the Allen factory. At this time, no other variations, such as a top hinge loading gate or wide grips, have been encountered but there is always a chance that one might turn up some day.

Chapter 34
32 CALIBER LIPFIRE REVOLVERS

The 32 caliber lipfire revolver is a rather unique pistol, with a six shot cylinder and an overhead rack and pinion ejector system. Made to chamber Allen's number 52 lipfire cartridge, it is standard with octagonal barrel lengths of four, five and six inches.

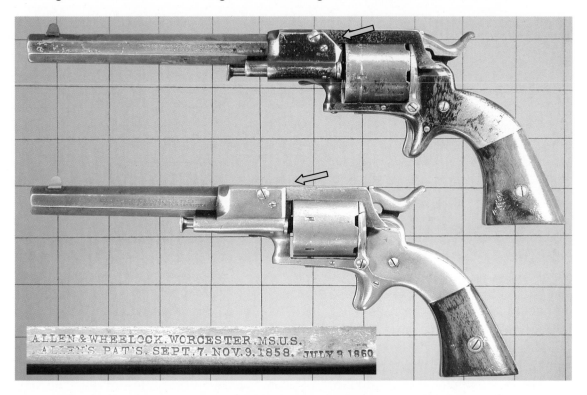

The revolver on the top has a six inch octagon barrel and a beveled ejector housing (see arrow). Number 132. The revolver on the bottom has a five inch octagon barrel and a square ejector housing (see arrow). Number 73. Barrel markings are the same as the 32 caliber rimfire revolvers. Note the added 1860 date.

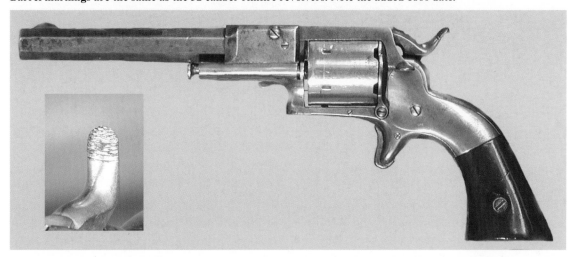

Pictured above is a late 32 caliber lipfire revolver that is marked E. Allen & Co. on the top barrel flat. Note that it has the square breech and the straight ejector tube. The only difference from the Allen & Wheelock marked 32 is the blade front sight, the slightly smaller grip escutcheons and a slash mark under the hammer knurling. (See arrow.) Number 442 from the Bart Richards collection.

Assembly numbers have been no help in determining which variation is late or early as both have been noted with high and low numbers. However, examples marked E. Allen & Co. appear to have the square breech, but not enough examples have been seen to form a definite opinion. As there does not seem to be any advantage of one design over the other, it is quite possible that Allen was buying his castings from more than one foundry that were using slightly different molds.

It has long been thought that the 32 lipfire was the first model of the lipfire series, but that cannot be true. Other than the ejector system, the 32 lipfire is basically identical to the late long cylinder 32 rimfire revolvers and has the same features and action. The 1860 patent for the inclined plane was originally designed for the 32 rimfire revolvers but later adapted to the 44, 36, and the 32 lipfire revolvers.

On February 4, 1862, Allen was granted reissue patent number 1,268 that had a better description of the original 1860 patent. The assumption that this was an early revolver came from the use of the July 3, 1860 patent die stamp rather than the 1862 date, which would have been correct, but it is obvious that Allen did not want to spend the money for a new die stamp so he simply used the old one. This is similar to the 1837 die stamp that was used for years after Allen had changed his pepperboxes over to the 1845 action. Allen was known for getting his money's worth from a die stamp as it is not unusual to see an 1837 date on a pepperbox that was struck by a fractured die.

It should also be taken into consideration that at that time in history Allen was contributing to the upcoming war effort, and already had an established line of smaller 22 and 32 caliber rimfire revolvers in his arsenal. As shrewd of a businessman as Allen was, he would have surely been directing his attention toward the manufacture of larger caliber revolvers, with a possible military contract in mind.

Regardless, there can be little doubt that the 1862 reissue of 1860 patent applied to the 32 lipfire, as it is the only revolver other than the 32 rimfire to carry that patent date.

The rack and pinion overhead ejector system is used on the 32 lipfire revolvers only and is a very reliable system and simple to operate.

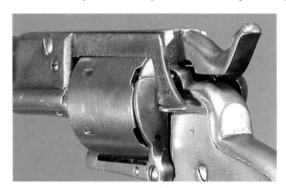 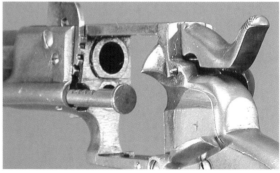

Shown above is how the ejector lever overlaps the loading gate to keep it in the closed position.

With the cylinder removed and the ejector lever raised, it's possible to see how the system works.

The internal workings of the 32 lipfire revolvers are illustrated in Allen's patent number 33,509, dated October 22, 1861, and is identical to the later type action used on 32 and 22 caliber rimfire revolvers. (See page 147.)

All parts are blued except for the hammer and trigger, which are casehardened, and the walnut grips are varnished.

Chapter 35
25 CALIBER LIPFIRE REVOLVERS

Designed to accommodate Allen's number 50 lipfire cartridge, there has been much speculation about the seven shot, 25 caliber lipfire revolver. For years it has been thought that none were marked, and some collectors have questioned if it was even a product of the Allen factory, as it had little resemblance to most of Allen's other firearms.

The question can be put to rest once and for all, as not only one but two have turned up with the correct Allen & Wheelock barrel markings and there are surely others.

Made without trigger guard or loading gate, it was necessary to remove the seven shot cylinder from the pistol for loading. The cylinder pin was used to punch out spent shells in the same manner as the 22 and 32 caliber rimfire revolvers.

Pictured above is one of the few Allen & Wheelock 25 caliber lipfire revolvers that have the correct barrel markings. Number 54.

These were very sleek looking little revolvers, but as the action is somewhat on the flimsy side, the reliability of the pistol would have been questionable at best.

Taking into consideration that Smith & Wesson was suing Allen for patent infringement at the same time the revolver was put on the market by Allen, it is surely no coincidence that the 25 has a very close resemblance to the small Smith & Wesson cartridge revolvers. This is more than likely why most of these revolvers were unmarked.

It is obvious that Allen had a considerable number of these little guns in various stages of manufacture, as well as a supply of parts, when the court ordered the firm to cease the production of cartridge revolvers in November of 1863.

Although it was well into the E. Allen & Co. era when the Rollin White patent expired in 1869, Allen nevertheless assembled these parts and they were eventually sold. It is not known if Allen continued to have castings for the pistol made or just assembled pistols until his supply of parts were exhausted.

Although mostly unmarked, the difference between the Allen & Wheelock and the E. Allen & Co. examples can easily be distinguished by examining the hammer knurling.

As with all other E. Allen & Co. cartridge revolvers that were carried over from the Allen & Wheelock period and retain the typical Allen & Wheelock square butt design, a double slash mark will be found directly under the knurling of the hammer. For some

182

unknown reason this is consistent with all 22 and 32 rimfire revolvers with square butts, as well as the 32 and 25 lip fire revolvers.

Before removing the side plate from a 25 caliber lip-fire revolver, it is necessary to relieve the tension of the main spring by using a "C" clamp.

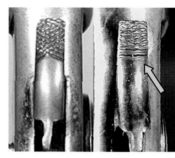

Although only a few 25 caliber lip-fire revolvers have been seen marked Allen & Wheelock none have been reported with E. Allen & Co. markings. The difference between the two revolvers can be seen by examining the hammer knurling. The Allen and Wheelock hammer on the upper left has the normal type saddle knurling but the hammer of the E. Allen & Co. pistol on the upper right has a hand filed double slash mark beneath the knurling (arrow). These slash marks are on all cartridge revolvers that were made with Allen & Wheelock parts. The only other difference is that E. Allen & Co. revolvers have smaller grip escussions.

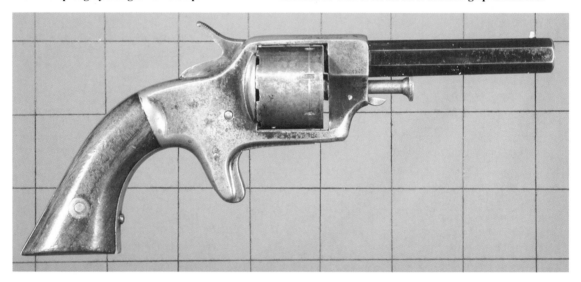

It is hard not to see a striking resemblance to the Smith & Wesson small frame revolvers of the time. There is little doubt that the 25 lipfire was an in your face gesture on Allen's part to get back at Smith & Wesson for suing him. This pistol is totally unmarked with the exception of the number 614.

After many years of researching these little revolvers, it appears that about as many were made by E. Allen & Co. as were made by Allen & Wheelock. It seems strange that Allen did not resume production of his 36 and 44 caliber cartridge revolvers when White's patent expired. After 1869, the largest cartridge handgun in the E. Allen & Co. arsenal was the 41 caliber rimfire single shot side swing pistol.

It is possible that after November of 1863 when Allen could no longer make cartridge revolvers, he had directed the majority of his attention to making cartridges. With his cartridge-making equipment reported to be superior to others and operating at capacity, Allen possibly decided not to get fully involved making very many handguns again. Allen's new hinge breech shot gun and steel shot shells were also selling well and with the increased competition in the gun making industry, this seems to be a logical theory.

Chapter 36
CARTRIDGE MAKING MACHINES

Although primarily noted for the manufacturing of firearms, it is a little known fact that Allen was an early inventor of cartridge making equipment that was superior to any other machinery of its kind, not only at that time, but also for many years to come.

Patent number 27,094, as shown below, was issued to Allen on February 14, 1860, and covered an improvement in machinery for the forming of a rimfire cartridge by using a process that Allen referred to as "bumping the rim." A copper slug about the size of a penny would be put through several drawing dies to form a cylinder that would resemble half of a medical capsule. When the capsules were put into his machine, his improvement would trim and form the swelled end of the cartridge to form the recess (rim) for the priming powder in one stroke. This system was quicker and more accurate than other cartridge making machines that used the method of spinning the case, which often caused unsatisfactory results making Allen's equipment superior to any other cartridge making equipment that was available at that time. It also appears that some of the basic principles that were used in his earliest inventions are still being used today.

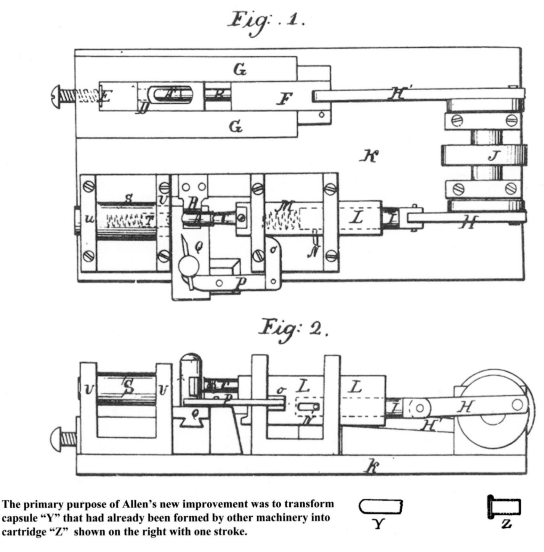

Fig. 1.

Fig. 2.

The primary purpose of Allen's new improvement was to transform capsule "Y" that had already been formed by other machinery into cartridge "Z" shown on the right with one stroke.

Allen and his successors would retain control of his cartridge making business until January 19, 1873, when Allen's widow, Sarah, sold the cartridge making machinery to U.M.C. for an undisclosed amount.

Allen's second patent for cartridge making equipment was patent number 31,695 and was issued to him on March 19, 1861. Simply put, his improvement consisted of a method of crimping the cartridge case to hold the bullet firmly in place and cutting the grooves in the head of the projectile to allow for the application of a lubricant.

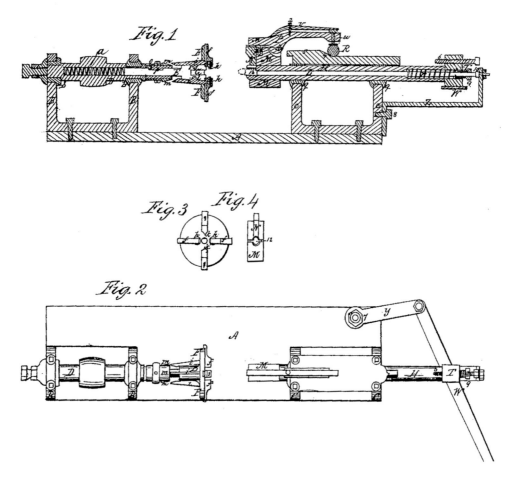

Allen's patent number 31,696 covers the machinery to crimp the case of the cartridge into the bullet to hold it securely and also creases the bullet for the lubricant.

This short chapter very briefly describes Allen's cartridge making machinery, and does not even scratch the surface of the true scope of the entire process.

It is obvious that a large part of Allen's later business consisted of the manufacturing of cartridges and cartridge making equipment. There is much more research that needs to be done before an accurate report can be made on this phase of his business.

As with the patents he obtained on the improvements on firearms, it is not possible to pinpoint the exact date when he actually started manufacturing cartridges but his patents did hold up in court.

In 1861, Allen & Wheelock had a very good rating with Dun & Bradstreet and in 1862, a slightly confusing report stated that Ethan Allen's company was producing as many as 20 thousands rounds of ammunition a day.

Chapter 37
BOXES AND BULLETS

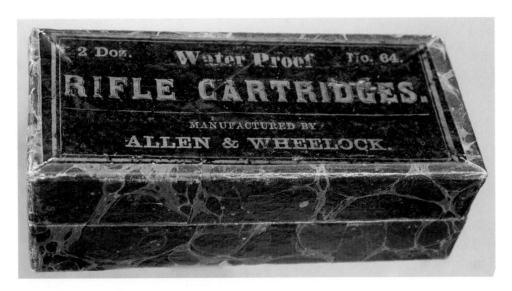

Pictured above is a fine, full box of Allen & Wheelock number 64 cartridges for the 42 caliber rimfire dropping block rifle. From the Perry Hansen collection.

To do any justice to the cartridges that were manufactured by the firm of Allen & Wheelock would require an entire book that has yet to be written. To the dedicated collector of early cartridges, there would be no better subject to write about as very little is known or has been written about this pioneer of the cartridge making industry.

Allen's cartridge making machinery was superior to his competitor's, and in January of 1862, it was reported that he was making 20,000 rounds a day to contribute to the upcoming war effort. This is quite an accomplishment for the time.

During Allen's span of business, he produced an amazing variety of different caliber rimfire, lipfire and even pinfire cartridges, which are listed below. The known designation that Allen had for his cartridges are in parenthesis.

- .22 short blank
- .22 short ball   (No 22)
- .22 short ball with raised A&W head stamp   (No 30)
- .30 short ball
- .32 short ball (No 32)
- .32 short ball with raised A&W head stamp. Also marked No 32
- .32 long ball   (No 32 Long)
- .35 rifle ball   (No 62)
- .38 short ball
- .38 long ball
- .41 short ball (No 41)
- .42 rifle ball (No 64)

- .44 short ball (No 44)
- .44 flat ball
- .44 long ball
- .46 short ball
- .54 Ballard Carbine
- .54 Starr Carbine
- .56/52 Spencer ball
- .56/56 Spencer ball
- .17 cal Shot shell primer
- 12 MM Lefaucheux pin fire
- .25 lipfire (No 50)
- .32 lipfire (No 52)
- .36 lipfire (No 56)
- .44 lipfire (No 58)

186

Shown above are some of the identifying tool marks found on the head of Allen Cartridges. Mouilesseaux, p. 85.

There is no doubt that Allen's invention of his lipfire cartridge was nothing short of ingenious. He was granted patent number 30,109 for improvement in metallic cartridges on September 25, 1860. In a portion of his patent, Allen made the following claim:

"The nature of my invention consists in constructing a projection or lip on a metallic cartridge for reception of a fulminate. By confining the fulminate to the projection C, I thereby save about seven-eights of the expense of this compound and lessen the liability in the same proportion of blowing off the cartridge end, which often occurs in exploding those in common use. I also make a stronger head, or end, to the cartridge, which obviates the difficulty of the swelling back of the head of the cartridge, as is common in other modes of construction."

E. ALLEN.
Cartridge.

No. 30,109.

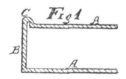   

Patented Sept. 25, 1860.

Shown above is an excerpt from the patent that Allen was granted for his lipfire cartridge.

On the far left is a 22 caliber short cartridge with a raised A&W head stamp, and the near left is a 32 caliber rimfire cartridge that also has the raised A&W head stamp. These appear to be the only two Allen cartridges that are known to have those marks. The box that contained the head stamped 22 cartridge is number 30, and the box containing the non-head stamped cartridges is number 22.

Shown above is a group of Allen's cartridges. From left to right they are 44 rimfire, 44 lipfire, 42 rim fire, 12 mm pinfire, 41 rimfire short, 38 rimfire long, 36 lipfire, 35 rimfire, 32 lipfire, 32 rimfire long, 32 rimfire short, 30 rimfire, 25 lipfire, 22 rimfire and a .17 primer for Allen's reloadable steel shot shell.

Allen cartridge boxes are highly sought after by collectors and are seldom seen. The following is an assortment of rare Allen & Wheelock black label cartridge boxes from the Perry Hansen collection.

This box originally contained 50 number 32, 32 rimfire cartridges with the A&W head stamp.

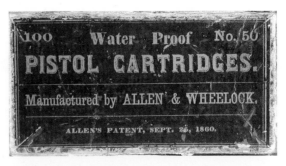

This box contained 100 number 50, 25 caliber cartridges. All lipfire cartridge boxes have the added words "water proof."

This very rare box held 100 number 32, 32 caliber rimfire cartridges.

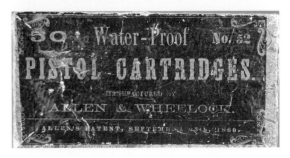

Number 52 was Allen's designation for the 32 caliber lipfire cartridges. It is not known what the purpose of his designate numbering system was.

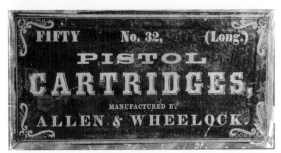

This fine box contained 50 number 32, 32 caliber long cartridges.

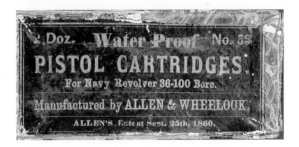

This box contained two dozen number 56 lipfire cartridges for the 36 caliber Navy revolver.

Number 64 was Allen's designation for the 42 caliber rimfire rifle cartridge.

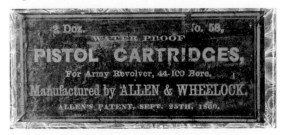

This box contained two dozen number 58 lipfire cartridges for 44 caliber Army revolvers.

188

"ALLEN'S" PATENT
BREECH-LOADING SPORTING RIFLE.

THIS cut represents "ALLEN'S" CELEBRATED "PATENT" BREECH-LOADING RIFLE, unsurpassed for force and accuracy in shooting, and for simplicity of mechanism. The barrel is easily detached from the frame by simply drawing out the connecting bolt, thus leaving it in a very compact form.

ONE OF THE PECULIAR FEATURES OF THIS ARM is the facility with which the set, or pull, of the trigger can be regulated; thus enabling the sportsman to have any degree of fineness he may desire. This is done by simply turning the set screw which passes through the tumbler, the head of which is exposed to view when the hammer stands at full cock.

Rifles on hand and made to order, with "Allen's Patent" and Globe Sights, any length of barrel and style of finish desired. Extra barrels fitted when required. Calibres, 35-100, 38-100, 42-100, 44-100.

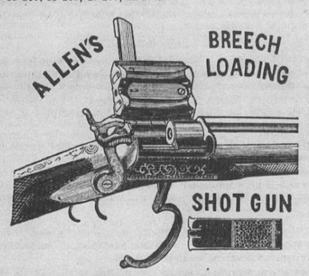

The above represents the gun with the lid open, the guard down, and a cartridge partly withdrawn; also a longitudinal section of a loaded cartridge shell, showing the conical or patent chamber form. The shells with which these guns are loaded being made of drilled steel, can be reloaded, lasting as long as the barrels of the gun; which fact, taken with its efficiency, simplicity, and neatness of finish, make it the most desirable shot-gun ever invented. Guns of the above patent on hand and made to order, of any length, crook of stock, and style of finish to suit. For sale by ONION, HAIGH & CORNWALL, SOLE AGENTS, 18 WARREN STREET, N Y., DEALERS IN GUNS, PISTOLS, RIFLES, GUN MATERIALS, AND FISHING TACKLE OF EVERY DESCRIPTION, SUITABLE FOR ALL PARTS OF THE COUNTRY. Please call and examine, or send for circular.

The ad for ONION, HAIGH & CORNWALL from the early 1870s advertises Allen's breech loading rifle and his breech loading double barreled shotgun. The cartridge era began during the time Allen & Wheelock were in business but their early cartridge rifles and shotguns remained in production for many years after the end of the Allen & Wheelock era.

Chapter 38
INTRODUCTION TO LONG ARMS

As with the pepperbox and percussion single shot pistols, the early percussion long arms were another carryover from the Allen, Thurber & Co. era, with only small changes.

The steel wrist and the steel forearm, or the absence of the forearm, easily identify the majority of early Allen & Wheelock percussion rifles and shotguns.

The bulk of the company's primary business of long arms leaned toward the manufacture and sales of field grade rifles and shotguns; but at the same time, they also produced some of the finest American-made long arms of their day.

Major production of long arms did not get into full swing until Allen & Thurber moved to Worcester, Mass. in July of 1847. There they produced an amazingly large line of long arms suitable for all types of shooting. This included single and double rifles, single and double shotguns, over-and-under, as well as side-by-side rifle / shotgun combinations and buggy rifles with detachable shoulder stocks. Later, Worcester production would include a percussion breech loading rifle, breech loading cartridge rifles in two different sizes and a breech loading double barrel shotgun which used patented reloadable steel shot shells.

It is hard to imagine how a relatively small manufacturing company like Allen's could carry such a large menu of long arms, along with his pistol and cartridge business.

Although long arms production was not a priority during the years at Grafton and Norwich, Allen did make a few rifles and at least one experimental bar hammer shotgun.

Although only a few rifles were made at Grafton, one example is pictured below.

Although not having the full steel wrist that is common on most Allen long arms, the overall appearance strongly resembles the typical Worcester manufactured side hammer rifles. The 46 caliber full octagon barrel is 30 inches long and is made without a forearm. The hammer and frame have some modest engraving. The left side of the frame is lightly marked ALLEN & THURBER / GRAFTON MASS. in two lines (see inset). The overall length is 45 inches. Number 29.

After the move to Norwich in 1842, the manufacture of a variety of pepperbox pistols, along with bar hammer single shot pistols remained the priority. This left little time to produce a line of long arms and only two rifles, one shotgun and whaling guns were mentioned during the nine month period the day book covers while the company was at Norwich. (The whaling guns sold for $35 each.)

Another one of Allen's major achievements that will not be covered in the following chapters of this book is his breech loading double barreled shotgun, commonly referred to as the hinged breech. Although not patented until August 22, 1865, during the E. Allen & Co. era, it is not only one of Allen's finest production firearms, but also one of the finest early American-made shotguns of its time. It was made to use Allen's reusable steel shot shell, for which he received a patent on May 16, 1865, three months before he received the patent for the hinged breech shotgun.

On Dec 15, 1868, Allen was granted another patent that not only covered improving the strength of the breech but also included a new steel shell that was made in a bottle-neck design and contained a rifle bullet that could be inserted into his shotgun giving it the same capacity as a rifle. (See patent on page 225.)

The shotgun was available in 12 or 10 gauge and in three different grades priced from $100 to $150, making it one of the most expensive American made shotguns of the time.

Grade one was a rather plain gun that had a minimal amount of engraving and good wood with a modestly checkered stock. Grade two had a considerable amount of engraving and a better grade of wood and checkering. Grade three was highly engraved with fine select wood that was finely checkered on both the stock and forearm.

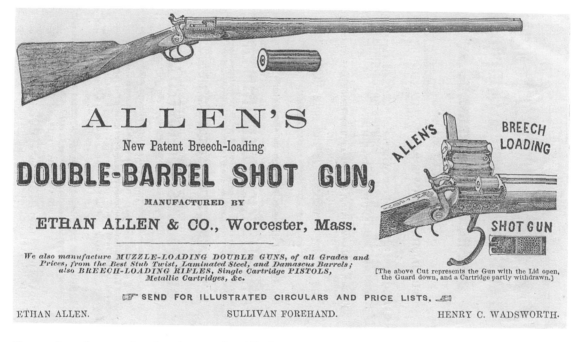

Shown above is an early advertisement for Allen's patented breech loading shotgun. It is shown with his reloadable steel shot shell which sold for $6.00 per dozen. Primers sold for $2.50 per hundred.

After placing both hammers at half cock and releasing the lock, the breechblock could be rotated to the left for loading or unloading as shown above. In typical Allen style, the trigger guard is used to activate the ejector system and by swinging the guard forward, the spent casings could easily be ejected.

It is interesting to note that on the bottom of the advertisement shown above, it lists not only Ethan Allen's name, but also that of his two sons-in-law, Sullivan Forehand and Henry Wadsworth, who were the "& Co." They would not only take over the business after Allen's death, but would later form their own company of Forehand & Wadsworth.

Chapter 39
MUZZLE LOADING PERCUSSION RIFLES AND SHOTGUNS

Early Allen & Wheelock muzzle loading rifles and shotguns were carried over from the Allen, Thurber & Co. period. They are distinguished from most other rifles by their steel wrist. Only the early Allen & Wheelock marked long arms have steel forearms.

Although no two rifles are exactly alike and have been seen in many different variations, two basic models were available. The most generic is the center hammer rifle that Allen referred to as the No. 10 inside cock. (Inside hammer.)

The field grade, side hammer single shot rifle was referred to as the No. 10 side cock. (Side hammer.) Both sold for around $10.00 per rifle and were available in a variety of calibers from 36 to 50.

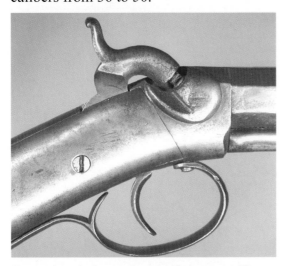

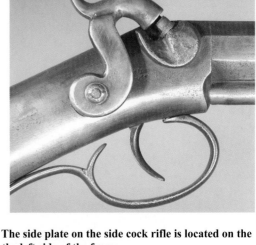

Shown above is the standard inside hammer rifle. The side plate is on right side of the frame.

The side plate on the side cock rifle is located on the the left side of the frame.

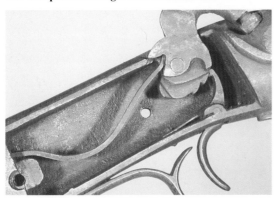

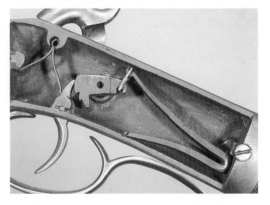

The action of the inside cock rifle has a curved main spring and a half cock position.

The action of the side hammer rifle has a hammer tumbler and a V-shaped main spring.

As shown above, the two rifles have entirely different actions. The action of the inside hammer rifle, in the upper left photo, has a very simple action while the action of the side hammer rifle, on the upper right, is more conventional. All better grade rifles and shotguns have side hammers. No center hammer shotguns have been observed.

Allen's better grade rifles have double set triggers and removable barrels. On early rifles, the internal parts are mounted to the inside of the frame. On later rifles, the action is mounted to the removable side plate and only the triggers are attached to the frame.

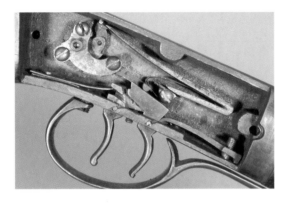 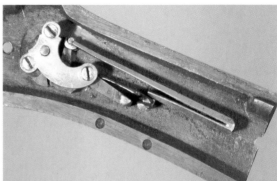

The double set trigger mechanism is attached to the inside of the frame on early models. **The double set trigger mechanism is attached to the right side plate on later models.**

Allen & Wheelock percussion rifles have several different types of forearms. Shown below are the three that are most often seen.

Only the very early field grade Allen & Wheelock muzzle loading rifles have steel forearms as shown above.

This high-grade bench rest rifle shown above has a steel ramrod tube merging into the lower portion of the barrel.

Later field grade rifles only have a ramrod tube on the bottom of the barrel. These are the most common.

Most Allen & Wheelock field grade rifles have solid frames, but the better grade percussion rifles had removable barrels that could be taken down by removing a threaded bolt that is located under the frame in front of the trigger guard.

Most of the take down bolts have a square head bolt that requires a special wrench to remove.

Most field grade percussion rifles have solid frames and the barrels are not removable.

Several different types of take down tools were available for Allen's rifles with removable barrels, as illustrated below. It is doubtful if Allen actually made these tools, but they were made to fit the take down screws on his long arms. The combination take down tool pictured below left is the only tool that could be considered as made by Allen.

 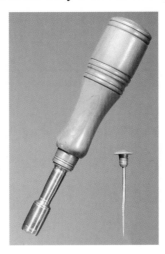 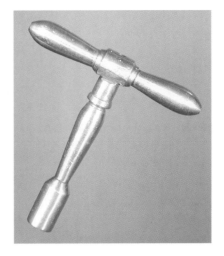

Combination take down tool, bullet mold and screwdriver.

This take down tool has a nipple pick in the handle.

This take down tool has a "T" type handle.

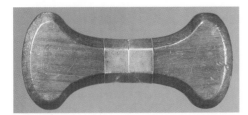 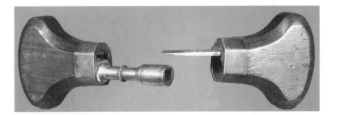

This cute little take down tool is in the shape of a bow tie.

When opened, it reveals a take down tool on one half and a screw driver on the other half.

SINGLE SHOT PERCUSSION RIFLES

This very early Allen & Wheelock inside hammer rifle has a 36 inch, 52 caliber octagon barrel that has deep rifling, a fancy type butt plate and a steel forearm. Overall length is 51 inches. Number 60.

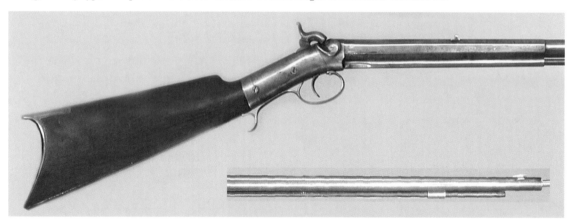

This is an early, small size inside hammer boys rifle that has a 28 inch octagon and round 44 caliber barrel. It is made with a crescent butt plate. Overall length is 44 inches. Number 4.

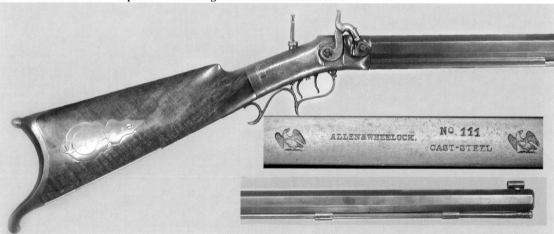

This 44 caliber bench rest rifle has a heavy, 28 inch octagon barrel. It has a contemporary adjustable rear tang sight with a globe front sight. It is marked with the double eagles (see inset), and has a heavy schuetzen style butt plate, double set triggers and a patch box. Overall length is 46 inches. Number 111.

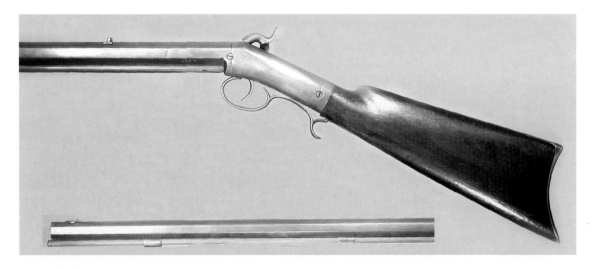

This no frill side cock field rifle has a 36 inch, 52 caliber, full octagon barrel and a solid frame. The overall length is 51 inches. Number 179.

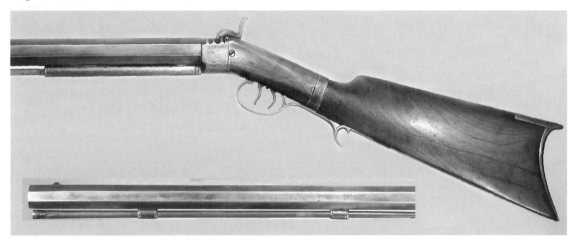

This is a little higher quality field grade rifle that has a solid frame and double set triggers. It has a full octagon, 38 caliber barrel that is 32 inches long. The overall length is 48 inches. The flutes on the top of the frame are for style. The barrel is marked ALLEN & WHEELOCK CAST STEEL, in one line. Number 10.

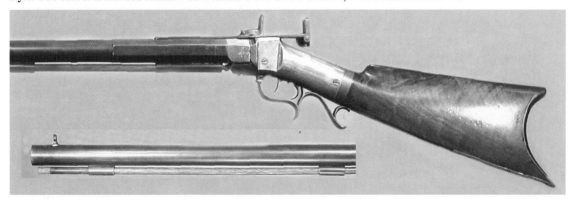

This carbine-style rifle has a 24 inch, 38 caliber, octagon and round removable barrel with double set triggers. A contemporary rear sight and a folding front sight were added after the gun left the Allen factory, as the rear sight covers the maker's name. Note the more typical Allen & Wheelock butt plate and absence of the steel forearm. The name C.A. Davis is stamped on the stock. The overall length is 40 inches. Number 4.

DOUBLE RIFLES

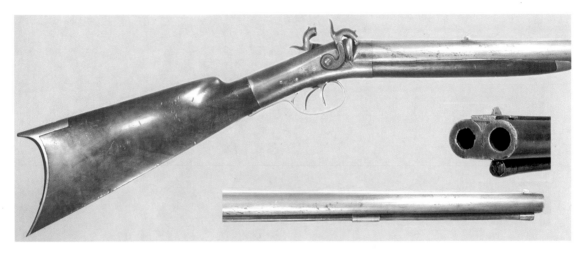

This unusual double barrel rifle has one 45 caliber smooth bore and one 42 caliber rifled barrel that are 30 inches long. Overall length is 41 inches and is number 1.

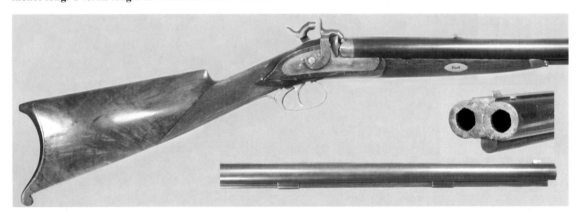

This high-grade double rifle has 30 inch, 45 caliber rifled barrels. It is unusual to see an Allen & Wheelock long arm with standard locks. Overall length is 47 inches and there are no numbers on the rifle.

SHOTGUNS

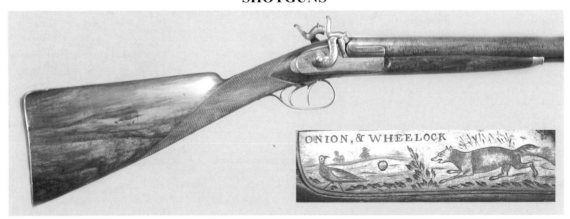

This is a rarely seen Onion & Wheelock-marked double-barreled percussion 12 gauge shotgun that is engraved and has Belgian proof marks. This is not an Allen-made shotgun but was one of the imported firearms offered by Onion & Wheelock in the advertisement shown in the history chapter. This is an exceptionally fine shotgun that is nicely engraved with checkered select wood and an ebony ramrod. No number.

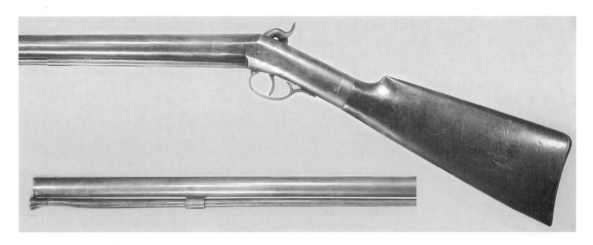

This 12 gauge, side hammer muzzleloader has a very long 38 inch round barrel. This is a typical Allen field grade, solid frame, single barrel shotgun that has an overall length of 54 inches. Number 18.

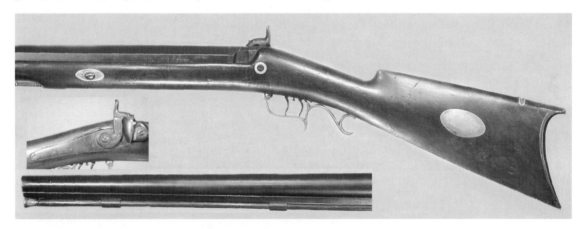

This massive 10 gauge, side hammer, single barrel shot gun has a tapered octagon and round 32 inch barrel that is one and three eighth inches wide at the breech. It is marked, ALLEN & WHEELOCK, with Allen's double eagle mark of quality. It has a conventional half stock style and a standard type lock plate (see inset). The overall length is 48 inches and there is a steel patch box on the right side of the stock. No number.

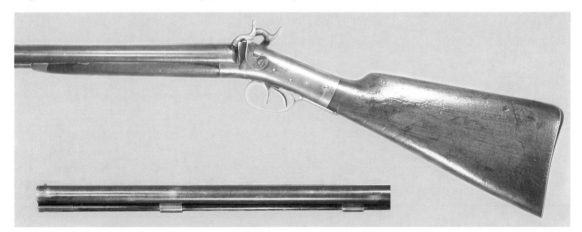

Above is a 16 gauge double-barreled shotgun with the typical Allen full steel wrist. The round, removable barrels are 28 inches long with an overall length of 45 inches. This gun was also made in 12 gauge and possibly 10 gauge as well. Number 6.

SHOT GUN RIFLE COMBINATIONS

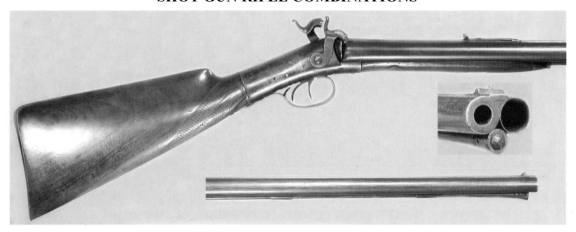

This side-by-side shotgun rifle combination is very rare, and possibly not a production model. The round, removable barrels are 26 inches long and are 38 caliber rifle on the right and 16 gauge shotgun on the left. Overall length is 43 inches. There is an X in place of a number on major parts.

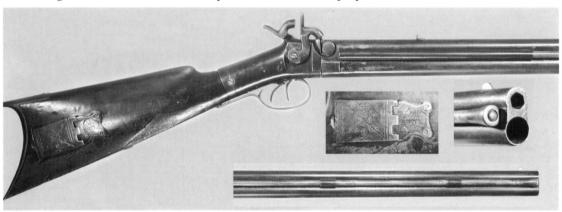

This is a better than average field grade, 44 caliber rifle over a 12 gauge shotgun combination with 30 inch round barrels. This is also a take down model. It has a patch box as well as a cap box that are located under the stock. Both were added later. The single ramrod has a ball rammer on one end and the shot tamper on the other end. The overall length is 46 inches. Number 8.

This high-grade 38 caliber rifle over a 16-gauge shotgun combination has 26 inch octagon and round barrels with two ramrods. It has a finely checkered stock with a patch box, a flip up rear sight and is marked ALLEN & WHEELOCK on the barrel with the double eagle mark of quality. Overall length is 44 inches. Number 4.

Chapter 40
THE TAP (FAUCET) BREECH RIFLE

On March 28, 1855, Allen applied for a patent that described a breech loading percussion rifle that would become known as the tap breech, faucet breech or monkey tail rifle. On July 3, 1855, which was during the Allen, Thurber & Co. period, he was granted patent number 13,154. It was a very sturdy and practical rifle that had a simple but efficient and strong action, but unfortunately arrived at the end of the percussion age and it is doubtful that more that 350 were made.

The rather uncomplicated design consisted of a rotating drum located in the breech that was activated by an operating lever. By raising the lever, a combustible paper cartridge could be inserted into the breech, or a loose ball and powder could be substituted. When the lever was brought down, it rotated the drum and closed the breech, while aligning the bullet with the barrel and exposing the powder to the nipple. A chamber at the breech end of the barrel was slightly larger than the bore, to allow the bullet to be inserted past the rotating drum and held against the rifling in the barrel when the breech was closed.

The operating procedure was actually quite simple. However, in his patent, Allen and his lawyers used two pages to describe the operation. The following is an excerpt from his original patent application.

"In using my improved firearm, the lever "e" is first to be raised above the stock, so as to bring the axis of the chamber "e" horizontal or into line with the bore of the barrel "a" and the passage "f". While the said parts are in such position, a cartridge may be laid in the passage "f" and pushed from thence into the charge-chamber "c" and the bore of the barrel "a". This having been done, the lever "e" is next to be turned down toward and upon the stock and so as to move the axis on the chamber "e" into an angular position with respect to that of the barrel "a". In consequence of the peculiar formation of the chamber "e", such chamber, during its return or last-described movement, will so act in conjunction with the bore of the barrel as to bend and break the cartridge and expose its contents or powder, so that it may readily be ignited when a percussion-cap is exploded on the nipple."

Translated, that simply means, *"Raise the lever, insert the cartridge and close."* It is obvious that Allen and his lawyers had to be very specific with their descriptions as this type of language was typical of most patent applications during that era.

In the excerpt from the patent, Allen refers to a combustible paper cartridge about two inches long, that he or someone else was making at the time. Although these rifles have been observed in 38, 42, 44, 48 and 54 calibers, none of the paper cartridges or the containers they must have come in, have ever been confirmed as being specifically made for these rifles.

It is evident that at least some parts for the gun were being made prior to the Allen & Wheelock period, (1856), as the letters "A, T. & CO." (Allen, Thurber & Co) were cast on the inside of the side plates on virtually all rifles.

It is not known why there was such a long delay in marketing, but one possibility is that Allen was trying to get these guns accepted by the government before putting them on the civilian market.

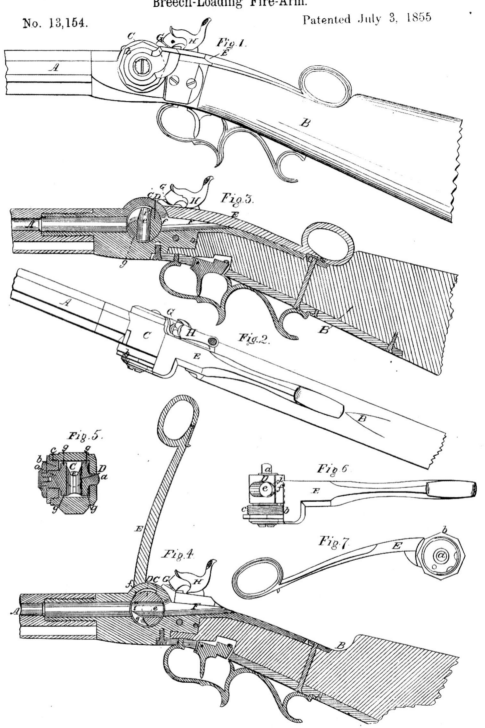

E. ALLEN.

Breech-Loading Fire-Arm.

No. 13,154.

Patented July 3, 1855

This is Allen's patent number 13,154, dated July 3, 1855. Although the principle of the action and the general design of the gun are basically the same, there is a considerable difference between the patent drawing and the final production model.

It was claimed by the noted Allen collector, Phil Van Cleave, that he had documented proof that one of these guns was fired in the field trials, but at this time, that has not been verified. Unfortunately, Phil passed away before he could publish his lifetime of research on Allen guns and much valuable knowledge died with him.

The following is a series of photos of what is possibly the only military-type carbine that was ever made by Allen. As the carbine shown below has a very strong military resemblance, there is little doubt that Allen had thoughts of a military contract, which might explain why there was such a lapse in time before these rifles were put on the market in civilian form.

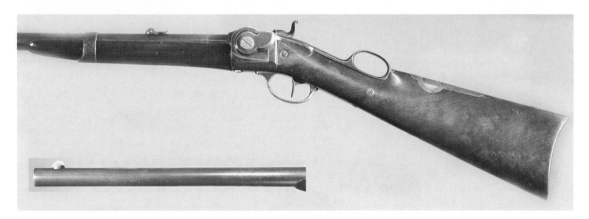

This is the left side view of the carbine that Allen supposedly fired in the Civil War field trials. A typical looking military carbine of 54 caliber with a 22 inch round barrel. There are no patent dates, and the only marks are E. ALLEN / WORCESTER, MA. that is engraved on the top of the operating lever and surrounded by some modest engraving. (See the lower left photo on the following page.)

Several different types of rear sights will be seen on the tap breech rifles. The most common is the conventional leaf sight with the adjustable ramp but others will be seen with military-type sights.

In *Fig. 1* of the patent drawing on the preceding page, the side plate is very short compared to standard production model but is nonexistent on the carbine.

Not mentioned in the patent is the take down feature that is standard on all tap breech rifles.

This close up of the left side of the carbine shows the absence of the side plate that is standard on all other tap breech rifles. The take down bolt can be seen at the bottom of the frame. (See Arrow.)

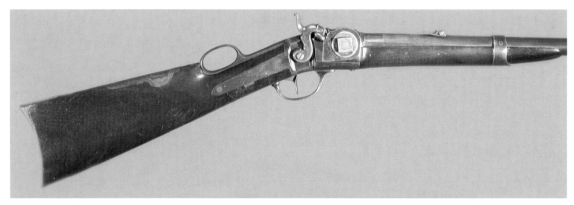

This is the left side view of the carbine. Note the typical carbine barrel band and the military-type rear sight. There is a conveniently placed receptacle for storage of a cleaning tool or spare caps set into the comb of the stock, directly behind the operating lever. There is no number on the gun.

A compartment to store a cleaning tool or spare caps is located in the comb of the stock.

The storage compartment has a flip up lid that gives the shooter easy access to caps or cleaning tools.

On the right is a close up of Allen's carbine. Note the military-style lock plate and trigger guard that is not used on standard production tap breech rifles. Note that the ring on the operating lever is much larger than normal.

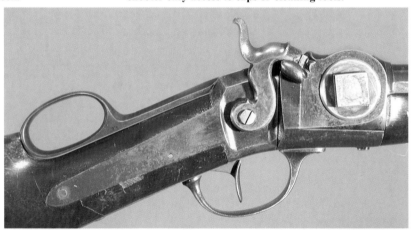

The only marking on the carbine is E. ALLEN / WORCESTER MS, that has been hand engraved on the top of the operating lever.

When the operating lever is raised, loading consisted of inserting a combustible paper cartridge or a bullet and loose powder into the breech.

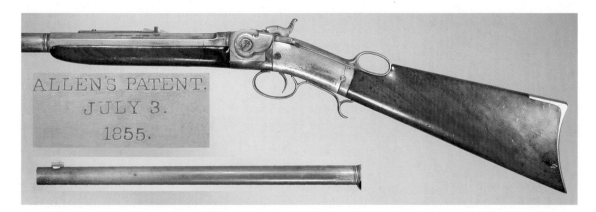

Shown above is a more conventional carbine style tap breech with what appears to be original nickel plating. The octagon and round 44 caliber barrel is 24 inches long and had a leaf type rear sight. The typical patent date **ALLEN'S PATENT / JULY 3. / 1855** is stamped on the operating lever (see inset). Number 268.

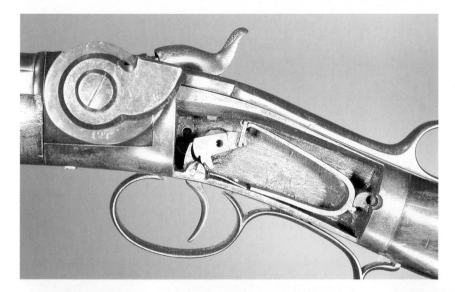

The action of the faucet breech rifle is simple but very reliable. This design is similar to the actions used on earlier Allen firearms. A "U" shaped main spring is connected to the hammer tumbler by an open link. The hammer tumbler has a half cock position.

The breech plug could easily be removed for cleaning.

The rear of the drum opens to allow for loading when the operating lever is raised.

The drum is designed so the chamber is always open to the barrel for loading or shooting.

On November 25, 1859, after a John Brown raid on Harpers Ferry, an Allen & Wheelock faucet breech rifle was found that had been carried by one of Brown's men.[1]

---

1. William B. Edwards, *CIVIL WAR GUNS,* Harrisburg, Pa, The Stackpole Company, 1962, p. 3 and 4.

This is an early 42 caliber faucet breech rifle with a 30 inch barrel and a patch box. It is marked ALLEN & WHEELOCK, WORCESTER, / CAST STEEL in two lines on the barrel. The operating lever is hand-engraved ALLEN'S PATENT / 1855. It is interesting to note that both N's in Allen's Patent are backwards. It is obvious that quality control was not one of Allen's priorities. Number 26.

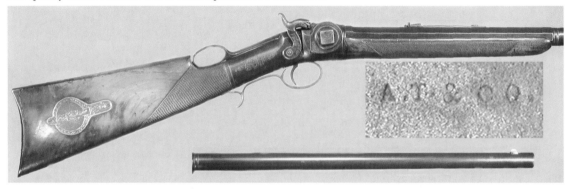

This is an early 42 caliber with a 28.5 inch barrel and adorned with typical Allen engraving on the frame, hammer, trigger guard, patch box and butt plate. The stock and forearm are finely checkered. On the inside of the side plate is stamped the letters A.T. & CO. (ALLEN, THURBER & CO.) Number 38.

This is surely one of the last rifles made. It has a 36 inch, 48 caliber barrel and has a patent date of Jan. 13, 1857 stamped on the operating lever, rather than the typical July 3, 1855 patent date. The only thing on this gun that could possibly apply to the 1857 patent would be the nipple with a special check valve to eliminate gas blow back, but unfortunately, the nipple has been replaced. Number 335.

These rifles were made in barrel lengths from 22 to 36 inches. It is certain that the rifles would have been more popular if Allen had not waited so long to put them on the open market.

Chapter 41
THE DETACHABLE BREECH TARGET PISTOL

Some of the finest arms to come out of the Worcester shops were Allen's target pistols. Often referred to as buggy rifles, these detachable breech target pistols were very expensive at the time, with a wholesale cost of about $60.

Most were made with detachable shoulder stocks that had ornate patch boxes. The barrel could easily be separated from the breech by removing a square headed screw at the bottom of the frame.

Although manufactured in very limited numbers, production started during the Allen & Thurber period and continued into the Allen & Wheelock era, with only modest changes. The most common caliber is 32.

Shown above is the Allen, Thurber & Co. marked detachable breech pistol with the stock detached. An extra set of conventional sights were also provided.

The target pistol shown above is in exceptionally fine condition and has a full length tube sight that is marked ALLEN, THURBER & C0. in one line. The pistol features an engraved casehardened frame, blued barrel, tube sight, and is equipped with a false muzzle. The stock is nicely checkered, with an engraved patch box and a storage area for the cleaning tool that is located in the butt plate overlap.

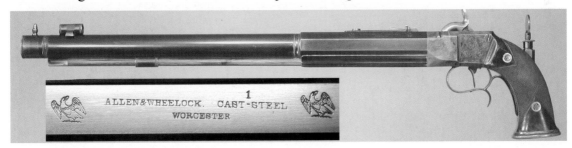

This later target pistol is marked; ALLEN & WHEELOCK, CAST-STEEL / WORCESTER, between two eagles. This pistol also has a false muzzle and a ball starter. It is cased as shown on the next page. Number 1.

There is no way of knowing how many buggy rifles were produced at the Allen & Wheelock factory, but production was obviously very limited, as only a few have ever been seen.

As these were very expensive guns at that time, they were more than likely made only as a special order item and were not a standard production model.

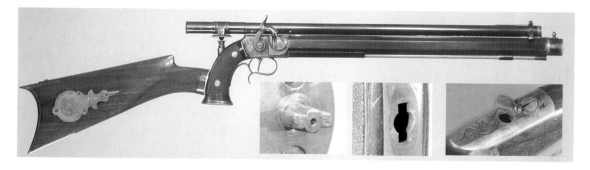

This Allen, Thurber & Company detachable breech target pistol appears to be the one mentioned in a letter from William Read to Allen, dated April 1, 1854, inquiring about a shipment of guns that they had ordered including one telescope sight for $25.00 and one detached breech pistol for $60.30 (Mouillesseaux, p. 108). The telescope is marked Allen, Thurber & Co. It has a 32 caliber 16 inch full octagon barrel. The detachable stock has a nicely engraved patch box and a storage area in the top of the butt plate over lap for a cleaning tool and attaches to the frame as shown in above photo. (See inset.) There are no numbers on the gun.

This later version is marked ALLEN & WHEELOCK on the barrel between two eagles and is virtually the same gun as the Allen, Thurber & Co., but with an octagon and round 15 1/2 inch barrel, and is cased with accessories as pictured below. It also has a storage compartment with a small trap to store the cleaning tool but it is located on the bottom of the stock. (See inset.) Number 1.

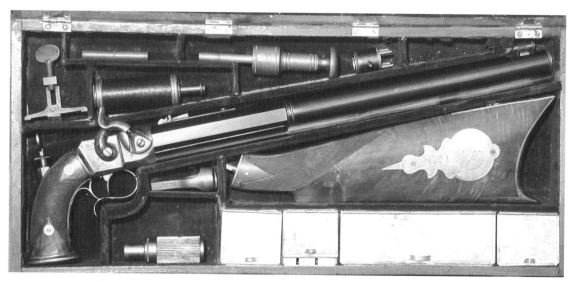

Above is the Allen & Wheelock target pistol in its case with accessories. On the bottom of the case is a row of four tin boxes with hinged lids for bullets, patches, primers, and cleaning supplies. The false muzzle, ball starter, and the tool for sizing the bullets are all numbered to the gun. Number 1.

Chapter 42
REVOLVING RIFLES

The rarest of all Allen & Wheelock production firearms are the revolving rifles. Made in 44 lipfire as well as 44 caliber percussion, only a few of each are known to exist. After more than 35 years of searching, less than ten can be accounted for. In addition to that total, there is known to exist a percussion rifle that has been crudely converted to rimfire and another one that has been made from a 44 caliber center hammer army revolver.

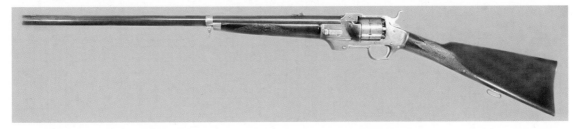

This 44 caliber Allen & Wheelock percussion revolving rifle has a 28 inch long, full round barrel with a checkered stock and forearm and is unmarked. Note the sling swivels and the steel nose cap. Number 7.

The cylinder of the percussion revolving rifle is actually three sixteenth of an inch longer than on the pistol. Like the 44 caliber Army revolvers, the triggerguard also serves as the bullet rammer. The frame shows the remains of what appears to be original nickel plate. The crank for removing the cylinder pin folds into the frame when not in use. (See arrow.)

By turning the crank, the cylinder pin is drawn forward so the cylinder can be removed.

The sensitivity of the trigger pull is adjusted by turning the screw located in the hammer. (See arrow.)

By use of a rack and pinion type system, the cylinder pin could be drawn forward until it had cleared the cylinder. The barrels of both guns can easily be removed by unscrewing a square headed screw, located in the top of the frame between the barrel and the cylinder. This is the same take down system described in patent number 33,033 dated September 18, 1860 for the dropping block rifle. One can only speculate as to why Allen was so vague and inconsistent with the applications of his patents. Both rifles have a trap door in the butt plate for storage of the take down tool.

This rare 44 caliber, Allen & Wheelock lipfire revolving rifle has a 28-inch octagon and round barrel. Although it is totally unmarked, there is no doubt about what it is. Number 11.

As with the 44 lipfire revolving pistols, the trigger guard activates the ejector. The take down screw is located on the top of the breech above the barrel (see inset). The length of the cylinder is identical to that of the pistol. The loading gate is attached at the bottom of the frame indicating it is of later production. A photo of the take down tool is shown on page 216.

The method for removing the cylinder is the same on both rifles.

Shown above is a close up of the snout that Allen refers to as the "projection" to vent the excess gas.

Although two of Allen's patents apply directly to the revolving rifle, no rifles have been seen bearing any patent data or the maker's name. Patent number 35,067 dated April

29, 1862, shows a section of a revolving rifle, and patent number 21,400, dated September 7, 1858, shows the gas deflector or snout. This feature is seen only on the revolving rifles.

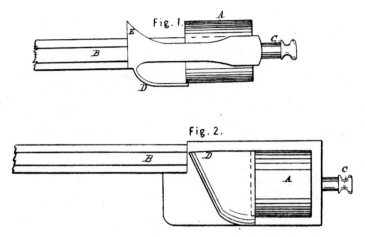

On the right is a portion of Allen's September, 1858 patent that basically covers the anti-fowling cylinder pin that is used on most of Allen's side hammer percussion pistols. But, in addition, it also describes a gas deflecting projection that he later used on all of his revolving rifles.

In a portion of Allen's original patent, he describes the purpose of his improvement as follows:

"To prevent that portion of fire and gas that finds its way out at the junction of the barrel and cylinder, when the piece is discharged, from injuring the hand or wrist when the piece is supported by the left hand in front of the cylinder and also to prevent any injure being done to the hand from an accidental discharge of the chambers not in range with the barrel, I form the projection D," etc, etc.!

The paragraph above is about one third of what has to be the longest sentence in the world, but it is enough to give us a general idea of what the purpose of that part of his improvement was for. The lengthy patent description was necessary and every word was reviewed by the other inventors' lawyers to make sure that there were no loopholes.

It is also interesting that in his ramblings, he makes a comment about the *"accidental discharge of the chambers not in range with the barrel."* As this improvement is only seen on revolving rifles, it becomes clear that he was referring to a percussion firearm since an accidental discharge was not a problem with cartridge revolvers. This might help answer the question of which came first, the percussion or the lipfire revolvers.

Patent number 35,067 of April 29, 1862, shows a cutaway view of the lipfire revolving rifle. Although several improvements had already been covered in other patents, Allen makes the comment that it can be *"loaded with a metallic or other cartridge with a tongue or lip."* This is the first time that the word *tongue* or *lip* had been used in any of Allen's patents relating to a firearm, although he had received a patent for the lipfire cartridge on September 24, 1860, over a year and a half earlier.

This patent also covers a type of action where the *"operating lever* (hand) *is placed nearly perpendicular to the rear face of the cylinder, thereby turning it with greater ease than by the common method."*

This is another great innovation, but the type action that is shown in this patent drawing is the same action that had been in use in all 44 and 36 caliber lipfire revolvers as well as the early 44 and 36 caliber percussion revolvers for quite some time. (See arrow in fig. 2 on the following page.)

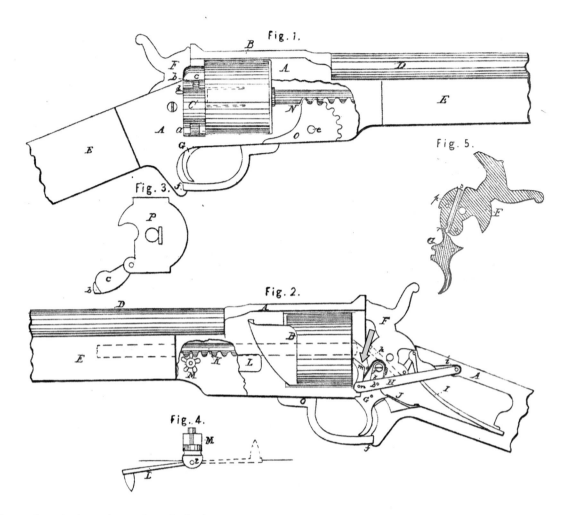

Shown above is the main portion of Allen's patent number 35,067 of April 29, 1862 that covers several major improvements. The arrow above points out the operating lever that Allen was referring to in his patent.

This is a poor picture of the cut-off patent model that Allen presented to the U.S. Patent Office when he applied for his patent number 35,067 that was issued on April 29, 1862. The photo is courtesy of the Smithsonian Institute.

About the only thing in the patent that is truly unique to the revolving rifle, other than the projection or snout, is the rack and pinion system that Allen has devised to withdraw the cylinder pin from the cylinder so it could be removed from the frame. The revolving rifles are the only firearms that used this improvement.

The method of adjusting the *"whole cock"* was a way to regulate the trigger sensitivity through a screw located in the hammer. Although this improvement is featured in the 1862 patent, it had been used on all production dropping block rifles for a year and a half and prior, but was not mentioned in the 1860 patent.

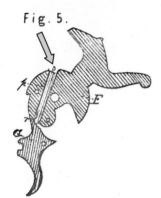

Fig. 5.

This was a simple, but ingenious way of adjusting the trigger pull without removing any parts. By placing the hammer on full cock, it is possible to adjust the long screw, which extends through the hammer (see arrow) and rests against the trigger to control its sensitivity.

After the hammer was at full cock, it was necessary to pull the hammer back beyond the full cock position to relieve the pressure of the hammer on the trigger notch. The adjusting screw could then be turned freely until the desired setting was found. This adjustment could be made any time and it is possible to set the trigger pull so lightly that the slightest bump could release the hammer and discharge the rifle. Although not mentioned in any of Allen's instructions, it would be advisable to make sure that the rifle was unloaded before making the trigger adjustment. This adjustment could be made with one of the screwdriver bits on the take down tool that was made for the dropping block rifle as well as the revolving rifles. (This was probably an extra cost item.)

The loading gate in the 1862 patent is shown hinged at the bottom, whereas the earlier September 24, 1861 patent for the 44 lipfire revolving pistol shows the loading gate hinged at the top. The cartridge ejector system that employs the trigger guard is also covered in the 1861 patent, but Allen has added the words:

"I also provide the sliding pin or plunger, which is used for the purpose of removing the cartridge-shells after being exploded, with a head of sufficient size to come in contact with the edge of the shell nearest to the front end of the cylinder and thereby save nearly one half in the action of the sliding pin over other models in common use, where the pin presses against the inside of the head of the cartridge-shell."

What that means is the head of the plunger on the ejector shaft is large enough to fill the chamber so it pushes on the front of the cartridge to eject it without having to go entirely through the empty case before coming in contact with the head of the spent shell. This feature was also used on the 44, 36 and 32 caliber lipfire revolvers as well. The over head ejector system that is used on the 32 lipfire is considerable different but the principal is the same.

As with many other firearms, amateur gunsmiths have always had the need to improve on the original design to suit their own needs or desires. The case in point is the little homemade revolving rifle shown below that has been converted from an Allen & Wheelock 32 rimfire revolver.

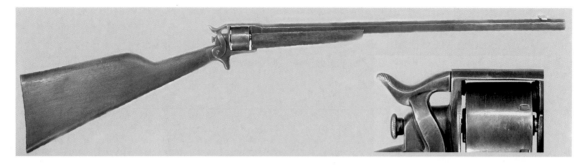

This is not a rare find or a lunch box rifle from the Allen & Wheelock factory, but in fact is a 32 caliber rimfire pistol frame that has been modified to accept a 17 inch section of a 22 caliber barrel and a homemade stock. The 6 shot cylinder has been sleeved down to chamber 22 caliber bird shot cartridges and is so marked on the barrel. A new cylinder pin that enters from the rear of the frame has been fashioned to replace the standard front entry pin (see inset above). Number 221.

Below is the envelope of a letter that was sent to Mrs. Fanny H. Kris, West Killingly, Conn. from Allen & Wheelock.

The envelope on the left has the Allen & Wheelock return address embossed on it. It dates between 1858 and 1864. Needless to say, items like this are very rare and seldom seen.

On the left is an enlargement of the return address from the envelope shown above. It reads: ALLEN & WHEELOCK. / MANUFACTURERS OF / FIREARMS / CARTRIDGES & C. / WORCESTER, MASS. The "& C." after the word "cartridges" means, "etc." (et cetera.) Note that cartridges were also a major part of the company at that time.

Chapter 43
BREECH LOADING CARTRIDGE RIFLES

Watch out for this mean looking old cuss. As a matter of fact, this is the author posing with one of his favorite dropping block rifles. It is a 44 caliber rimfire with a rare 24 inch round barrel. Number 30.

214

Most commonly referred to as the dropping block or drop breech rifle, it is a good looking rifle that came standard with a blued barrel and frame, casehardened hammer, trigger and trigger guard. The prices were from $20 to $40 depending on the extras that were added. A casehardened frame was available at extra cost and Allen's patented tang sight was an extra $5.00. Varnished or oiled walnut stocks were standard but select wood was also available. Steel nose caps randomly appear on large frame models only.

Although no government contracts for the rifle are known, all large frame dropping block rifles are considered to be secondary military by most collectors. There is no question that these rifles were at least considered for military use as references made in the Pitman notes on *U.S. Martial Small Arms and Ammunition, 1776 to 1933, Volume 1* shows two schematics of an Allen dropping breech rifle.[1]

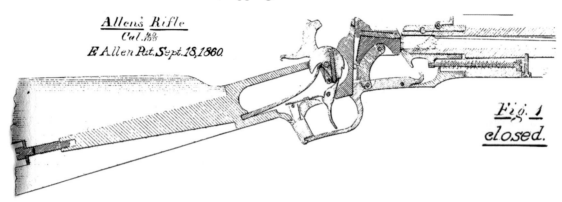

The drawing above from the Pitman Reports shows a schematic of a 44 caliber Allen dropping block rifle in the closed and cocked position.

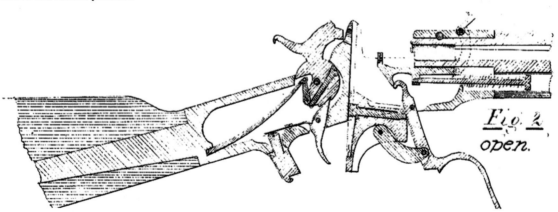

The second view of the Allen dropping block rifle shows the breech lowered and the ejector activated.

All Allen & Wheelock rifles observed have been 35, 38, 42 or 44 rimfire. The addition of the 22 and 32 rifles and center fire system came later, during the E. Allen & Co. and Forehand & Wadsworth period. Conversions to centerfire are not unusual.

Patent number 30,033 was granted to Allen on September 18, 1860, for improvements in breech loading firearms. The patent describes a breech-loading firearm with a removable barrel that will accept a metal cartridge case. The patent covers the

---

1. John Pitman, General U.S. Army Ordnance *THE PITMAN REPORTS,* Tacoma, Washington, Armor Publication 1987, p. 81.

method of ejecting a fired shell by use of the trigger guard, and a rear sight with a 0 to 10 scale of adjustment. Allen made the following claim regarding the safety of his firing pin.

"As the hammer can only strike the rod (firing pin) when the piece D (breechblock) is raised sufficiently high to cover the cartridge, there is no danger of an accidental discharge of the piece occurring from the fall of the hammer while the breech-piece is down, thus avoiding danger to the person using the gun."

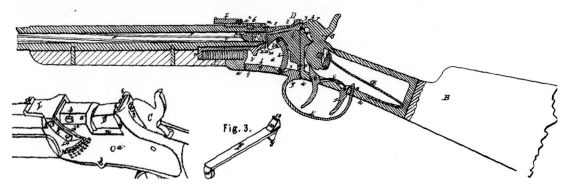

Shown above is an excerpt from Allen's patent number 30,033 for the dropping block rifle. The drawings show a second trigger that acts as the trigger guard latch. It is doubtful that any production models were made with the second trigger. The ejector is shown in *fig 3* above.

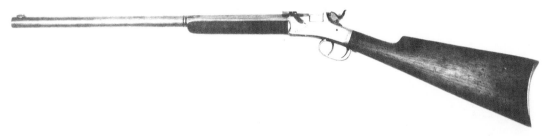

This is the rifle that Allen presented to the U.S. Patent office to obtain his patent number 30,033. Photo is courtesy of the Smithsonian Institute.

Allen & Wheelock dropping block rifles were made in two different frame sizes. The 44 and 42 calibers were on the large frame and the 35 and 38 were on the small frame. The small frame rifle would be discontinued at the end of the Allen & Wheelock era.

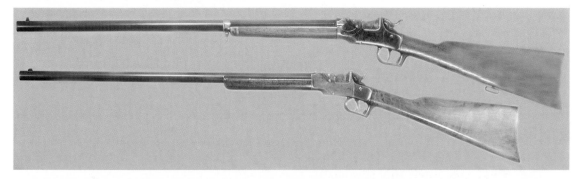

Shown together for size comparison is a large and a small frame model. The large frame rifle is a 42 caliber that has sling swivels and a steel nose cap on the forearm. Number 85. The small frame rifle has neither but does have the rear swing sight. Number 210. Small frame rifles were only made during the Allen & Wheelock era.

The 10-position adjustable rear sight was used on most Allen & Wheelock dropping block rifles, but would be discontinued on later large frame models and replaced with the more generic ramp type sight located on the barrel.

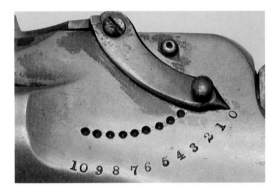

Allen's adjustable rear sight has elevation numbers graduated from 0 to 10. The sight would be replaced later with a leaf type sight.

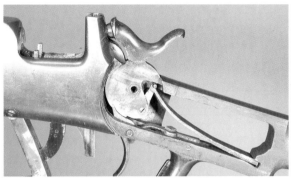

After putting the hammer on the half cock, the trigger guard could be rotated forward to lower the block and activate the ejector.

The barrel could easily be separated from the frame by removing a small tapered pin located near the rear sight. Small frame models and a few very early large frame rifles have an unthreaded tapered round pin that could be removed by simply knocking it out. This method remained in use on the small frame rifles throughout production. The large frame rifles, however, soon had a tapered square head threaded screw that had to be removed with a special take down tool that was stored in the rear of the stock and was accessible through a trap door that is located in the butt plate. (See page 218.)

The take down tool has two screwdriver bits of different sizes as well.

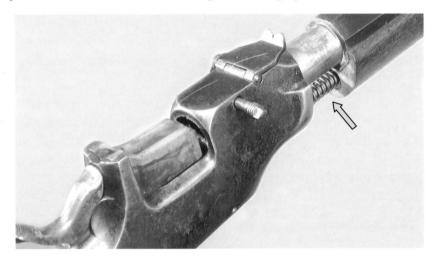

With the takedown screw removed, the barrel can be easily slid forward and removed for cleaning or storing. Care must be taken when separating the barrel from the frame as it is possible for the ejector to fall out (see arrow).

The Allen takedown tool shown in the above left photo has two different size screwdriver bits. The smaller bit is used to adjust the trigger sensitivity on dropping block rifles as well as both the percussion and lipfire revolving rifles.

ALLEN'S PATENT BREECH-LOADING RIFLE,

FOR METALLIC WATER PROOF CARTRIDGES.

This arm is very simple in construction; can be fired rapidly; shoots with great accuracy and force; easily taken apart and kept clean.

TO LOAD, set the lock at half cock, drop the lever, insert the cartridge, and replace the lever. After firing, the exploded cartridge is withdrawn by pressing the lever forward. To detach the barrel, draw out the pin back of the sight, and slide it out. The lever and slide can be detached by removing the screw that holds the lever. The part that throws out the exploded cartridge can be taken out by removing the barrel.

TO REGULATE THE SET OR PULL OF THE TRIGGER, cock the piece and turn the screw that passes through the cock. To detach the stock, open the lid in the butt plate, take out the screw at the bottom of the hole, and slide it off.

This advertisement for Allen's patent breech loading rifle from the early 1860s, reads as follows:

"This arm is very simple in construction; can be fired rapidly; shoots with great accuracy and force; easily taken apart and kept clean. To load, set the lock at half cock, drop the lever, insert the cartridge and replace the lever. After firing, the exploded cartridge is withdrawn by pressing the lever forward. To detach the barrel, draw out the pin back of the sight, and slide it out. The lever and slide can be detached by removing the screw that holds the lever. The part that throws out the exploded cartridge can be taken out by removing the barrel. To regulate the set or pull of the trigger, cock the piece and turn the screw that passes through the cock. To detach the stock, open the lid in the butt plate, take out the screw at the bottom of the hole, and slide it off."

So widely known. Remodelled and for either Rim or Central Fire Cartridges. For quality of workmanship it is not surpassed, and for accuracy of shooting, made in the following calibres, viz.: 22-100, 32-100, 38-100 and 44-100.

PRICE LIST.

A Rifle made with any of the above calibres, 24 inch Barrel, Plain Finish, Octagon Barrel $21.00
"   "   "   "   "   "   "   "   "   Half Octagon Barrel 20.00
Common Peep and Globe Sights, extra . . . . . $1.50   Swivels and Slings, extra 1.50
Hinged or Tip-Down Peep and Globe Sights, extra . . . 3.00   Extra Quality Rifle, fancy stock, varnished, case-hardened frame   40.00
"Allen's Patent" Hinged or Tip Down Peep and Globe Sights, extra 5.00   All Barrels above 24 inch, 50 cents per inch extra.

DISCOUNT TO THE TRADE.

In this 1870s period ad, (during the E. Allen & Co. era) Allen breech loading rifles were advertised as: *"So widely known. Remodeled for either rim or center fire cartridges. For quality of workmanship it is not surpassed and for accuracy of shooting, made in the following calibers: 22, 32, 38 and 44 calibers."* Retail price was $20 with a 24 inch octagon and round barrel and $21 for a full octagon barrel. Longer barrel lengths were offered at 50 cents an inch extra. Also offered were Allen's patented tip down rear peep and globe front sights for $5.00 extra; sling swivels were $1.50 and a gun with extra fancy stock and casehardened frame was offered at $40.00; discounts were offered to the trade. Although not mentioned, nickel plating was also an option.

The vintage of a dropping block rifle can be determined in several different ways, some of which have been covered earlier in this chapter. Another way is by evaluating the butt plates as shown below. The majority of these rifles have butt plates like the one shown in the left photo. It is rather thin, covers only the end of the stock and the trap door is hinged at the top. The intermediate variation is slightly thicker, has a two inch overlap on top and the trap door is hinged at the bottom. The third type on the right has a more distinctive curve and a two and a half inch overlap. There is no trap door in the butt plate as it is from the cased rifle shown on the next page. The take down tool that would normally go in the storage area in the stock is part of the casing. This eliminated the need for the trap door. Nearly all small frame rifles have the early type butt plate shown in the left photo.

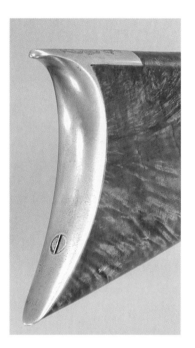

This is the most common type early butt plate door.

The intermediate butt plate overlaps the top of the stock.

Late butt plates have a pronounced curve and no trap door.

The most common caliber of the Allen & Wheelock-marked large frame rifle is the 42 rimfire, but occasionally a 44 will be seen. The most common caliber in the small frame rifle is 35 caliber rimfire but 38 is not uncommon. Since the 42 will often be mistaken for a 44 and the 35 will often be mistaken for a 32 or 38, it presents a problem when attempting to determine the exact caliber, as standard bore gauges are normally not that accurate.

On the right are the markings found on all Allen & Wheelock dropping block rifles.

ALLEN & WHEELOCK
ALLEN'S PAT SEP 18 1860

Most Allen & Wheelock dropping block rifles are normally marked on the top barrel flat as shown above but some very late models that were made without Allen's rear swing sight are marked on the breech where the swing sight would normally be.

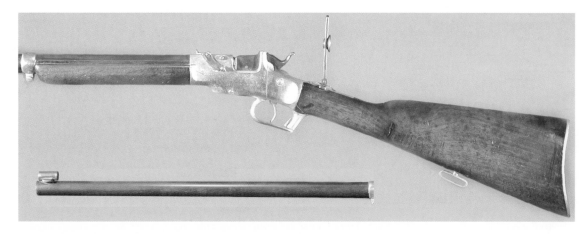

This 38 caliber small frame dropping block rifle has a nickel plated frame and a blued octagonal and round 24-inch barrel with a globe front sight and a non-Allen tang sight. The overall length is 41 inches long and is one of the few small frame rifles with sling swivels. Number 273.

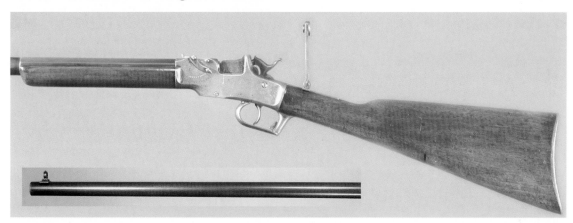

Above is a small frame 35 caliber rifle. It also has a non-Allen rear tang sight, as well as the typical Allen swing sight. It has a 22 inch octagon and round barrel with a flip-up front sight. Number 70.

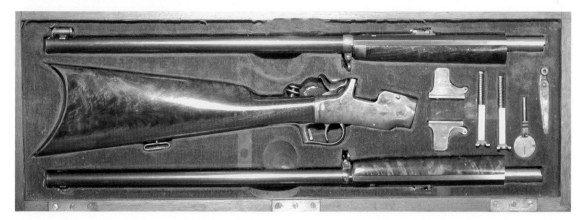

This dropping block rifle is in a French-type casing and has one frame, with one 42 caliber barrel and one 35 caliber barrel. Included are two breech blocks, two ejectors, a take down tool and an Allen's patent rear tang sight. A cleverly designed cap covers the opening in the sight base when the tang sight is not on the gun. This is a high grade rifle with casehardened frame and select wood. Note the late style butt plate, the absence of the typical swing sight and the presence of a conventional rear sight on each barrel. Number 3 on the frame and one barrel, block and ejector and number 2 on the other barrel, block and ejector.

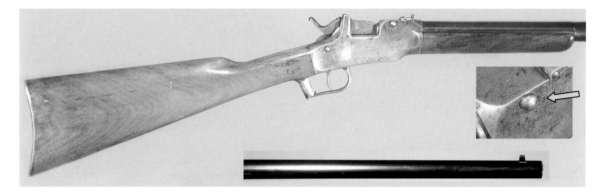

Pictured above is a very early 42 caliber, large frame dropping block rifle. Early rifles have a round headed tapered pin (see arrow in inset) that must be knocked out from left to right before the 24 inch octagon and round barrel can be removed. Number 320.

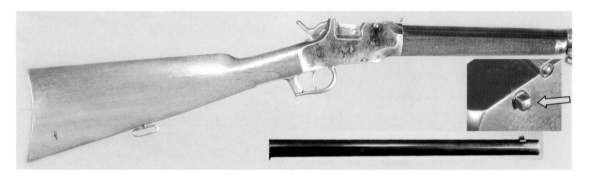

This is the most common Allen & Wheelock dropping block rifle. It has an octagonal and round 24 inch, 42 caliber barrel, sling swivels and a steel nose cap. The wood has an oiled finish and is of field grade quality. A standard type take down screw that can be removed with Allen's take down tool is used on all subsequent rifles. (See arrow in inset.) Number 85.

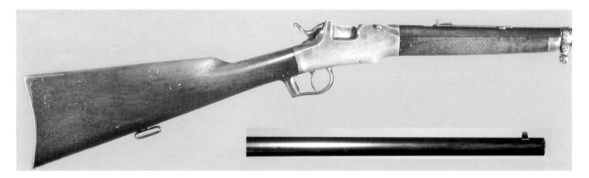

Above is a rare 44 caliber rifle with a 22 inch full round barrel. This is a very late model that has a military-type rear sight that is mounted on the barrel and does not have the typical Allen rear swing sight. This rifle also has sling swivels and a steel nose cap. The maker's name is on the top of the breech and there are no marks other than the number on the barrel. Number 30.

Although not covered in Allen's original patent for the dropping block rifle, the method of regulating the trigger pull by adjusting a screw that *"passes through the cock"* is standard on all dropping block rifles. This improvement was not featured in a patent until April 29, 1862 in patent number 35,067. (See patent on page 210.)

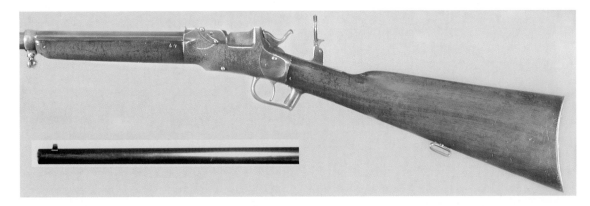

This early 42 caliber dropping block rifle is equipped with Allen's patented tang sight that is attached to the rifle with a mounting bracket cast into the top tang of the frame. This was obviously a very good method of attaching the sight but a special frame had to be cast for rifles equipped with this sight. Number 713.

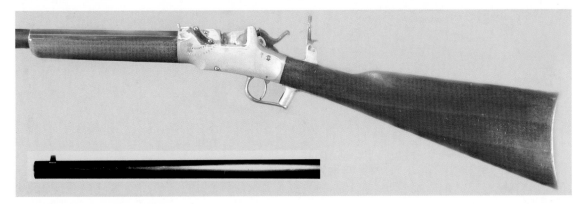

This extremely rare brass frame 42 caliber rifle has a 24 inch octagon and round barrel. The rifle is identical in size to the steel frame rifle pictured in the preceding plate, except for the brass frame. It also has Allen's tang sight that has the attaching bracket cast into the frame. Number 4.

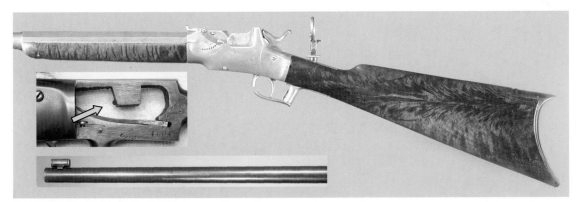

This 35 caliber barrel is mounted on a large frame dropping block rifle and has an Allen's patented rear tang sight. It is very unusual to see a small caliber barrel on a large frame. It is of late production and was obviously made after Allen & Wheelock discontinued their small frame model. It has a 24 inch octagon and round barrel with a globe front sight and select wood. The tang sight has the later type of mounting that is inserted into a hole in the back strap. The back strap was made with a reinforcement that was cast to the inside of the frame. The arrow in the inset illustrates the reinforced area and the setscrew that holds the base of the sight in place. Number 1371.

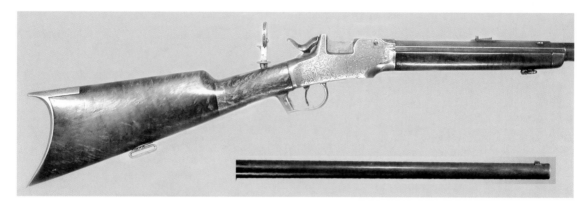

This 42 caliber dropping block rifle was engraved by L.D. Nimschke. It is illustrated on page 10 of R.L. Wilson's book, *L.D. Nimschke, Firearms Engraver.* Number 2.

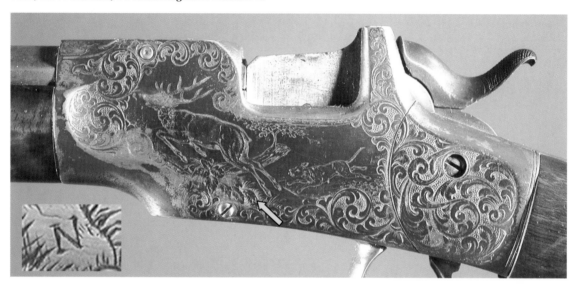

On the left of the frame shows an elk being chased by a dog. Nimschke's initial is on the side of the frame just above the arrow but is hardly visible (see inset). Late rifles such as this one do not have the rear swing sight.

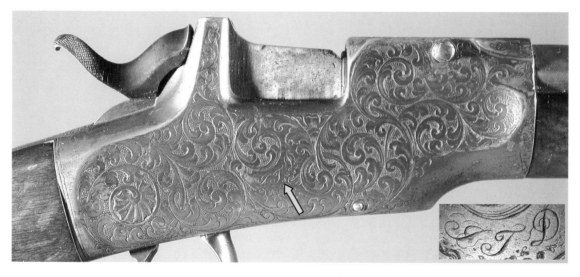

Although this photo does not do the engraving justice, the engraving itself is very sharp and well done. The initials *J.T.D.* are etched on the right panel just above the arrow (see inset).

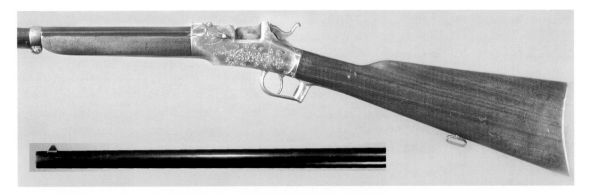

This is another 42 caliber dropping block rifle that has a more conventional type of engraving. Although the number of the rifle is much higher than the previous rifle, it was made much earlier. Number 776.

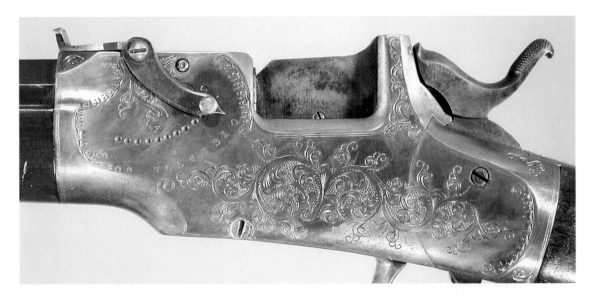

This rifle is equipped with the typical rear swing sight but does not have Allen's patented tang sight.

Although nicely done, only the frame is engraved. This is the more typical type of engraving that is seen on the few Allen & Wheelock firearms that were engraved.

It was mentioned earlier in these writings that an Allen collector should never say never, because just about the time that you think you have seen them all, something new pops up. In this case, it was a huge, oversized dropping block rifle that is over 50 inches long, has a full stock with two barrel bands, and a round 32 inch, 56 caliber barrel.

There have been several interesting theories from other collectors about what it is and what its intended use was. One suggestion was that it could have been one of Allen's experimental models and was an attempt to make a two-band musket. That is a possibility, as it has a rail at the muzzle end that extends down the barrel for about three and a half inches, which could have been for a bayonet. Although it looks like a military-type rifle, no information has been found to confirm this.

An interesting point is that the gun has never been finished. Although the metal parts are smooth, no care has been taken to round off some of the edges or to put elevation numbers for the rear sight or put a knob on the adjusting lever on the sight.

Despite all of that however, the gun has been well used and as Allen was making 56 caliber cartridges at that time in history, the possibility exists that it was used to test fire cartridges, which seems to be the most popular theory.

Whatever its purpose, it is the only one that has ever been noted, and it weighs over seven pounds.

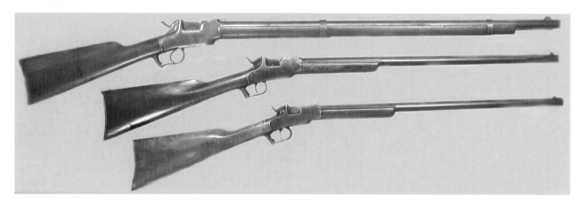

Arranged for size comparison are three Allen & Wheelock rifles. On the top is an unmarked and unnumbered 56 caliber rifle with a 32 inch round barrel and an overall length of just over 50 inches. In the middle is a standard large frame 42 caliber Allen & Wheelock dropping block rifle with a 26 inch, 42 caliber barrel that is 43 inches overall length and marked B. Kittredge & Co on the top of the barrel. Number 393. On the bottom is a 35 caliber small frame rifle with a 24 inch barrel and is 40 inches overall in length. Number 210.

Other than size, there is little difference between this and the standard size rifle.

The rifle has the typical Allen rear swing sight but does not have elevation numbers.

On October 28, 1862, Allen was granted patent number 36,760 for *"IMPROVE-MENT IN BACK SIGHTS FOR RIFLES."* The improvement consisted of a disk with 16 different peepholes, each representing a different elevation. The disk was locked in place by a spring loaded latch. (See "E" in *Fig 2* below.)

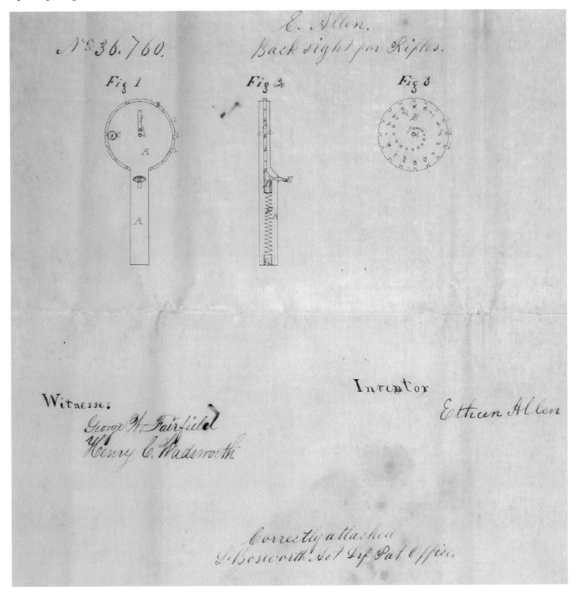

This is the original of patent No. 36,760 for the rear adjustable tang sight that was issued on October 28, 1862. It is signed by Ethan Allen and witnessed by George W. Fairfield and Henry C. Wadsworth.

Allen explains has improvement as follows; *"The nature of my invention consists in so arranging a series of holes in a revolving disk, between two plates of metal, with a vertical slot cut through each, that as the disk is turned from one notch in the periphery to the nest a new hole appears in the slot a little higher of lower than the last, according to the direction the disk is revolved."*

The operation is as follows: The part A of the sight is secured to the breech of any ordinary rifle, and disk B is turned until "1" is seen through the opening C in plate A', when one of the holes in disk B is brought opposite slot F at its lower extremity, as seen

226

at K, Fig. 1, producing the required opening for a sight at the shortest distance. Then, as it is found necessary to elevate the piece, the disk is revolved, bringing each figure in succession to view through the opening C, which raises the sight higher, up to "16," when the opening in slot F will be found to be at the highest point.

Although Allen uses an entire page of his patent application explaining how it works , the preceding excerpt is paragraph three and five, which gives a fair assessment of the contents of the patent.

Allen writes that the sight could be *"attached to any ordinary rifle"* but to this date, no rifles other than Allen rifles have been reported with the sight.

There are two different ways of attaching the sight to the rifle. The mounting seen below left is the early method, where the base for the sight is cast into the frame. Shown below right, it would appear that a hole was simply drilled in the back strap and the shaft of the tang sight inserted. In reality, the later rifles that were made for this application have a rather large block cast into the underside of the tang strap, to reinforce the hole where the sight goes through the frame. This would be the standard method of attaching the tang sight on all subsequent models to the end of production.

Patent No. 36,760.

The mounting base for the early tang sights is cast into the back strap.

This is the most common way of mounting the tang sight and is used on late model rifles.

No small frame dropping block rifles have been reported with Allen's tang sight but that is not saying that it is not possible that they do exist.

Chapter 44
EPILOGUE

Production of the dropping block rifle continued, with little change, well into the Forehand & Wadsworth era. A few center hammer percussion 44 and 36 revolvers were made during the E. Allen & Co. era for a short time and were probably replaced by the five shot Providence Police Revolver. The remaining parts for the rimfire and lipfire revolvers that were in the process of assembly in November 1863, when the injunction was handed down, would eventually be completed and sold after White's patent expired in 1869. When the existing supply of Allen & Wheelock frames were depleted, a new frame with a bird's head grip was introduced. This classic style would continue in use to the end of production.

With the gain in popularity of more practical percussion and cartridge revolvers, the pepperboxes had become the victim of Allen's own success and died a slow death.

In 1868, the Canadian government acquired 34 of the 44 caliber lipfire revolvers and verbal information was given to the author that a small quantity of 36 and 44 caliber lipfire pistols were sold to the Montreal, Canada Police Department at about the same time, but that has not been confirmed. However, it has been confirmed that the 44 lipfire revolver is considered as a Canadian military revolver.

Production of the 22 and 32 rimfire single shot, side swing pistols were not affected by the injunction and continued through the Forehand & Wadsworth era with only a slight frame change. An ejector system was added to the 22 rim fire single shot and production began on a 41 caliber derringer about 1865. It was available with either a full octagon or an octagon and round barrel, and would remain popular for many years. In contrast to the 41 rimfire single shot, Allen also introduced a small, brass frame vest pocket 22 single shot derringer, with a two inch octagon and round barrel that was marked E. Allen & Co Makers.

In 1865, Allen added his new hinge breech double-barreled shotgun and reloadable steel shot shell that would have a lasting effect on the gun making industry. On December 15, 1868, he was granted patent number 84,929 for improvements on the hinge breech shotgun. Included in the patent was a bottleneck steel cartridge that made it possible to fire a rifle bullet from the shotgun. This was the last patent that Allen was issued.

When Allen's first brother-in-law, Charles Thurber, joined the company, it was apparent that he brought some much needed operating capital with him. It appears that Thurber was from a wealthy family and probably knew very little about the gun manufacturing business, but in 1837, he gave up his job as a schoolteacher to become Allen's partner until 1856 when he retired. He died in 1886 at the age of 83.

Thomas Wheelock was Allen's other brother-in-law and held a prominent position with Allen & Thurber for many years. He and Allen's sister Mary were married in 1839 but it is not known if he was working for Allen & Thurber at that time or joined the company later. It appears that he was more involved in the every day business of the company rather than the actual manufacturing part of the business.

After Wheelock's death in 1864, the company continued to prosper until Allen's death but it would never be the same as it was during the golden years of Allen & Wheelock (1856 to 1865).

228

Ethan Allen died on January 7, 1871. After his death, his friend and former pastor, The Reverend H.L. Wayland, made the following remarks:

"*All of his creations were characterized by the extreme simplicity that seems one of his highest marks of truly great invention. It was illustrative of the grasp and tenacity of his mind that he never put his conception upon paper. He carried them in his head until they were perfected; the models and castings were then made after his verbal directions.*

"*By his inventive skill, his resolute perseverance and his unwearied industry, Mr. Allen acquired a handsome property. Perhaps the most marked trait in his character was his fearlessness. He was not merely brave; it seemed that the element of fear had been left out.*

"*He was a friend, warm and unchanging. He was unalterable in his attachments. He was a fond father, indulgent almost to a fault. He was an affectionate and devoted husband, strongly attached to his home and enjoying it very keenly. He was a kind brother and a grateful and tender son.*"[1] (Copied as written.)

Allen's two sons-in-law, Sullivan Forehand and Henry Wadsworth would continue to run the business for another 30 years.

Above is the factory that Forehand & Wadsworth occupied from 1876 to 1902. It was formally known as the Old Tainter Mill on Gardner St. From F. P. Rice's book *The Worcester of 1898.*

Shown on page 5 of the History chapter, is a drawing of the factory that Forehand & Wadsworth occupied from 1871 to 1876. That was the same factory that Allen & Thurber built in 1854 after the Merrifield fire. It had been the home of Allen & Thurber, Allen, Thurber & Co., Allen & Wheelock, E. Allen Makers and E. Allen & Co. In 1876, Forehand & Wadsworth relocated their factory at the Stone shop at the Junction, known as the Old Tainter Mill on Gardner Street. After Henry Wadsworth died in 1990, the company became Forehand Arms Co. until 1902 when it was sold to Hopkins & Allen.

Although the Allen & Wheelock Company's main business was the manufacture of firearms and cartridges, the machinery that Allen invented would revolutionize cartridge making for many years to come.

And so it ends. The company that Ethan Allen started with $12.00 and survived for nearly 65 years has long been history, but the legacy that Ethan Allen and Thomas Wheelock left for the gun making industry can still be felt. It cannot be calculated how many people that were connected with Allen, either directly or indirectly, learned their trade and business skills and later went on to their own success.

---

1. F.P. Rice, *The Worcester of 1898,* F.S. Blanchard & Co, Publishers, Worcester, Massachusetts, p. 545.

Chapter 45
PATENTS

Listed below are all of the known patents that were granted to Ethan Allen from November 11, 1837 to December 15, 1868. Allen was granted a total of 25 patents, and six reissues of existing patents. **Patents that were issued to him during the Allen & Wheelock era are in bold type.**

PATENT NUMBERS:	DATE:	DESCRIPTION:
461	November 11, 1837	Double action pistol.
2,912	January 16, 1843	Engraving machine.
60	January 15, 1844	Reissue of patent number 461, Double action pistol
64	August 3, 1844	Reissue of patent number 461, Double action pistol.
3,998	April 16, 1845	New action for pepperbox and bar hammer revolvers.
13,154	**July 3, 1855**	**Faucet breech rifle.**
15,454	**July 29, 1856**	**Minie ball bullet mold.**
16,367	**January 13, 1857**	**Bullet rammer for percussion side hammers, the method of attaching a barrel of a four shot pepperbox to the frame, and a nipple with a gas check valve.**
18,836	**December 15, 1857**	**Action for percussion side hammer revolvers.**
21,400	**September 7, 1858**	**New anti-fouling cylinder pin for side hammer percussion revolvers, and gas vent for revolving rifles.**
22,005	**November 9, 1858**	**Method of attaching a side hammer to a revolver with bored through cylinders. (22 rimfire)**
633	**December 14, 1858**	**Reissue of patent number 3,998, new action for Pepperbox and bar hammer revolvers.**
27,094	**February 14, 1860**	**Cartridge making machinery.**
27,415	**March 13, 1860**	**Machine to cut the rotation teeth on revolver cylinders.**
28,951	**July 3, 1860**	**Inclined plane for cartridge revolvers.**
30,033	**September 18, 1860**	**Dropping block rifle.**
30,109	**September 25, 1860**	**Lipfire cartridges.**
31,695	**March 19, 1861**	**Machine for crimping cartridges.**
33,328	**September 24, 1861**	**Cylinder pin locking device. (44 lipfire revolver)**
33,509	**October 22, 1861**	**New action for revolvers.**
1,268	**February 4, 1862**	**Reissue of patent 28,951, inclined plane for cartridge revolvers.**
35,067	**April 29, 1862**	**New action for 44 and 36 lipfire and percussion pistols and revolving rifles. Also included in this patent is a method of adjusting the trigger sensitivity and a bottom hinged loading gate for lipfire revolving rifles and pistols.**

PATENTS, CONTINUED

PATENT NUMBERS:	DATE:	DESCRIPTION:
36,760	October 28, 1862	Peep sight for rifles.
1,737	August 16, 1864	Reissue of patent number 21,400, anti-fouling cylinder pin for percussion revolvers and gas vent for revolving rifles.
46,617	March 7, 1865	Ejector system for single shot cartridge pistols. (Last known Allen & Wheelock patent)
1,949	May 9, 1865	Reissue of patent 27,094, machine to cut rotation teeth on revolver cylinders.
47,688	May 16, 1865	Reloadable steel shot shell and primer.
48,249	June 20, 1865	Method for making Damascus twist shotgun barrels.
49.491	August 22, 1865	Hinge breech double barrel shotgun.
55,596	June 19, 1866	Method of soldering gun barrels together.
84,929	December 15, 1868	Improvement on hinge breech shot gun. This patent also includes a barrel insert that makes it possible to fire a bottle neck rifle bullet from a shot gun.

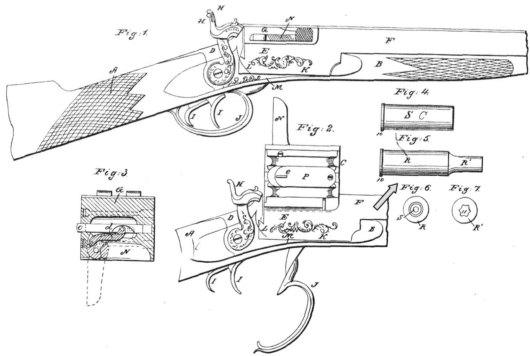

Above is patent number 84,929, issued December 15, 1868. This was the last patent granted to Allen. It is basically an improvement of his earlier patent for the hinge breech shot gun. Note that the triggerguard activates the extractor. Of special interest is the barrel insert that is actually a reloadable bottle neck steel rifle case that can be fired from a shotgun. (See arrow.)